HUMAN COMMUNICATION: THEORETICAL EXPLORATIONS

EDITED BY ALBERT SILVERSTEIN

UNIVERSITY OF RHODE ISLAND

LEA LAWRENCE ERLBAUM ASSOCIATES, PUBLISHERS
HILLSDALE, NEW JERSEY
1974

DISTRIBUTED BY THE HALSTED PRESS DIVISION OF

JOHN WILEY & SONS
New York   **Toronto**   **London**   **Sydney**

Lawrence Erlbaum Associates, Publishers
62 Maria Drive
Hillsdale, New Jersey 07642

Distributed solely by Halsted Press Division
John Wiley & Sons, Inc., New York

Library of Congress Cataloging in Publication Data

Silverstein, Albert, 1935-
  Human communication.

  Includes bibliographical references.
  1. Communication—Psychological aspects. I. Title.
BF637.C45S55   1974   153   74–14880
ISBN 0–470–79172–1

Printed in the United States of America

CONTENTS

PREFACE

One would be hard pressed to find a subject area more consistently fascinating and currently crucial to contemporary thinkers than that of human communication. Certainly there is no topic which has more profound significance for the human condition, for it is that process (or configuration of processes) that has allowed man to survive in his current form despite his being singularly unsuited to survive in any particular environment. Beyond that, it is clear that man's current form (i.e., his most distinctly human characteristics) is granted to him through communication, which provides humans with the basis for their societies and the richness of their cognitive worlds. So it is scarcely surprising that scholars across so many different disciplines have confronted this subject in the hope that it will yield answers to many of the most fundamental and vexing questions concerning human existence. Today's investigators of that realm are like Yossarian, the hero of Heller's *Catch-22,* collectors of good questions. But while Yossarian used questions like ''When is right?'' and ''Where are the Snowdens of yesteryear?'' to disrupt educational sessions, the questions articulated by the international brigade of communications researchers are stimulating more high level pedagogy than virtually any other single group.

The flowering of empirical and theoretical explorations of communication has brought as part of its fruit an enormous quantity of books dealing with the subject in one form or another. And yet, of this vast array of published volumes, there is none that can be considered truly introductory. That is, no current book treats the whole spectrum of problems related to human communication from the different viewpoints of creative scholars within the various disciplines that address those problems. There are certainly textbooks that attempt to survey ''the field'' as the author sees it. But even when these texts are eclectic in design (which is seldom), the limitations of the author's perspective and his desire to survey the important empirical findings interact to slight many significant questions and innovative approaches. More often, the attempt to deal with the entire realm of communication results in some idiosyncratic integration of the issues that the author believes will yield the most penetrating set of insights. There are also many books of readings in communications, many quite narrow in scope, some covering a wide spectrum. But whatever the scope of such books, the selections are usually quite brief and are addressed to very specific problems, often having been excerpted from prior publications. And, of course, the majority of the published works dealing with communication are monographs that deal with a very limited set of issues. An increasing number of these have an interdisciplinary flavor and are authored by scholars of varied backgrounds, but their greatest value cannot be for the new reader. Indeed the new reader in communications will find it a complicated matter to come into contact with a representative array of the fascinating questions that have been collected by the community of investigators interested in communication. There are certainly college courses offered to that very end, in which the teacher has judiciously culled the resources at his disposal for a collection of writings that will fill this bill, but such a collection does not exist within the covers of one volume. And where can the intelligent student or layman who wants to become introduced to communication outside of a college course turn?

This book is an attempt to fill the gap previously described. Each chapter has been written especially for this volume by an eminent theorist in one of the disciplines dealing with communication, and both surveys the range of issues within its domain and presents the author's personal theoretical approach. A guiding principle for all the authors was that an introduction need not be an oversimplification. So that while they attempted both to be representative in their discussions and to avoid unnecessarily technical terminology, they were equally careful to avoid any semblance of the pre-digested formula used in elementary textbooks. In addition, each author presents an original thesis within the context of his survey which provides the reader with a first-hand glimpse of what scholarly work is like in that discipline. A consequence of this overall strategy is that the reader can see clearly the great diversity that exists among the different approaches and levels of analysis used in the study of communication. The authors also stress those points of articulation that are found between the concepts used in the different chapters.

The scope of topics covered in this book is restricted to basic processes in communication in the hope that they would provide the intelligent student a means of finding out what the study of human communication is really all about. More specific day-to-day topics regarding communication are generally well covered in the popular press and literature and tend to lead one's attention away from the basic issues and questions that make this study such an exciting one today. Thus issues like ''how television can distort the news'' and ''trends in movie-making in the 70's'' were not included. My first attempt to provide intelligent students with this sort of vehicle came when I was designated Coordinator of the University of Rhode Island Honors Colloquium for the 1971–72 academic year. I chose the topic of human communication for the year's theme and promptly found that no volume existed which was appropriate to our needs. The series of topics selected for that year and the speakers who were invited to address them formed the basis for many of the chapters in this book, and the idea for organizing and producing a volume like this one took shape toward the end of that year. The support I received as Honors Colloquium Coordinator from the University's administration and the Faculty Senate's Honors Program Committee, especially its chairman Dr. Charles Nash, was very generous and I would like to express my thanks for it at this point. I am also very grateful to Dr. George Miller for his valuable suggestions in organizing both the colloquium and this book and for his advice on the selection of authors. The staff of LEA have been consistent and enthusiastic supporters of this volume from its first inception and I owe them much gratitude for their continuing good advice. But my deepest debt for this work is to my wife, Myrna. From the moment that I accepted the position of Coordinator of the Honors Colloquium to the last page of edited manuscript, there has been no way to find the point at which her contribution ended and mine began (although I suspect the most intelligent decisions were always hers). Beyond that, our communications on this project have been such an exciting adventure to me that no expression of gratitude could constitute an adequate message regarding their value.

August, 1974   Albert Silverstein

To Myrna
"let me see thy countenance,
let me hear thy voice;
for sweet is thy voice,
and thy countenance is comely."

1
PSYCHOLOGY, LANGUAGE, AND LEVELS OF COMMUNICATION

George A. Miller
Rockefeller University

The most general place to begin is with the concept of communication itself, before we move on to the study of linguistic communication. ''Communication'' is a very abstract word. Communication can be accomplished by an endless variety of means.

The general framework for studies of communication were set down more than 20 years ago by Norbert Weiner (1948) and Claude Shannon (1948, 1951) as a basis for their mathematical theory of communication. If we try to say in the most general terms what all the different kinds of communication have in common, it comes down to something like this: Communication occurs when events in one place or at one time are closely related to events in another place or at another time. For example, the vocal sounds I make in a lecture are, I hope, closely related to the sounds produced at the ears of my audience. One familiar and important instance of this general definition is the creation of a correlation between the acoustic waves impinging on a microphone at one place and time and the acoustic waves generated by an earphone or loudspeaker at another place and time. The practical implementation of this particular kind of correlation has been the subject of enormous technological effort. Any physical process that has this capacity to span space or time can be used as a communication system. Human speech, which provides a way for events in my nervous system to affect events in your nervous system, is one kind of communication, but it is only one of many different ways the abstract concept of communication can be realized in a practical form.

It is in this abstract sense that we can talk about communication between machines, or the communication of diseases, or the hereditary communication of traits from parents to their offspring. I say we *can* talk about all these different

1

kinds of communication, but I am not going to. My topic is "Psychology, Language, and Levels of Communication," which means that I am only going to talk about the kinds of communication that go on between animals in general, and between human beings in particular.

I have now defined what I mean by "communication," but I still owe you definitions of "psychology" and "language."

The word "psychology" also covers a great variety of things, but I think that most psychologists would accept a rather abstract definition along the following lines: *Psychology is the science that attempts to describe, predict, and control mental and behavioral events.*

I must confess that this definition hides a certain amount of disagreement among those who call themselves psychologists. Some would say that they are interested only in *behavior,* and others would reply that you cannot ignore *mental events.* And some psychologists would say that they only want to *describe* what people do, whereas others believe their major responsibility is to *predict* what people are going to do, and still others argue that the real test of psychology as a science is its ability to *control* what people do. Rather than try to settle all these arguments, therefore, I have included all points of view in my definition.

I want to put my definition of communication and my definition of psychology together, but before I do that I think I should devote a few words to the possible use of psychological science to *control* mental and behavioral events. Many people get upset when they hear that psychologists are trying to control them. They do not want to be controlled; they do not want to be "brainwashed." They want to be free to think and do whatever seems right to them. They get very worried that these scientists are developing in their laboratories some new and monstrous technology that will reduce human beings to mechanical robots. So the whole question of control as a scientific objective is clouded by moral and political overtones.

What is the current state of this question? Do we in fact have techniques that enable us to control people? The answer is "yes." There does exist a behavioral technique that can exert powerful control over people's thoughts and actions. This technique of control can cause you to do things you would never think of doing otherwise. It can change your opinions and beliefs. It can be used to deceive you. It can make you happy and sad. It can put new ideas into your head. It can make you want things you do not have. You can even use it to control yourself. It is an enormously powerful tool with a wide range of applications.

Now, the behavioral technique I have in mind was not invented by psychologists. This particular technique of control has been around at least as long as human beings have existed. Far from thinking of it as an evil or threatening thing, most people regard this particular method of control as one of the great triumphs of the human mind, indeed, as the very thing that raises man above all other animals.

The technique of control that I am talking about, of course, is human speech. Speech is the most subtle and powerful instrument we have for controlling other people. Nothing that psychologists can invent in their laboratories is likely to be nearly as influential in controlling people. My point is very simple, namely, that it is not necessary to think of all techniques of control as essentially evil or immoral. Some are essential for the existence of civilization as we know it.

I said I wanted to put the definitions of psychology and communication together. Let me do that now. Communication is a process that occurs when different events are closely related; psychology is concerned with mental or behavioral events. The *psychology of communication,* therefore, must be concerned with *relations* between different mental or behavioral events. In the most common and familiar case, what a speaker says is one set of events, and what his listener understands is another set; if these are closely related, we say that communication is occurring. But the psychology of communication is not limited to talking and listening. Other kinds of events, intentional or unintentional, can also serve the purpose of communication.

In its broadest form, therefore, the psychological study of communication includes not only the study of spoken communication between people, but also the many kinds of unspoken communication that go on constantly when people interact. It even includes the kind of communication that goes on between animals. A complete survey of this subject would have to include all these kinds of communication.

As a practical matter, however, spoken communication between people is the most interesting kind of communication, and probably the most important. So I shall address the remainder of my remarks to this particular case.

Interest in the nature of human speech and language is a very general characteristic of twentieth-century thought. This century has seen the emergence of descriptive linguistics as one of the most rigorous and analytical of all the social sciences, but interest in language has not been confined to linguists alone. Anyone who, in the spirit of this century, tries to understand the intricacies of human thought finds it necessary to understand first the intricacies of the symbolic systems through which human thought makes itself manifest. Thus logicians, philosophers, and psychologists must share the linguist's concern with language.

Moreover, in parallel with this broad study of language has run an amazing revolution in our technology of communication. In this century the telegraph, telephone, phonograph, radio, television, and communication satellite have accustomed us to instantaneous communication from the most distant corners of the world.

These two developments—the scholarly study of language and the creation of a vast technology of communication—seem to have begun as independent manifestations of the spirit of our times. But with the emergence of digital computers as language-processing systems, the world of the academy and the world of technology joined forces in their attempts to understand the nature of language and communication. Indeed, in order to communicate with our computers, a whole new class of artificial languages had to be invented. Each decade seems to bring some new advance, to open some new possibilities.

Thus, psychologists interested in language and communication feel themselves to be part of a much larger army of workers contributing to the purification of ideas that rank among the great triumphs of the modern mind. This feeling lends an excitement to the field that is often difficult for outsiders to comprehend. It means that the zoologist who records the grunts and gestures of the great apes, or the psychologist who analyzes the almost unintelligible utterances of young children, or the neurologist who studies aphasia or stimulates the centers in the brain that control speech, or the engineer who designs telephone circuits to transmit the human voice more efficiently, or the grammarian who states rules for forming grammatical sentences, or the logician who analyzes the way we should use words like "some," "all," and "none," or the philosopher who tries to untangle linguistic sources of philosophical confusion, or the sociologist who measures social effects of mass media of communication — all these workers and many others can see themselves as participating in and contributing to one of the great intellectual adventures of the twentieth century. Seen in isolation, any one of these studies might seem uninteresting, even pointless. Taken all together, they point to a concern for language and communication as among the principal intellectual preoccupations of our time.

The central object of all this interest and excitement, of course, is human language. Since I have carefully defined "psychology" and "communication," I must now try to say what "language" means.

There seem to be at least two different ways to define what a language is. According to one definition, a language is a socially shared means for expressing ideas. I would call this a *functional* definition, because it is stated in terms of a function that language serves. Another definition says that a language is all the well-formed sentences that could be generated according to the rules of its grammar. I would call this a *formal* definition, because it is stated in terms of the forms of sentences. The formal definition tells us how to decide whether or not a particular utterance is a sentence in the language; the functional definition tells us what the sentence is used for. Both definitions reflect important aspects of language.

According to the formal definition, a language is defined by its grammar (Chomsky, 1957, 1965). So that moves the problem one step deeper. What is a grammar? Let me put it this way: A sentence is a string of sounds that has a meaning to the people who know the language. The basic problem, therefore, is to understand how the sounds and the meanings are related. A grammar is a set of rules that describes how the realm of sound is related to the realm of meaning.

Considered abstractly, a grammatical sentence is a highly complex and structured thing, and it faces in two directions. On the one hand it must have a semantic interpretation, a meaning, and on the other hand it must have a phonological realization, a pronunciation, an acoustic shape. The formal problem for the grammarian, therefore, is to describe this abstract concept in such a way that both its sound and its meaning are explained.

Anyone who speaks a language, of course, must know how its sounds and its meanings are related. That is to say, he must know the grammar of his language. When we say this, however, we do not mean that he could explain the grammar to someone else; we say he knows it because he uses the language appropriately. His knowledge of grammar is implicit. Only when he studies grammar in school does he begin to make this grammatical knowledge explicit and communicable to others. One of the fascinating problems for a psychologist interested in human communication is to explain exactly what it is that a person knows implicitly when he knows a grammar, and how this information is organized and stored in his memory.

In order to be able to use a language effectively, of course, a person must know much more than its grammar. I like to think of this knowledge as organized on six distinguishable levels (Miller, 1964). On the first level, he must be able to hear acoustic signals. On the second level he must have *phonological* information about the sounds of his language. On the third level he must have *syntactic* information about the formation of sentences. On the fourth level he must have *lexical* information about the meanings of words and combinations of words. On the fifth level he must have *conceptual* knowledge of the world he lives in and talks about. And on the sixth level he probably has to have some system of *beliefs* in order to evaluate what he hears.

Grammar, of course, deals with only the first four of these levels — acoustics, phonology, syntax, and lexicon — and with relations between them. A psychologist interested in language, however, must also remember that a person's concepts and beliefs play an essential role in his use and understanding of linguistic messages.

The sort of thing I have in mind when I talk about levels has already been incorporated into the theory of communication in terms of a critically important distinction between the *signal* that is transmitted and the *message* that the signal conveys. The need for this distinction becomes obvious as soon as one recognizes that the same message can be encoded by many different signals. Indeed, in the course of a single transmission from source to destination a message may be recoded several times into acoustic, electrical, or printed forms; the nature of the signal will change with each recoding, but the message should remain invariant throughout. Without some concept of the message as different from the signal, we would have no way to talk about what should remain invariant under transformations of the signal. And without some notion of what should remain invariant, of course, we would have no way to characterize tolerances for noise or distortion, that is to say, we could not define a "fidelity evaluation function." In short, the distinction between message and signal is fundamental to modern communication theory.

I would like to point out, however, that there is something disturbingly asymmetrical about this dichotomy between signal and message. We have a very concrete, physicalistic notion of what a signal is, but it is much harder to say with equal confidence what a message is. Messages are something that must remain invariant. They are something that the transmission system mustn't mutilate. In the case of linguistic communication, they are what a person should understand when he receives an appropriate signal. In short, the concept of a message is very abstract, to say the least, and some might be tempted to call it downright vague. For most technological applications, of course, this vagueness is of no concern, since all actual operations are performed on the signal, and everyone knows what that is. But for a psychologist like myself, the message conveyed by the speech signal is the principal object of interest, and its abstract character can be a source of considerable inconvenience.

I see no way to make the concept of a message any less abstract, but something can be done to make it a bit less vague. The messages that are communicated by speech, at any rate, can be characterized in several different ways. These different characterizations are related in a hierarchical manner, or, as I prefer to say, by a sequence of levels such that a given level presupposes all the operations involved at lower levels. Another way to say it is that I want to generalize the signal-message distinction in such a way that messages are regarded as signals at the next higher level.

I think the best way to get at these levels is to consider the different ways that linguistic communication can fail. Linguistic communication can fail if we don't hear it, or if we perceive or remember it incorrectly. But even if we hear it correctly, it can fail due to misunderstanding. The more serious problems arise at the higher levels and require more powerful explanations. In short, there are a great variety of ways that communication can fail. We need some kind of scheme for categorizing them, and I believe that a series of levels is the sort of scheme that can do it.

With that much of an introduction to what I am up to, let me outline again the levels we must distinguish. Table I summarizes the levels of linguistic processing that I think we must distinguish.

At the lowest level of all, a person simply listens to a spoken utterance. Even if the language is incomprehensible, you can still hear an utterance as an auditory

TABLE 1

Levels of Processing

Process	Unit	Sample theories
Hear	Auditory stimulus	Detection theory
Match	Phonemic pattern	Information theory
Accept	Grammatical sentence	Generative grammar
Interpret	Meaningful sentence	Semantic markers
Understand	Speech act	?
Believe	Basis for action	? ? ?

stimulus, and can respond to it as present or absent, loud or soft, slow or fast, long or short, on the left or on the right, as a masculine or a feminine voice, and so on. If a person is deaf, of course, spoken communication will fail at this level, and therefore at all subsequent levels. In society at large, however, most of our failures of communication cannot be attributed to everyone's being deaf. Our problems of understanding one another are far more complicated than that.

At this first level, in other words, a person responds to the signal itself, not to the message it conveys. Thus, psychologists have found it possible to use various theories that engineers have developed—signal detection theory is a good example — to describe how people function as signal-detecting and signal-transforming devices. That is to say, when people are asked to function as signal-processing systems, they can be described by the same theories that describe all such systems, animate or inanimate. I will not attempt to review the very extensive work that has been done on auditory psychophysics, or even to illustrate it by example. It is good science and psychologists are proud of it, but for my present purposes I want to mention it only to establish what I mean by the lowest level of linguistic processing.

At the second level, given that an utterance is heard, a person who knows the language can match it as a phonemic pattern. This distinction between the first and second levels resembles a traditional distinction that psychologists have drawn between sensory and perceptual psychology; in sensory psychology a person responds independently of the meaning of the stimulus, whereas in perceptual psychology he is allowed to interpret the stimulus in the light of his previous experience. It also resembles a distinction that linguists draw between phonetics and phonemics; in phonetics an attempt is made to provide a universal, physicalistic description of all the possible segments of a spoken utterance, whereas in phonemics the description is given in terms of the features that are significant in particular languages.

A phoneme is a class of spoken sounds—or "phones"—that are judged to be perceptually identical, although the actual acoustic signals may be very different. The most obvious example in English is the phoneme /k/, which is very different in the words *keep, cup,* and *coop,* yet which all speakers of English will recognize as the "same" sound. A more interesting example is the phoneme /p/, which speakers of English aspirate in initial positions, but do not aspirate as part of a consonant cluster. That is to say, the /p/ in *pin* and the /p/ in *spin* are very different acoustic signals, yet speakers of English do not perceive the difference, and most of them are surprised when it is pointed out to them. (To experience the difference, speak these two words with the back of your hand held an inch in front of your lips.) In other languages, the presence of aspiration might signify a phonemic distinction, and speakers of that language would hear those two phones as very different phonemes.

When I say that at this second level a person who knows a language can match its phonemic patterns, I mean he can use his own phonological skill as a speaker of the language to code a variety of different acoustic signals into the intended phonemic classes. This ability to match—that is, to repeat—a spoken input has been studied intensively in experiments on speech perception. The initial studies of speech perception were conducted at the Bell Telephone Laboratories by men who called them "articulation tests" because they wanted to study how well an inanimate machine like the telephone was able to "articulate" the sounds of speech (Fletcher, 1929). Since then, of course, the test methods have been widely used, not only to test the quality of voice communication systems, but also to study psychological processes involved in speech perception.

I should point out that most of the original articulation tests were conducted with nonsense syllables constructed by stringing the phonemes of English together in ways that were perfectly pronounceable, but which did not happen to form English words. That is to say, at this level of information processing, people are able to use their phonological skills to match the received input, even though they may be unable to assign any meaning or significance to the patterns of phonemes they perceive. The pattern of phonemes can be regarded as an input signal to a higher level of processing, where meanings are assigned. We will come to this higher level in a moment; at this second level, however, all we require is that the person be able to echo the signal he receives.

The difficulty of this task depends very critically on the size of the set of alternatives that the listener expects. In order to illustrate this fact, I would like to describe very briefly an experiment that I conducted twenty years ago (Miller, Heise, & Lichten, 1951).

Listeners were told in advance what the set of alternative words would be. All of the words were English monosyllables. They knew they would hear one of the words in the given set. The size of the set was varied: 2, 4, 8, 16, 32, or 256 words, or they were told simply that they might hear any English monosyllable, a condition I estimate to be the equivalent of a vocabulary size of about 1000 words. The words were spoken into a microphone, the speech signal was mixed with measured amounts of random noise, the noisy signal was fed to the listeners through high-quality earphones, and the accuracy of their responses was then scored. The results are summarized in Fig. 1.

Here the per cent of words correctly matched by the listeners is plotted as a function of the signal-to-noise ratio, with the size of the vocabulary as the parameter. In all cases, of course, as the speech signal increased in intensity relative to the noise, the accuracy of the listeners' responses increased. I think that the interesting way to look at these data is to compare the several curves at a given signal-to-noise ratio. Take the -12 dB level as an example. At -12 dB a particular speech signal—the word *boy*, for example—could be perceived correctly 90% of the time when it was known in advance to be one of two possible signals that might occur, whereas *exactly the same acoustic signal* could be perceived correctly only 3% of the time when the listener was expecting any one of a thousand different monosyllables. I emphasize that the acoustic signal in both cases was the same. The only difference was what the listener expected.

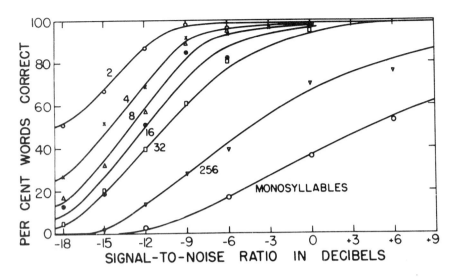

FIG. 1.1. The rate at which intelligibility increases as speech becomes louder (relative to a masking noise) depends on the number of alternative words that the listener expects to hear. (From Miller, Heise, & Lichten, 1951.)

The fact that a better signal-to-noise ratio is needed in order to discriminate among a larger number of messages is, of course, exactly what the Shannon-Weiner theory of selective information would lead us to expect. For experiments such as this one, therefore, psychologists were again able to borrow a theory developed originally for engineering purposes and to show that when human beings are asked to select among a set of alternatives, their performance could be described by the same theories that describe all such systems, animate or inanimate.

I should add, however, that when a delay is inserted between the input and the response—that is to say, when we test memory instead of perception—the simple and direct application of information measurement proves to be inadequate (Miller, 1956). But that, too, might have been expected from the original theory, which was explicitly formulated for memoryless systems. The memory experiments are a bit complicated in this respect, and since the complications add little or nothing to our understanding of differences between levels of processing, I will not try to review them here.

In the context of linguistic communication, therefore, the simplest possible interpretation we can give to the signal-message distinction is that the signal is the acoustic wave that impinges on the ear, and the message is the string of phonemes that the listener is able to produce in order to match what he hears. It should be perfectly obvious, however, that this definition of the message is not adequate to cover everything that goes on when people use speech in social interaction. As an audience listens to me they are, I hope, doing something more than merely matching the strings of phonemes that I am generating. Therefore, we need still another, more abstract definition of the message, so let's press on to the third level.

If an utterance can be heard as an acoustic stimulus and matched as a phonemic pattern, then the next level of processing is to accept or reject it as a grammatical sentence in the language. Grammatical processing presupposes phonological processing of the input. Otherwise said, we can regard the phonemic pattern as the input signal and the grammatical evaluation as the message at this level of processing. If you think of the relation between the levels in that way, however, I should issue a word of warning. Speech perception is a complicated process, and we do not really know whether the information processing required for the lower levels must actually *precede in time* the processing required for the higher levels, or whether processing at all levels could be going on simultaneously. I tend to think that the message is being processed at all levels simultaneously, and that sometimes the results obtained at the more abstract levels can be used to facilitate the processing at the lower levels. If I am right, of course, then there must be enormously complex interactions between levels. However, it will be easier to talk as if the simpler processing had to precede the more complicated processing, even though you and I both know that the actual machinery may operate very differ-

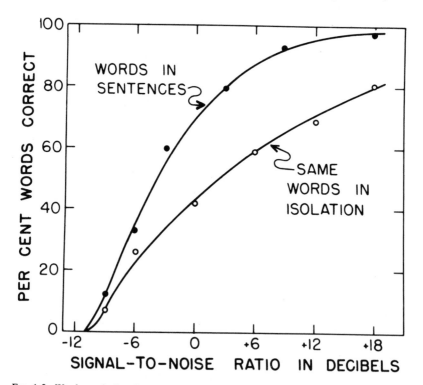

FIG. 1.2. Words can be heard more easily if they are part of a grammatical sentence than if they occur in a haphazard order. (From Miller, Heise, & Lichten, 1951.)

ently. All we really know is that simpler processing can be carried out successfully even when the more complicated processing cannot, but not the other way round. With that warning out of the way, let us return to a consideration of the level of grammatical processing.

We have known for many years that words are easier to hear when they occur in grammatical sentences than when they occur in random order. Figure 2 indicates the magnitude of this difference. At a level of accuracy of 50%, these two curves are about 9 dB apart. That is to say, grammatical sentences like "Peat is cut in the bogs and used for fuel. The woman wore a small pink scarf," etc. can be perceived correctly at much lower signal-to-noise ratios than can the same words heard in haphazard order: "bogs, small, cut, wore, fuel, scarf, peat, woman," etc. The words in isolation are the same acoustic signals, and the same phonemic patterns, as the words in sentences, yet the words in isolation are harder to hear.

There are (at least) three different kinds of explanation that can be offered for this difference. One explanation says that words in sentences are easier because the sentences are "redundant" in the technical sense defined by Shannon. Another explanation says that they are easier because the sentences conform to familiar syntactic rules. And the third explanation says that they are easier because the sentences are meaningful. In my opinion, all three explanations are correct.

A precise definition of the concept of redundancy was one of the most important conceptual contributions of Shannon's theory of communication. In a redundant signal, the message is effectively repeated more than once, which makes the signal longer than it would have to be if the coding were more efficient, but which has the advantage that the message is not necessarily lost when parts of the signal are distorted or masked by noise. That is to say, redundancy is a great antidote against communication failure. Since sentences are indeed more redundant — that is to say, more predictable — than are haphazard strings of words, it is easier for a listener to guess what the words must have been in this redundant context.

Now, the reason sentences are redundant is that there are rules known both to speakers and listeners that constrain our freedom in permuting the order of the words we use. Shannon characterized these rules in terms of transitional probabilities between consecutive segments of the signal, and for engineering purposes that was a very powerful approach. As a psychological theory of what the human listener was doing, however, an explanation of redundancy in terms of transitional probabilities is not satisfactory. The major objection is that the number of transitional probabilities that a person would have to learn in order to speak grammatically far exceeds what anyone could even hear, much less learn, in a finite childhood (Miller, Galanter, & Pribram, 1960, Ch. 11). In order to understand how a person could predict the future of a grammatical sentence, therefore, psychologists turned to a less powerful but more plausible explanation in terms of syntactic rules. The redundancy that Shannon had defined was then viewed simply as the statistical consequence of the operation of these syntactic constraints on word order.

Thus the first two explanations, in terms of redundancy and in terms of syntax, come down to the same thing. The explanation in terms of meaningfulness, however, introduces something new and intrinsically more complicated. Nevertheless, it is quite correct, because the sentences were indeed meaningful in a way that the isolated words were not; the original experiments do not enable us to parcel out the contribution of syntactic rules from the contribution of semantic rules. In order to suggest how this might be done experimentally, I want to describe another experiment I did almost ten years ago (Miller & Isard, 1963).

Let me first describe how we constructed our test sentences. Suppose you take two sentences like "The odorless liquid became a filthy mess" and "The academic lecture attracted a limited audience." Since they have roughly the same syntactic structure, we can construct two new strings of words having the same syntactic structure by simply taking alternate words from each sentence. In this way we obtain "The academic liquid attracted a limited mess" and "The odorless lecture became a filthy audience." These derived strings are still syntactically similar to the original sentences, but they are semantically anomalous. That is to say, they obey syntactic rules, but they violate semantic rules. Finally, as a control, we scrambled the words in a haphazard order. This gave us three kinds of test materials: grammatical and meaningful, grammatical but semantically anomalous, and neither grammatical nor meaningful. Note that the words were the same acoustic stimuli and the same phonemic patterns in every case.

We then used these materials in tests of speech perception and obtained the results shown in Fig. 3. The top and the bottom curves are, of course, just a replication of the results shown in Fig. 2. The new result is the middle curve, obtained for the sentences that obeyed syntactic rules but violated semantic rules. As you might have expected, both kinds of rules contribute to the redundancy of meaningful grammatical sentences, but syntax alone can make a significant contribution to speech perception.

I might point out, just in passing, that the transitional probabilities between successive words in the anomalous sentences were quite low, so the redundancy predicted on that basis would not be sufficient to explain their superior intelligibility to the random string of words. If, however, the redundancy is thought of in terms of transitional probabilities between parts of speech, as constrained by syntactic rules, rather than between particular words, the results are much more comprehensible.

I have paid considerable attention to the first three levels because we know most about those levels. Experimental studies of how we hear acoustic signals are at least 100 years old; experimental studies of how we match phonemic patterns are at least 50 years old; and experimental studies of how we accept grammatical sentences are now about 10 years old. So we have something to say about them. For the remaining three levels, however, the going is much more difficult. This is especially unfortunate, since most of the really serious failures of human communication occur at the levels of interpretation, understanding, and belief.

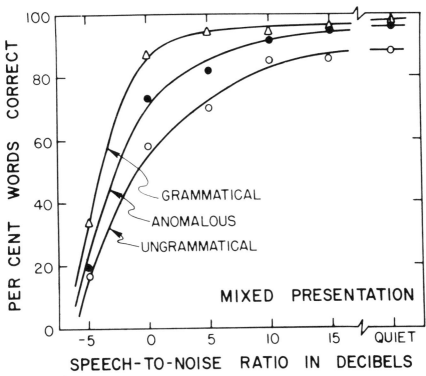

FIG. 1.3. Words are heard more easily in grammatical sentences than in haphazard order, even when the sentences are semantically anomalous. (From Miller & Isard, 1963.)

At the fourth level, beyond hearing, matching, and acceptance, comes the level of semantic interpretation. Here again, with the proper warnings against presuppositions about temporal order, one can think of grammatical strings as the input signal to a system that assigns semantic interpretations. Semantic interpretation is a highly complex skill that humans perform at very rapid rates, yet one which we have only the dimmest notion of how to explain in such a way that computers could arrive at the same interpretations. Not only does the meaning of each word have to be looked up in some internal equivalent of a dictionary, but the interpretation of each individual word is affected by the company it keeps. The theoretical problem is to systematize the interactions of the meanings of words and phrases within their linguistic contexts.

At this level we are interested in the semantic interpretations that people can give to a sentence in what has been called the ''zero-context'' situation (Katz & Fodor, 1963). Zero context is exemplified as follows: You find an unmarked envelope and open it; inside there is a piece of paper that is blank except for one grammatical sentence that is written on it. You have nothing to work on but the sentence itself. You have no contextual information about who wrote it or what motivated him to write it or what events preceded or followed it. Simply on the basis of your knowledge of the language, you will be able to assign an interpretation to the sentence, to say what other sentences have a similar interpretation, to say whether it is anomalous or ambiguous, to say something about what it entails and what it presupposes. These are some of the performances that a theory of semantic interpretation should be able to explain.

Although we are not yet in any position to suggest a satisfactory formal theory for the cognitive apparatus that carries out such operations as these, it is obvious that we will need something fairly complex and abstract. I suspect we will need a theory that can deal with the construction of mental representations, of mental images — a theory about how we convert the spoken symbols into some kind of abstract, internal model of what the message conveys. The theories of semantic interpretation that have been suggested to date stop far short of this goal, and before we can extend them appropriately we will have to do many experiments aimed at discovering the various constraints and degrees of freedom in the mental apparatus we are trying to describe.

The fifth level is included because it is necessary to distinguish between interpreting a sentence and understanding it. To utter a sentence in social interaction is to perform a speech act (Searle, 1969), and how that act is understood is far more complicated than how it is semantically interpreted. I remember one evening when I came home from work and my wife greeted me at the door with the following sentence: "I bought some light bulbs today." Now, you can hear this utterance, and you can match it, and you can describe its grammatical structure, and you can even interpret it or paraphrase it, but you would not really understand what she meant unless you happened to know that the lights had burned out in our kitchen the day before. What the sentence meant to me was that if I wanted any dinner, I'd better go to the kitchen and replace those burned-out bulbs. You had to know more than the language in order to understand her speech act; you had to know something about the situation as well.

Let me give another example: Suppose someone were to say, *Mary and John saw the mountains while they were flying to California.* If we consider this sentence simply from a grammatical point of view, we must classify it as ambiguous. It has at least two meanings. According to one meaning, it could be paraphrased, *While Mary and John were flying to California they saw the mountains.* According to the other meaning, it could be paraphrased, *While the mountains were flying to California Mary and John saw them.* There is nothing that we know about phonology or syntax or the meanings of the words involved that will help us decide between these two meanings of *Mary and John saw the mountains while they were flying to California.*

But that is ridiculous! Everyone knows that mountains don't fly. Anyone would know immediately that the sentence *Mary and John saw the mountains while they were flying to California* means that Mary and John were flying, not the mountains. But how do we know this? Is it part of the lexical meanings of the word *mountain*? Certainly not. You can look up the meaning of *mountain* in any dictionary you like, and it will not tell you that mountains don't fly. Such knowledge is part of your conceptual information about the world you live in, not part of your lexical knowledge about the meanings of words. So in order to understand how people understand language, we must recognize that they use their general conceptual information as well as their specific lexical information.

But suppose, just for the sake of argument, that we were wrong. Suppose that in the subsequent conversation it turned out that the speaker really did intend to say that the mountains were flying to California when Mary and John saw them. What would we say to that? I don't know what you would say, but my response would be, "I don't believe you." In the final analysis, I would appeal to my system of beliefs in order to evaluate what the speaker was saying. So beliefs, too, must play a role in linguistic communication.

Our conceptual knowledge and our system of beliefs are not really part of our linguistic knowledge, but they play an important role in the way we understand language in actual use. This brings us back to the other definition of language, the functional definition, which says that language is used to express ideas. When we use conceptual information or our beliefs to interpret a sentence, we are going beyond the linguistic form of the sentence and are evaluating it and interpreting it in terms of the plausibility of the ideas it expresses, and in terms of the way it is being used in the social situation in which it occurs.

Lest you think that concepts and beliefs are relatively unimportant in the way we use language, let me give another example. Suppose I tell you, completely out of context, that *John drinks wine*. How would you understand this sentence? Suppose you know who John is, and suppose you know what wine is, and suppose you understand what it means to drink wine. Suppose you know all these words, and you understand the grammatical structure of the sentence perfectly well. You still would not be certain what I meant. You would not know why I said such a thing to you. You would not understand my intentions.

When I say *John drinks wine* I might be doing any of several things. I might be warning you. I might be informing you. I might be making a prediction. I might be making a promise, or an accusation, or a joke. I might be telling a lie, or asking permission, or expressing criticism. I might be doing any one of a number of different things, and unless you knew which one I intended to do, you would not really understand the meaning of my speech act.

Most of our misunderstandings of other people are not due to any inability to hear them, or to parse their sentences, or to understand their words. Such problems do occur, of course. But a far more important source of difficulty in communication is that we so often fail to understand a speaker's intentions.

Because such failures are so common, most languages have special verbs that a speaker can use to make his intentions clear (Austin, 1962). For example, if I say *Let me warn you that John drinks wine,* it would mean something entirely different from saying *Let me assure you that John drinks wine. Warn* and *assure* are intentional verbs. In many situations, of course, special verbs of intention are unnecessary, because the social context makes it perfectly clear what a speaker's intentions must be. But sometimes, when they are omitted, confusion and misunderstanding can result.

I believe that most of our failures to make our intentions clear are innocent. We are not trying to be deceitful or confusing; we simply are not clever enough or quick enough to think of the best way to express the meaning we really wish to communicate. Our listener, if he knows the context and can infer something about our intentions, can frequently correct our clumsiness. He can understand what we meant, even though a literal interpretation of what we actually said might have been very different.

At lower levels of communication processing, the ability of a listener to correct the signal he receives can usually be attributed to his knowledge of the phonological, morphological, grammatical, and lexical constraints our language imposes on grammatical utterances. That is to say, at the lower levels we attribute this resistance to distortion to the listener's familiarity with the linguistic sources of redundancy in spoken messages. In those cases it is reasonably obvious how redundancy operates as an antidote against communication failure.

I would like to suggest that something analogous is also occurring at the more abstract levels of communication processing. At the higher levels, of course, the mechanisms are different; they have more to do with well-formed thoughts than with well-formed sentences. However, I think it is possible to recognize some of the constraints that we place on admissible sequences of units at these higher levels. Logic is one of our highest level mechanisms for introducing redundancy (i.e., predictability) into our messages. Intentional verbs are another. And there are probably many more. Discovering and analyzing these abstract constraints is one of the most challenging and exciting tasks in this field of research.

My purpose here will have been served, however, if I have persuaded you that human communication, like the human body, is an extremely complicated and delicate thing, and that in order for it to work at all we must have available a wide variety of error-detecting and error-correcting redundancies, just as the body must have a wide variety of defense against disease. The redundancies that we have evolved to make linguistic communication more resistant to infectious errors are not limited to those that can be characterized acoustically, but extend even to the most abstract levels of understanding and belief.

REFERENCES

Austin, J. L. *How to do things with words.* Cambridge, Mass.: Harvard University Press, 1962.
Chomsky, N. *Syntactic structures.* The Hague: Mouton, 1957.
Chomsky, N. *Aspects of the theory of syntax.* Cambridge, Mass.: MIT Press, 1965.
Fletcher, H. *Speech and hearing.* New York: Van Nostrand, 1929.
Katz, J. J., & Fodor, J. A. The structure of a semantic theory. *Language,* 1963, **39**, 170–210.

Miller, G. A. The magical number seven, plus or minus two: Some limits on our capacity for processing information. *Psychological Review*, 1956, **63**, 81 – 97.

Miller, G. A., Galanter, E., & Pribram, K. H. *Plans and the structure of behavior*. New York: Holt, Rinehart & Winston, 1960.

Miller, G. A., Heise, G. A., & Lichten, W. The intelligibility of speech as a function of the context of the test materials. *Journal of Experimental Psychology*, 1951, **41**, 329 – 335.

Miller, G. A., & Isard, S. Some perceptual consequences of linguistic rules. *Journal of Verbal Learning and Verbal Behavior,* 1963, **2**, 217 – 228.

Searle, J. R. *Speech acts: An essay in the philosophy of language*. Cambridge: University Press, 1969.

Shannon, C. E. A mathematical theory of communication. *Bell System Technical Journal,* 1948, **27**, 379 – 423, 623 – 656.

Shannon, C. E. Prediction and entropy of printed English. *Bell System Technical Journal*, 1951, **30**, 50 – 64.

Weiner, N. *Cybernetics, or control and communication in the animal and the machine*. Cambridge, Mass. and N.Y.: Technology Press and Wiley, 1948.

2
INFORMATION AND MOTIVATION[1]

D. E. Berlyne
University of Toronto

Students of communication have, naturally enough, paid a great deal of attention to the content and the form of messages, to what they communicate and how. They have studied the effects of the medium through which a message is transmitted and of the style in which it is framed. But there are times when it is useful to consider how much is being communicated, to have some way of measuring, or at least estimating and comparing, the quantities of information imparted through different messages. This might help us, for example, to decide how successfully a communication process is doing what it is meant to do and to look for ways of improving its effectiveness. At other times, we might want to ascertain the maximum amount of information that can be conveyed through a particular kind of message, so that ways of increasing the maximum might be sought or so that communicators might be prevented from wasting time and effort through misguidedly trying to exceed the maximum. And, above all, as psychologists interested in human behavior, we want to know how people are affected by the amount of information coming from a particular source, quite apart from what the information is.

However, it is not at all easy to determine how much information there is in a particular message. It is obviously unsafe to base an estimate solely on the length of a message or on how many words or other elements it comprises. It certainly seems reasonable, on the whole, to suppose that one could say more, and convey more information, in a longer message than in a shorter one, but this is not always the case. We all know from painful experience how some writers and speakers

[1] The preparation of this chapter and the research reported in it have been supported by Research Grants A-73 from the National Research Council of Canada and S70–1570–X2 from the Canada Council.

19

have perfected the art of using many words to tell us nothing. On the other hand, there are times when a single word, or a single event of some other kind, can produce a shattering revelation. We may feel that we have learned more from it than from listening to hours of talk, or from reading many books, at other times.

As an alternative approach, it might be thought possible to measure amount of information by counting up the number of facts that a message announces. But this lands us in several difficulties immediately. First of all, can the information residing in a message be identified solely with its factual content? Do we not often receive information from material that does not describe objects or events? Even a factual message can surely give us a great deal of information—e.g., about the originator of the message, his tastes, his level of education, his emotional concerns—that is not explicitly stated. It may be implicit in the style, the vocabulary, the tone of voice, etc., in which the message is couched. Quite apart from that, how do we count facts? If I tell you that a certain object is green and circular, is this one fact or two facts? If I tell you that I saw Mr. X this morning, you can deduce, even if you are not acquainted with Mr. X, that I saw a creature with two eyes, a nose, and a mouth, not to mention two lungs, an esophagus, and a spleen. If you know Mr. X, there is a great deal more that you will know about what I saw. How many facts does this information embody? What about a meteorologist's message that tells us that there will be either snow or rain tomorrow. How many facts are to be found in it? One might argue that complex facts like these could be broken down into a number of elementary facts, e.g., facts each attributing one characteristic to one object. Some years ago, Bar-Hillel and Carnap (1953) tried to develop measures of information based on the attempts of philosophers like Carnap and Wittgenstein to analyze the elementary facts that make up the meaning of a complex factual statement. But their techniques, ingenious and interesting as they were, do not seem to have won widespread application during the years that have since elapsed.

The greatest complication of all lies in the fact that the quantity of information in a message cannot be estimated without taking into account who the recipient is and what goes on inside him. One and the same message may very well convey different amounts of information to two different people or to the same person at different times. For example, a native speaker of Chinese will receive much more information from a message written in Chinese than somebody who has no knowledge of that language, and a message that was highly informative the first time I heard it may add nothing to what I know when I hear it for a second time soon afterwards. What is particularly crucial is the way in which a message interacts with the existing beliefs and expectations of the recipient or, in other words, with information already stored inside him. A message telling him something that fits in very well with other messages he has received in the past, or that follows logically from them, will, one would suppose, supply less information to him than a message that jars with what he has previously assumed and causes him to reorganize his view of certain matters from top to bottom.

So, all things considered, it seems that, in looking for a measure of the information embodied in a message, one must consider what the message does to a human being receiving it. One must ask how deeply it affects or changes him. One must, in other words, compare the state he was in before he received the message with his state after the message has done its work. No message about a particular topic gives information to somebody who already knows everything there is to know about that topic. Similarly, if somebody holds false beliefs about a topic so firmly that he will not admit of any possibility that he is wrong, he will be impervious to information about it. The only questions about which we can be informed are questions about which we do not feel completely sure. In other words, information implies prior uncertainty. The best way to define information is as something that reduces uncertainty. The quantity of information received from a message can then be equated with the degree to which uncertainty is reduced through its receipt.

INFORMATION THEORY

Psychologists interested in communication, perception, thought processes, skills, and motivation might very well sooner or later have developed measures of information in keeping with the view that has just been outlined. But as it happened, scientists, mathematicians, and engineers working outside the bounds of psychology originated measures of a rather different nature shortly after the Second World War.

Psychologists recognized their applicability to their own area of interest, as well as to a much broader range of questions. It was seen that measures reflecting the psychologically significant aspects of information transmission and reception could be derived from these other measures. There was the additional advantage that processes of interest to the psychologist could be seen as special cases of phenomena that take place throughout nature, both animate and inanimate, and it is, of course, one of the fundamental aims of science to find unifying concepts and principles.

So we must now look at the main measures introduced by what has come to be called information theory. This is a mathematical theory introduced by C. E. Shannon in an article first published in 1948. As is usually the case, some of his ideas had been anticipated by earlier workers. They have since been elaborated and applied to different kinds of subject matter in hundreds of books and articles. Shannon, who was then working at the Bell Telephone Laboratories, was concerned with some technical problems facing telecommunications engineers, but it soon became apparent that his innovations had a much wider scope than that. They are, in fact, capable of illuminating virtually every process in the universe. This means that they have a vast integrating power, as great as, if not greater than, that of the concept of energy that physical scientists worked out from the early part of the nineteenth century onwards. Whenever anything happens in the universe, energy either must be transferred from one object to another or must change its form, and the mathematical laws governing energy changes must be obeyed. Similarly, every occurrence in the observable world involves production or transmission of information, in the broad technical sense introduced by Shannon, and must obey the mathematical principles to which information is subject.

Psychologists are, of course, interested in what goes on inside human and animal organisms and in how they are affected by events in the environment, including messages, that impinge on them. But information as discussed by information theorists is something that can pass between two human or other living creatures, between a living creature and some region of the nonliving world or vice versa, or between two regions of the nonliving world. It is a matter solely of what kinds of events occur and how often. In other words, the measures introduced by information theorists depend on objective probabilities. These are the kinds of probabilities that mathematicians and scientists generally deal with. According to their usage, probability is defined as "relative frequency." How probable a particular kind of event is means the proportion of times when it hypothetically *could* occur that it actually *does* occur.

Uncertainty

The first information-theoretic measure that we must look at is commonly called *uncertainty*. It has sometimes been called "entropy," a term denoting a concept in thermodynamics to which it bears close mathematical relations. Nevertheless, the information theorist's measure of uncertainty does not refer to a psychological state of uncertainty, such as we were discussing earlier. It is more accurately regarded as a measure of variability. Variability in the physical world is usually what causes human uncertainty, but it can, nevertheless, exist independently of whether anybody is made uncertain by it or not.

Objective uncertainty (as we may call it to distinguish it from the subjective uncertainty existing in animals or human beings) is a measure that can be applied whenever we repeatedly encounter a particular kind of situation in which several alternative, mutually exclusive events occur at different times. Each event can then be assigned a probability value, which, as we have noted, represents its relative frequency of occurrence. Anybody who can list the alternative kinds of events and specify the probability of each can then calculate uncertainty (U).

The essential characteristics of such a measure are as follows. First, if the number of alternative events is held constant, uncertainty is greater the closer their probabilities come to being equal. Secondly, if their probabilities are equal, uncertainty will be greater, the greater the number of alternatives. As we shall see, information-theoretic measures do not always agree with everyday usage of the terms with which they are labeled, but in this case, there is a reasonable degree of accord. To take one topical example, there is obviously a great deal of uncertainty about who will be a party's candidate for the Presidency of the United States when a dozen politicians are campaigning for the nomination. We would surely agree that there is less uncertainty a few months later, when the possibilities are narrowed down to two or three, and that uncertainty has been eliminated altogether when the candidate has finally been chosen. Similarly, we would say that things are more uncertain when there are two candidates with comparable chances of success than when one of the two candidates is much more likely to win than the other.

The actual formula for uncertainty *(U)*, introduced by Shannon, takes into account both the number of different alternatives *(n)* and the probability of each of them *(p_i)*:

$$U = - \sum_{i=1}^{n} p_i \log_2 p_i \qquad (1)$$

This will give a value in "bits." The "bit" (abbreviated from "binary item") is a convenient unit. It represents the uncertainty that exists when there are two equally likely alternative events (the highest uncertainty that can exist with two alternatives). The point can perhaps be most easily understood if we think of the game of Twenty Questions. Uncertainty about the object that one player is thinking of is gradually reduced as the other player puts questions to him that can be answered either "yes" or "no." The most efficient way to play the game is to select questions that are equally likely to be answered affirmatively or negatively, i.e., questions that divide the range of possible objects remaining into two equal halves. Each such question will eliminate one bit of uncertainty, and the number of bits of uncertainty in any situation corresponds to the number of *efficient* yes-no questions that could narrow the alternatives down to a single one. A question that, on the other hand, is much more likely to be answered "yes" than "no," or vice versa (e.g., "Is it the Eiffel Tower?"), reduces uncertainty by less than 1 bit, which means that it is inefficient and wasteful.

Information Content

A measure of uncertainty can be worked out, then, whenever we have what, in probability theory, is called a "sample space," or what engineers call an *ensemble*. This is a situation in which we can enumerate what kinds of events might occur, and how probable each one is, but have no way of knowing which one will occur (or is occurring, or has occurred). As soon as we know which of the alternative possibilities is realized, we can assign a measure of *information content*. This is also customarily stated in bits and is defined by the equation

$$I = - \log_2 p \qquad (2)$$

Information content *(I)* is greater, the more improbable an event is, ranging from zero, when there is only one kind of event that could occur, to infinity, when an impossible event occurs. The uncertainty associated with a sample space is actually equivalent to the average information content of the various events that occur in it over a long period.

This technical concept of information diverges in at least some respects from what the term connotes in everyday usage. Suppose, for example, we are listening to a friend who is telling us over the telephone how he spent his vacation; and suppose that, in the middle of his account, without warning, he utters some nonsense syllables. According to the ordinary use of the word, we would say that his speech was very informative until he changed over to nonsense syllables, whereas the nonsense syllables conveyed no information whatever. But as far as the technical measure of information content is concerned, the opposite would be true. The nonsense syllables would have a much greater information content than sentences describing exciting experiences on the beach, because nonsense syllables occur much less frequently in the course of telephone conversations. Information content can be regarded as a measure of the degree to which an event is unexpected. It comes quite close to everyday concepts like surprise and news value. For example, it is a hoary old adage in journalistic circles that "Man bites dog" is news, whereas "Dog bites man" is not. This is, of course, because the former occurrence is relatively improbable, whereas the latter happens every day. Similarly, newspapers do not announce that the sun has risen because, in the light of previous experience, the probability of this event is 1. On the other hand, a total eclipse of the sun will be reported, because there are very few days on which it happens.

Rate of Information Transmission

The next important information-theoretic measure, namely *rate of information transmission (T)*, is applicable whenever we have two sample spaces, A and B, i.e., whenever we have two situations in which several alternative events can occur. We can then speak of an information channel linking sample spaces A and B, whether or not there is an actual physical connection between them. T represents the average amount by which uncertainty about what is happening in one sample space is reduced by knowledge of what is happening in the other sample space. In other words, it is a measure of the degree of correspondence or association between events in the two sample spaces. This makes it a useful measure of correlation comparable to chi-squared, product-moment correlation and other familiar statistical devices. There are several algebraically equivalent formulas for T, of which the most generally useful is probably

$$T = U(A) - U(A \mid B) \tag{3}$$

Here, $U(A)$ represents the initial uncertainty of sample space A, while $U(A \mid B)$ is the conditional uncertainty of A, also known as the "residual uncertainty." This is the uncertainty about what is happening in A that exists when a particular event is known to occur in B. If transmission is perfect, the conditional uncertainty will be equal to zero, so that transmitted information will equal the initial uncertainty, $U(A)$, which is the maximum value it can assume. If, on the other hand, the residual uncertainty is as high as the initial uncertainty, the transmitted information will be zero. The uncertainty about A cannot then be reduced at all by knowing about B. In well-functioning telephone lines and other efficient communication systems, perfect transmission of information can be achieved. After hearing the sound that comes out of the earphone, one can predict with complete precision and certainty what was said into the microphone at the other end. But in faulty telephone lines, and in most of the communication channels that occur in the natural world, the amount of transmitted information is somewhere between zero and the maximum. That is to say, conditional uncertainty is somewhere between the initial uncertainty and zero. On knowing what is happening in B, one is in a somewhat better position to guess what is happening in A, but there is still a chance of being wrong. This advantage, partial as it is, is far from worthless. There are many occasions when complete elimination of uncertainty is too much to hope for, and some uncertainty reduction is better than none. For example, it would be easy to make a fortune at the race track if one could guess with even a little better than chance success which horse will win a future race.

It is worth pointing out that information transmission in this sense is always symmetrical, and the average measure, T (which is, as we have noted, the usual measure), must have the same value, in whichever direction the information is considered to be going. For example, in a well-functioning telephone line, the listener is in a position to tell from the sounds he hears what the speaker is saying, but somebody stationed near the speaker is also able to deduce from what the speaker is saying what sounds will be heard at the other end. The average amount by which uncertainty about the input is reduced, on knowing the output, and the amount by which uncertainty about the output is reduced, on knowing the input, must always be equal whether information transmission is perfect or not.

Once again, we have a way of looking at things that make sense in terms of everyday linguistic usage in some respects but not in others. Suppose, for example, we had a telephone wire with a strange deficiency, such that whenever the speaker said "yes" into the microphone, the word "no" was heard in the earphone and vice versa. For the information theorist, this would be just as good a transmitter of information as the usual kind of line, which produces a close resemblance between the sounds that go into the input and the sounds that come out of the output. This may seem a little startling until it is realized that, once one had discovered the changes produced by this strange information channel and how regular they were, one could be just as well off as somebody fortunate enough to possess a normal telephone connection. One could still predict the input from the output, and vice versa, by deciphering the code. If, on the other hand, there were a telephone line that was equally likely to produce "yes" and "no," regardless of whether somebody said "yes" or "no" into the input end, information transmission would be zero, and the channel would be useless. On hearing the word "yes," the listener could deduce only that the speaker may have said "yes" or "no," which is exactly the position he would have been in without hearing what came out of the earphone at all.

Redundancy

The final information-theoretic measure that we must consider is *redundancy*. Suppose that we have a source of information capable of originating messages, each consisting of a certain number, n, of signals or elements. Suppose, further, that each signal can take any of m different forms. We could regard this source as a combination of n sample spaces, each having m alternative kinds of events. The maximum uncertainty that could be associated with such a source would be achieved if every one of the n signals took on every one of its m possible forms equally often. The uncertainty associated with each signal would then be $\log_2 m$ bits (the power to which 2 must be raised in order to obtain m), producing a total uncertainty of $n\log_2 m$ bits for the whole message.

However, the actual uncertainty attributable to a source of information, or system of sample spaces, is often considerably less than the maximum. This could happen in either of two ways. First, as we observed, uncertainty is maximal when the alternate events are all equally likely. So, uncertainty would be lowered if certain events occurred more often than others. This state of affairs, known as "distributional redundancy," is found in any message written in English or another natural language. If any letter of the alphabet or a space were equally likely to occur at any point, the uncertainty would equal $\log_2(27)$, or 4.9 bits; but certain letters occur much more frequently than others, so that the actual uncertainty is considerably lower. A person who, knowing nothing else, guessed that an e occupied a certain position in a sentence would be right more often than if he chose from the 27 possibilities at random.

Secondly, and perhaps more important, we can have "correlational redundancy." Suppose that, just after a particular signal has occurred, certain signals are more likely than others to follow. Identification of the first signal would then improve one's chances of guessing what the following signal would be. One could, in fact, regard two adjacent signals as belonging to two sample spaces between which there is information transmission. Uncertainty about the second is reduced by knowing what the first will be (and, of course, vice versa). This kind of interdependency is likewise characteristic of natural languages. For example, if one is receiving the letters making up a written message one by one and q has just appeared, there is very high likelihood the next letter will be u. As a result of both distributional and correlational redundancy, the actual uncertainty of messages written in normal English is about 50% of what it would be if all letters were used equally often and if each letter were equally likely to be followed by any other letter. Of several ways of measuring redundancy (R), the commonest, and probably the most useful, is to express it as a percentage of maximum uncertainty (i.e., as relative redundancy), i.e.,

$$R = \frac{U_{\max} - U}{U_{\max}} \times 100 \qquad (4)$$

Here, U_{max} means "maximum uncertainty" and U means "actual uncertainty."

Redundancy obviously runs counter to economy. To convey the same information, a message with 50% redundancy has to be twice as long as a message using the same vocabulary of signals with maximum uncertainty. But this is compensated by the advantage of protection in case of error. The presence of redundancy means that there is some degree of overlap or duplication between the information conveyed by different elements of the message. Consequently, if one element were misread or altered in transit, the recipient would encounter, and recognize, an improbable combination. This would tell him that there is probably something wrong. So he would perhaps take steps to recover the missing information by having the message transmitted a second time. Frequently, this is not necessary. If there is redundancy, clues supplied by the context can help him to work out what the incorrect element should have been. If, for example, somebody sees the word "qzick" in a written document, he can tell that the second letter is not what it should be, and he can readily correct the mistake. He may, in fact, not even notice the mistake, as proofreaders know to their cost. The perceptual processes in the brain make use of redundancy in constructing an image of print or other material that the eyes are examining and in following spoken words.

We can contrast this situation with what happens when numbers are used instead of letters. There is then generally no redundancy at all. Every one of ten numerals is usually just as likely as another to appear in a particular place in a multidigit number. As a result, there is no way of knowing whether a number has been transmitted accurately or not, and, even if one digit is known to be wrong, there is no way of finding out from neighboring digits what it should have been. If, for example, you have a friend who lives in a house with a four-digit number, the erroneous replacement of one single digit by another leaves you as badly off as if you did not know the number at all. When it is more important to save time and space than to guard against dangers of error, numbers are often used to replace letters and words, e.g., the number corresponding to an item of merchandise may be placed on an order form instead of a verbal description, and numbers sometimes replace phrases or sentences in telegraphic codes.

EARLY APPLICATIONS OF INFORMATION THEORY IN PSYCHOLOGY

In their attitudes to the new conceptual tools provided by information theory, psychologists went through a succession of phases, which are often found with theoretical innovations. First, there was a phase of exaggerated expectations. Some went so far as to believe that information theory could solve all the problems of psychology and that its language would be adequate for saying everything that needed to be said about psychological phenomena. Then came a phase of disillusionment, when some went to the opposite extreme and asserted that information theory had nothing of substance to offer to psychology. Now there are signs of a more balanced and sober appraisal. We can see that information theory offers us some conceptual analogies and measuring techniques that can be useful and even indispensable in some circumstances but that, like every other device used in scientific research, have their limitations.

As we have seen, information-theoretic measures can be used whenever a sample space of any sort is being considered, and there are at least two sample spaces that are of interest to the psychologist. One is the stimulus space consisting of the events that are perceived through sense organs. These can obviously take any of a large number of forms at any moment, and every combination or succession of perceived events (stimuli) can be considered as a message in the broad sense. Some of them will also be messages in the narrow and more usual sense, i.e., they will have been constructed by human beings for the express purpose of conveying information to other human beings. Secondly, there is the response space. The bodily movements that a person performs and the words that he utters at any particular moment are likewise selected from a wide range of alternative possibilities. Consequently, uncertainty values can be attached to aspects or portions of the environment and to the behavior of individuals in particular situations. When particular stimuli and particular responses occur, we can attach measures of information content to them. Furthermore, there is clearly some degree of information transmission between the stimulus space and the response space. If one knows what a person is seeing or hearing, one is in a better position than one would be otherwise to guess what he will do or say. But transmission along this channel will not be perfect; it will rarely be possible to predict the response with complete confidence and precision. The usual symmetry will also hold: knowledge of a person's responses will help one tó guess what stimuli he is perceiving.

Whenever somebody has to discriminate objects or events and describe them verbally or perform some act depending on them, information is being taken in from the external environment and transmitted through the nervous system to emerge incorporated in behavior. Psychologists were therefore excited quite early about the possibility of measuring the information that is transmitted through such processes as perception, manual skill, and thinking. Similarly, they have sought to measure the information that is stored when something is committed to memory and retrieved when what is remembered is recalled. They were particularly interested in the upper limits to the amount of information that the human nervous system can conduct. Like all information channels, the nervous system must have a maximum channel capacity, and errors and confusions must result when this capacity is overstepped. They were also eager to determine how long the nervous system took to process information, finding evidence that human subjects take longer to respond to a stimulus, the greater the initial uncertainty and therefore the greater quantity of information that has to be extracted from it before it can be identified.

With regard to the first problem, one interesting finding emerged from evidence reviewed by G. A. Miller (1956) in a famous article entitled "The Magic Number Seven—Plus or Minus Two." It appears that human beings can generally classify

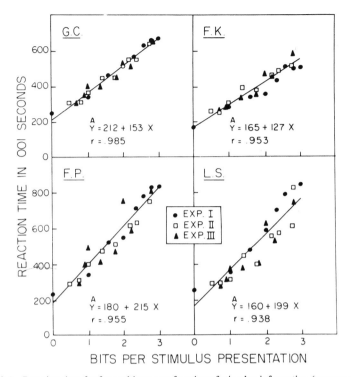

Fig. 2.1. Reaction time for four subjects as a function of stimulus information (expressed in bits) when amount of information was varied in different ways in three experiments. (From Hyman, 1953.)

stimuli into about seven categories with reasonable accuracy. This means that the information-transmitting capacity of the nervous system is somewhere between 2 and 3 bits per signal. If required to make finer discriminations than this, subjects are liable to show errors and inconsistencies. The limitation seems to hold whether subjects are required to estimate loudnesses of sounds, degrees of saltiness of liquids, numbers of points on a briefly exposed line, or the characteristics of many other sensory qualities. In this connection, it is worth noting that musical systems of all known societies use scales or modes of between five and seven pitches at once, and we are accustomed to talking about the seven colors of the rainbow, even though the number of discernible hues in the spectrum is much greater than that.

To turn to the second problem, Fig. 1 shows the results of an experiment carried out by Hyman (1953) on choice reaction time. Subjects had to note which of several lights came on in each trial and utter an appropriate syllable. Uncertainty was manipulated by varying the number of possible lights and their relative frequencies. As the graphs show, the time taken to utter the syllable after the lights became visible increased with stimulus uncertainty, and the points came close to fitting a straight line.

After a while, psychologists became a little less enthusiastic about information-theoretic measures, as they turned out not to maintain such stable values from situation to situation as at first seemed likely. Moreover, the graphs relating information-theoretic variables to stimulus and response variables did not always produce smooth, simple curves.

Nevertheless, measures of uncertainty, information content, and the like, continue to prove useful. How accurately objects can be discriminated, how quickly they can be recognized, how precisely a skilled movement can be timed and directed at a target, how much of something seen or heard can be recalled later, how readily the combination of characteristics denoted by a certain concept or word can be identified — all these are regularly found to depend, among other factors, on how much information is contained in each stimulus and on how much information has to be transmitted through the nervous system.

Perhaps even more important is the way in which psychologists have adopted a way of thinking derived from information-theoretic measures, even when they do not compute precise values for them. For example, several areas of research have been revolutionized by the recognition that the effects of a stimulus on behavior often depend on the sample space to which the stimulus belongs, i.e., on what other stimuli might have appeared in its place (Broadbent, 1958). Perception, memory, and reactions to stimuli in general are seen to be affected by how the stimuli are "coded," i.e., how possible stimulus events are divided up into alternative classes and how the alternative classes are labeled. Any coding invariably means taking into account certain characteristics of a stimulus and ignoring others, and this, in information-theoretic language, means transmitting part of the information content while discarding the rest. Analogies between human psychological functioning and operations of computers, which are, of course, machines for analyzing and processing information, are particularly popular at present.

INFORMATION-THEORETIC MEASURES AND MOTIVATION

In recent years, a completely different way of using information-theoretic notions in psychology has been establishing itself. I am referring to the use of measures and concepts derived, directly or indirectly, from information theory in the study of human motivation. Naturally enough, these problems concern behavior through which human beings seek access to information.

Here, in contrast with areas of research that we have just been discussing, the objective measures introduced by Shannon are less useful than their subjective counterparts. As we have observed, the objective measures depend on objective probabilities or relative frequencies. They denote mathematical and logical relations. They describe events that actually occur and what an observer could legitimately deduce from them. But motivation theorists must consider factors inside human beings that make particular kinds of information welcome and the impact (including the emotional impact) that information has when it is received. The measures of greatest interest to them must therefore depend on subjective probabilities. By the subjective probability of an event, we mean how likely a person judges an event to be, how confidently he would predict that it will take place, how strongly he is inclined to expect it, how much he would bet on its occurrence. Subjective probabilities can sometimes be estimated by asking subjects to state in some form how much chance they think there is of a particular event happening in a particular situation; but an event may have a subjective probability for an individual without his knowing it or being able to specify it. So, subjective probabilities have sometimes to be assessed more indirectly through behavior. One kind of procedure to which decision theorists have given a great deal of study, including mathematical analysis, involves asking people which of several alternative wagers they would prefer to accept.

So, if we substitute subjective probabilities for objective probabilities in Shannon's formula, we should obtain a serviceable concept of *subjective uncertainty*. This will increase with the number of alternative contingencies that the subject recognizes as possible in the situation of interest and with how close he comes to judging them equally likely. There will, of course, be a tendency for subjective uncertainty to be higher when objective uncertainty is higher. Our expectations are naturally very much affected by what kinds of events have occurred and, how often, when we have encountered comparable situations in the past. But they depend on other factors as well. Consequently, our estimates of probability may be seriously wrong, and we may fail to think of some possibilities that could materialize.

Uncertainty means psychological conflict, since a person who expects one of several things to occur, without knowing which it will be, must hold several competing forms of behavior in readiness. Since these are appropriate to mutually exclusive contingencies, they must interfere with one another in some way. Furthermore, a response appropriate to an event that may or may not take place must both be mobilized, in case it may have to be used, and held in check, as the corresponding event may not materialize. Thus, further conflict results.

The subjective equivalent of information content must be *surprisingness,* i.e., the extent to which a perceived event contradicts an expectation. Here, once again, there must be some degree of conflict between a response that was held ready for what was expected to occur and a different response, called forth by what happened in its place.

Finally, motivational phenomena may sometimes depend on the average amount of uncertainty reduction due to information received along a particular channel, which would be the subjective equivalent of the usual objective measure of transmitted information. But the *actual amount of subjective uncertainty reduction* consequent on perception of a particular stimulus will, one would imagine, be of more direct importance for motivation theory.

Curiosity

The term that has dominated discussions of motivation over the last half century is "drive." There is no general agreement among psychologists on the precise connotations of this term, and there are many who feel uncomfortable using it at all. Nevertheless, we can do our best to skirt contentious issues by recognizing that at least some human behavior, as well as animal behavior, seems clearly enough to conform to the following pattern.

First, there is some condition—it may be an external irritant (e.g., something pricking the skin, or excessive heat or cold) or a shortage of some vital commodity (e.g., food or water) — that upsets the organism's equilibrium and ultimately threatens its well-being and survival. This leads to a state of agitation, in which the organism is mobilized and alerted. Its capacities for taking in information through the sense organs, for processing information through the brain, for taking action through the muscles and glands, are raised to abnormally high levels that could not be maintained for long without stress. The organism may be highly restless and active. It may, on the other hand, be unusually motionless to outside view, while a great deal of ferment is taking place inside it. This is what psychologists have traditionally called a state of "heightened drive," although the term "arousal" has more recently been coming into use to denote these phenomena. A state of heightened drive is also a state in which certain kinds of behavior are likely to come to the fore, namely, kinds of behavior that are likely to eliminate the disturbance and reduce drive. Furthermore, events that relieve the drive state promote the learning of new responses that might be useful when similar conditions are encountered in the future.

Conditions like hunger and pain certainly seem to fit this picture. Animals and human beings suffering from them become aroused and excited. They tend to indulge in appropriate forms of behavior, namely, food seeking and flight, respectively. Responses that are followed by the appearance of food when the animal is hungry, or by the termination of pain, will be learned, so that they come to be performed relatively promptly when the same kind of problem recurs.

There have, during the last 10 years, been indications that subjective uncertainty and surprise (the subjective equivalent of high objective information content, i.e., low probability) can, like hunger and pain, induce a state of heightened drive with the kinds of consequences we have just been reviewing. This broadens our view of human motivation considerably. The newly recognized kinds of drive states we have been talking about are known both in technical writings and in everyday speech as "curiosity." A state of curiosity can be relieved by receipt of relevant information, capable of reducing the uncertainty that precipitated it. Furthermore, responses through which the relevant information can be obtained are likely to oust other forms of behavior and to undergo a learned strengthening, at times when curiosity is strong.

Let us look very briefly at some of the kinds of experimental evidence that have provided support for this view. Changes indicative of fluctuations in arousal can be detected, with the help of powerful amplifying equipment, in several systems of the body. Among the most useful of them are changes in the electrical activity of the brain, recorded through the electroencephalograph (EEG), and changes in the electrical properties of the skin (particularly a short-lasting drop in resistance known as the galvanic skin response or GSR). One way to induce subjective uncertainty is to present the human subject with a blurred picture. If the degree of blur is moderate, the subject is unable to identify the object depicted, but he can discern some of its properties and think of several possibilities without being sure which is the right one.

In one of our experiments (Berlyne & Borsa, 1968), we found that blurred pictures of familiar objects evoked EEG waves indicative of an alerted brain for a longer time than the clear versions of the same pictures. It was, of course, conceivable that this effect was caused by the blur as such, rather than by the uncertainty resulting from the blur. So we carried out a second experiment, in which a blurred picture sometimes was followed by the corresponding clear picture and sometimes was preceded by it. In the former case, the superior alerting power of the blurred picture still appeared, but when the blurred picture came after a clear picture of the same object, so that the subject knew what the object was and the blurred picutre was robbed of its ability to induce uncertainty, the effect was absent. So we are entitled to conclude that uncertainty was the responsible factor.

Another experiment was designed by Nicki (1968, 1970) to verify that uncertainty increases the likelihood of seeking information capable of lessening the uncertainty in preference to other information. He put his subjects through a number of trials, on each of which they first saw a blurred picture projected on a screen for 5 seconds. The blurred picture then disappeared, and the subject could press either of two keys, one of which caused a clear version of the same picture to be projected while the other one produced an unrelated clear picture. Subjects showed a gradual increase in the probability of performing the response exposing the relevant clear picture, i.e., the one providing information capable of removing the uncertainty. Once again, it was necessary to make sure that uncertainty was the operative factor. Nicki confirmed that it was in two ways. First, he found that if the related clear picture was projected before the blurred picture, which did not therefore generate uncertainty, the preference for pressing the key exposing the related clear picture was no longer in evidence. Secondly, he tried his procedure with different degrees of blur and obtained the effect only with a moderate degree of blur. This was the only degree that had been found in preliminary experiments to occasion a relatively high level of subjective uncertainty. In a variant of his procedure, Nicki used 20 general-knowledge questions (e.g., "What is the capital of Lithuania?") instead of blurred slides. The two key-pressing responses would then produce either a sentence recognizable as an answer to the question ("Vilnius is the capital of Lithuania") or a statement answering a quite different question (e.g., "The spider has eight eyes"). The subjects came, of course, to perform the former response more often than the other.

Blurred pictures were used once more in an experiment (Berlyne & Normore,

1972) designed to find out whether reduction of uncertainty would favor learning. This should be the case if curiosity is comparable to other forms of drive that receive more study. The experiment was concerned with what is called "incidental remembering": subjects were given no warning that they would be asked to recall anything later, so that they had no reason to make any special effort to commit the material to memory. Electrodes were, in fact, attached to their hands, and they were told falsely that GSR would be recorded, so that the true aim of the experiment was disguised. The subjects went through three kinds of trials, which were intermingled. In one kind, a blurred slide was exposed on a screen for 5 seconds, followed by the corresponding clear picture for 5 seconds. In another kind of trial, the clear picture appeared after a 5-second interval during which the screen was blank. In a third kind of trial, the clear picture appeared for 10 seconds.

Afterwards, subjects were asked to name as many of the objects depicted in the slides as they could recall. The objects that had appeared in a clear slide preceded by a blurred slide were remembered significantly more often than the others. This means that the sequence of uncertainty induction and uncertainty reduction produced better learning than exposing the clear slide for twice as long. That uncertainty was the crucial agent was verified by showing that the effect did not occur when a blurred picture came after the corresponding clear picture (precluding the induction of uncertainty) or when a blurred picture was followed by an unrelated clear picture (precluding the reduction of uncertainty).

Comparable results were obtained in other experiments (Berlyne, Carey, Lazare, Parlow, & Tiberius, 1968; Parlow, 1970) using different material and a different technique for generating uncertainty. These experiments studied "paired-associate learning." Subjects were shown a Turkish word (or what purported to be a Turkish word) next to an English word representing its meaning. They were later shown the Turkish words (without having expected a memory test) and asked to supply the English words that went with them. When subjects had been shown the Turkish word alone and been asked to guess its meaning before seeing the Turkish and English words together, recall scores were higher than when the Turkish and English words had appeared without the prior guessing phase. Instructions to guess must engender uncertainty regarding the correct answer and consequently conflict among alternative guesses. The effect did not appear if subjects were asked to guess the meaning of one Turkish word and were then shown a different Turkish word with its English translation. Then, uncertainty was induced but not relieved. It would appear, therefore, that both the initial phase of uncertainty and the subsequent phase of uncertainty reduction are necessary for incidental learning to be facilitated in this way.

Many other experiments have provided slightly less direct evidence for the connection between uncertainty and curiosity by studying exploratory or stimulus-seeking behavior. It can be assumed that the uncertainty attendant on the initial contact with a visual or auditory stimulus pattern will increase with the pattern's degree of complexity. Several experiments have shown that patterns tend

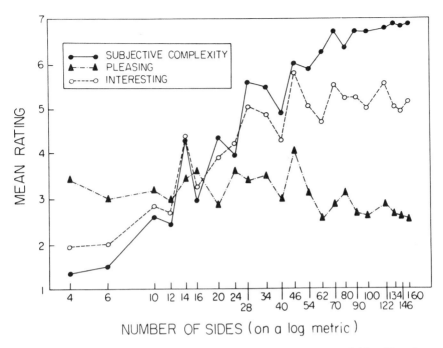

FIG. 2.2. Mean ratings on three scales of polygons with differing numbers of sides. (From Day, 1967.)

to be rated more complex the more elements they contain. Fig. 2 illustrates this with data from an experiment by Day (1967). He presented subjects with randomly constructed polygons having different numbers of sides. As the graph shows, the mean complexity rating went up steadily as the number of sides increased. Figure 3, taken from a doctoral dissertation by Crozier (1972), displays mean complexity ratings for tone sequences. Every sequence consisted of 40 tones, each lasting about .5 sec. Every tone had a pitch, a duration, and a loudness allocated to it at random. The number of alternative values from which these properties were selected varied from sequence to sequence, so that the total amount of uncertainty per tone could be worked out by adding the uncertainty values for the three properties. As can be seen from the figure, the curve relating mean complexity ratings to uncertainty per tone comes remarkably close to a perfectly straight rising line. Yet other experiments have demonstrated reductions in judged complexity when there is symmetry, or other forms of similarity or interdependence, among the elements of a pattern.

So, subjective complexity depends on the two factors that determine uncertainty, namely, the number of possibilities and the degree of redundancy. The more complex a pattern, the more information a subject has to absorb before its characteristics have been fully identified and his initial uncertainty about it has

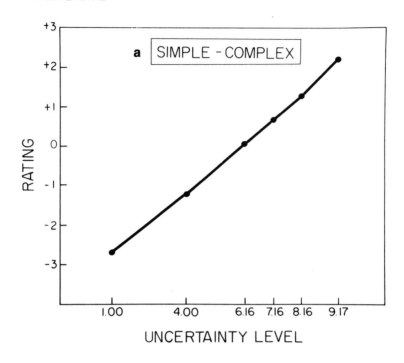

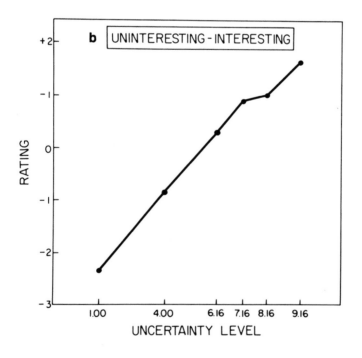

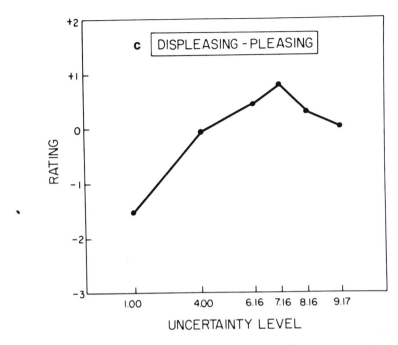

FIG. 2.3. Mean ratings of randomized tone sequences of differing uncertainty levels for *(a)* complexity, *(b)* interestingness, and *(c)* pleasingness. (From Crozier, 1972.)

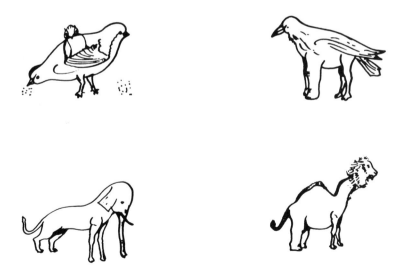

FIG. 2.4. Examples of incongruous pictures used in various experiments. (From Berlyne, 1958.)

been disposed of. It is therefore understandable that when people are allowed to look at, or listen to, a series of patterns one after another for as long as they wish, they invariably spend more time inspecting more complex patterns. Furthermore, when patterns of differing complexity are displayed side by side, the more complex pattern is more likely to attract the subject's gaze.

Then again, there are indications that surprising stimuli, i.e., stimuli with a high subjective information content, induce curiosity and exploratory behavior with particular effectiveness. When something happens that differs from what has usually been experienced in a certain context and contrasts with what was expected, we cannot feel comfortable until we have gathered more information about it to find out exactly what it is like and how it came about. The same applies to incongruous patterns (see Fig. 4) in which elements or properties that we do not expect to find together appear in combination. Experiments have shown that surprising and incongruous stimuli are looked at for a longer time than others. They have also been found to induce heightened arousal more markedly than other stimuli, as revealed by EEG and GSR recordings.

Boredom

The research we have just been discussing implies that, when a human being has insufficient information about some object or event that is presented to him, or when he receives information from it that jars with other information that he is receiving at the same time or that past experience has stored inside him, he has a desire or "drive" or (in one sense of the word) a "need" for information. But he is not then inclined to seek out just any kind of information. What he wants and what will assuage his uncomfortable state of uncertainty is relevant information, i.e., information coming from particular sources or with particular content, because such information alone can relieve the uncertainty. There are, however, other conditions in which we can talk about a desire or need for information that is quite different in origin. Furthermore, these are conditions in which the source and content of the information are of little account. More or less any kind of information will be welcome. What matters is the amount of information.

The conditions we are now considering constitute what we call "boredom." This is a state of discomfort that can arise either in an environment where little or nothing is happening or in an environment where what is happening is extremely monotonous. The intake of information is inordinately low in environments of both these kinds, because there can be little information entering through sensory inlets where there is little stimulation, and because repetitive stimulation leaves little room for surprise and uncertainty. In the 1920s Anitra Karsten (1928), a Finnish lady working with the famous psychologist Kurt Lewin in Berlin, reported some imaginative experiments on what she called "mental satiation." Subjects were kept at tedious tasks, such as covering sheets of paper with vertical strokes for hours on end. Sooner or later they found the situation intolerable, and many of them resorted to diabolically ingenious ways of circumventing the imposed monotony by varying their behavior surreptitiously.

Karsten's experiments formed an isolated attack on this important area of research, until the topic of "sensory deprivation" or, as it is sometimes called, "sensory restriction," was opened up by Bexton, Heron, and Scott (1954). These experimenters kept subjects in an almost silent room wearing translucent goggles, so that there was as little external stimulation as could be contrived. After this experience, various disturbances of perceptual and intellectual functioning, fortunately all of them temporary and reversible, were detected. But from our present point of view, the most interesting finding was the disagreeable nature of sensory deprivation. Despite the generous payment they received, it was difficult to persuade subjects to prolong the experience for more than a day or two. Some of them relished stimulation that they would normally disdain, such as recordings of stock-market reports and a talk designed for children. The absence of external stimulation was frequently compensated by rich internal stimulation in the form of imagination and reminiscence.

The craving for variable stimulation that sensory deprivation induces has been investigated most thoroughly by Jones (1966). After spending several hours in sensory deprivation, subjects were allowed to press buttons that produced random sequences of colored lights or sounds with varying degrees of unpredictability. More unpredictable sequences will, of course, yield a greater average information content per element. Subjects showed themselves more inclined to press a button, the more unpredictable the pattern it produced and the more time they had spent deprived of stimulation before they were allowed access to it.

Experiments like these point to a mounting eagerness for information intake when hours or days are spent in an impoverished environment. It is also known that information overload, due to an environment that is excessively and bewilderingly rich in unpredictable variation, can be disturbing. So there seems to be a moderate level of incoming information that human beings strive to maintain, taking corrective action when the information content of the environment exceeds it or falls short of it.

Some more recent experiments suggest that even a few seconds of low information influx can make a difference and that human beings take steps to regulate their level of information processing even over very short periods. One group of experimenters (Leckart, Levine, Goscinski, & Brayman, 1970) allowed subjects to look at slides, displaying random polygons, for as long as they wished. They varied the duration of darkness between two consecutive slides from 2 to 44 seconds and found (see Fig. 5) that the longer the preceding spell of "perceptual deprivation," as the experimenters called it, the longer the polygon was kept on the screen. In some of our own experiments (Berlyne, 1972; Berlyne & Crozier, 1971), subjects had to press either of two keys, one exposing a more complex visual pattern and the other a less complex pattern, on each of a succession of

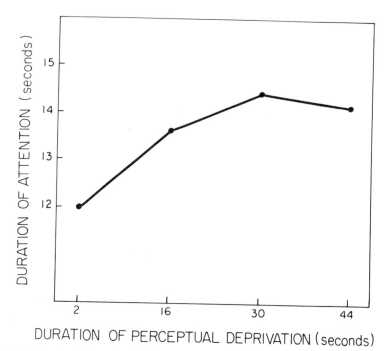

Fig. 2.5. Duration of inspection of polygons ("attention") as a function of duration of immediately prior perceptual deprivation. (From Leckart et al., 1970.)

trials. The two patterns between which they could choose were the same trial after trial. If the few seconds before the response was occupied with stimulation of low information content, they chose preponderantly to expose themselves to the more complex pattern. This was so if this prechoice period was occupied by darkness, by visual patterns that had been seen repeatedly, by white noise (a hissing sound), or by light music. If, on the other hand, subjects were presented during the prechoice period with stimulation that made demands on their information-processing capacities, i.e., colored slides of tourist attractions or excerpts from a recorded story, the preference for the more complex pattern disappeared.

Aesthetics

Information-theoretic concepts promise to be especially useful in the study of motivational aspects of behavior connected with the arts. Experimental aesthetics, the application of the methods of experimental psychology to aesthetic problems, is over 100 years old, but it was not pursued very intensively until recent years. Now there are abundant signs that it is entering a new phase of unprecedented vigor, and the influence of information theory is one of several developments that have given rise to the so-called "new experimental aesthetics" (Berlyne, 1971, 1972).

There are at least three ways in which information-theoretic analyses can be of value to the psychological aesthetician. First, they enable us to view a work of art as a fabric of interwoven pieces of information traceable to various sources. Every element of a work, whether it be a word, a musical note, a dab of color, or a ballet step, is selected from a set of alternatives with varying frequencies of occurrence, so that the work can be regarded as a message in the information-theoretic sense. Paintings sometimes depict scenes or objects. Novels and poems often describe events. In such cases some of the information content of a work is transmitted from environmental stimulus patterns that the artist has perceived at one time or another. He may do his best to depict them faithfully, or he may rearrange their ingredients to construct a fictitious story or an imaginary situation. But the impact of a work of art depends also on the way in which its subject matter is presented, on style or form as well as on content. This is the point made by the Rumanian mathematician, Marcus (1970), when he says that "the language of science admits many synonyms, but the language of art does not." In poetry, as compared with prose, what is said is, if anything, less important than how it is said. If the statements in a poem are couched in different terms, e.g., when the poem is translated into another language, it becomes a different, and probably inferior, poem. This means that part of the information content of a work of art is embodied in the manner in which the artist expresses himself. Some of it is information transmitted from (or, in ordinary language, "information about") processes going on inside the artist that may be peculiar to him or characteristic of some special group with which he identifies himself. The artist's work reflects his "feelings" about particular matters, or about the world in general, the way he "sees" them, what he thinks about them, his tastes, and what he regards as important and worthy of attention. Styles and schools of art differ in how much of the limited information-transmitting capacity of a work is taken up by information from these various competing sources.

A second application of information theory arises because the appeal of a work of art depends, at least partly, on "form," "structure," or "composition." In some artistic *genres*, such as absolute music, nonrepresentational painting, and concrete poetry, what these terms designate constitutes the whole substance of a work, but it is at least one important constituent of any artistic product. Philosophical aestheticians of previous centuries, as well as more scientifically minded theorists of the twentieth century, have used expressions like "uniformity in variety," "unity in diversity," and "order in complexity" in attempting to specify the essentials of formal beauty or aesthetic value.

We need some way of defining the factors named in these phrases, and ultimately of measuring them, since they can all exist in different degrees and the precise degree to which each of them is present is crucial. Information theory holds out hope of accomplishing this. The more "complexity," "variety," or "diversity" there is in a class of patterns, the greater the uncertainty associated with it and, consequently, the greater the information content of a particular pattern belonging to the class. When we say that one pattern has more "structure" or "organization" or "order" or "unity" than another, we mean that there are similarities, or, more generally, recognizable relations linking its elements, or that elements are readily grouped into subdivisions of the overall pattern. This implies that, when parts of a pattern are perceived, expectations are formed with regard to what other parts will be like. There is therefore transmission of information from one part of a pattern to another, which is precisely what is called redundancy. The expectations that are aroused in this way are often fulfilled, as when a work of art conforms to the rules governing a particular style or art form, but artists sometimes depend for their effect on violating them and doing something unexpected, which would not succeed if the expectations were not confirmed in most instances.

Lastly, there has been a great deal of experimental work on some of the verbal evaluations that seem pertinent to aesthetic appreciation. These have invariably turned out to be closely related to complexity and other properties of patterns that are bound up with uncertainty and information content. Such experiment have been carried out with a great variety of material, including visual patterns and arrangements, paintings and photographs, random sound sequences, musical passages, and pieces of poetry and prose.

The evaluative judgments that have been studied fall into two principal groups. How *interesting* a stimulus pattern is rated generally goes up steadily as complexity, novelty, and uncertainty increase, although there is sometimes a leveling off, or even a slight decrease, when these attributes reach extremely high levels. In contrast, when subjects are asked to indicate how pleasing, pleasant, beautiful, or good they deem a pattern to be, or how much they like it, intermediate levels of complexity, uncertainty, and novelty receive the highest ratings. These are evidently the levels that avoid the undesirable extreme of banality and tedium, on the one hand, and confusion and surfeit, on the other. Figures 2 and 3 provide illustrative graphs from Day's (1967) work with polygons and from Crozier's (1972) with random tone sequences.

THE BIOLOGICAL ROOTS OF INFORMATION SEEKING

The contemporary experimental psychologist, unlike the philosophical psychologists of this and previous centuries, is a psychobiologist, i.e., he inquires into the ways in which psychological phenomena are related to biological adaptation. He knows that human behavior depends on characteristics of the brain and other parts of the body that evolved because they enhanced our ancestors' chances of survival.

In line with this biological orientation, we must consider how the profound motivational importance of information may have originated in the course of evolution. There are two quite distinct lines of argument that can help us to answer this question and seem capable of throwing light on two distinct kinds of information-seeking behavior.

On one hand, we must recognize that subjective uncertainty is, from a biological point of view, a situation of great potential danger. When an organism cannot tell which of several occurrences may be imminent, when it is confronted with something whose nature, antecedents, and sequel are not clear, it is usually unable to tell what course of action to perform or to hold in readiness. Several conflicting modes of reaction will, in all likelihood, be initiated at once, and they will interfere with one another, causing disruption and maybe paralysis. It is therefore essential that animal organisms should have forms of behavior at their disposal through which the missing information that could relieve uncertainty is likely to be obtained. This information is needed, in the first place, to guide the behavior of the moment. But it must be borne in mind that the behavior of higher animals, including ourselves, is governed to a very large extent by learning, i.e., by stored information. Consequently, a further benefit of a strong tendency to chafe at uncertainty, and to seek ways of putting an end to it, is the likelihood that something will be learned, that information will be taken in and retained that could supply clues to appropriate behavior on future occasions.

So far, what has been said applies to behavior aimed at specific items of information, including what has been called "specific exploration" and other manifestations of curiosity. We have, however, noted that information is sometimes sought regardless of content or source, which means that specific uncertainties and curiosities are not at work. The behavior that then emerges has been called "diversive exploration." It is most clearly in evidence at times of boredom. To account for it, we must look for quite different biological requirements. One that comes to mind is the fact that sensory deprivation, or confinement to environments lacking in information and uncertainty, can impair various psychological functions. The same applies to environments that flood our sense organs with an excess of uncertainty and information. It seem that a situation requiring a moderately high level of information intake is the kind of situation that the human nervous system was made for and the kind in which it works best. It would appear, therefore, that we are so constructed that we feel uncomfortable when too much or too little information reaches us. We are then impelled to take remedial action, either by moving to a more satisfactory environment or by constructing a more satisfactory environment in our vicinity. The latter is, of course, what the artist or the interior decorator does, but it seems clear that the setting up and overcoming of uncertainty also plays a major part in aesthetics.

Finally, there is an argument that has been developed with supporting evidence by the outstanding animal psychologist, Schneirla (1959). The world is a dangerous place for most animals. It is full of creatures that are eager to pounce on them and devour them, as well as other threats of calamity. If, however, animals played safe by keeping away from stimulation, they would never gain access to biologically vital objects, such as food, water, and mates. They must therefore strike a balance between approaching sources of stimulation too readily and not approaching them enough. To a large extent, they receive guidance in resolving this dilemma from cues that function, whether through heredity or through learning, as signals of potential danger or of potential gratification. But these clues can scarcely be sufficient when unfamiliar objects are encountered. On the whole, highly novel, startling, or puzzling events—in other words, events productive of extremely high uncertainty or information content—are more likely to be harmful, whereas events possessing these properties to a lesser degree tend more often to be associated with beneficial conditions. We can, in the light of all this, understand why a tendency to seek out the former and shun the latter has become implanted in the constitution of the higher animals, including ourselves.

REFERENCES

Bar-Hillel, Y., & Carnap, R. Semantic information. *British Journal for Philosophy of Science*, 1953, **4**, 147–157.

Berlyne, D. E. The influence of complexity and novelty in visual figures on orienting responses. *Journal of Experimental Psychology*, 1958, **55**, 289–296.

Berlyne, D. E. *Aesthetics and psychobiology*. New York: Appleton-Century-Crofts, 1971.

Berlyne, D. E. Experimental aesthetics. In P. C. Dodwell (Ed.), *New horizons in psychology 2*. Hammondsworth, Eng.: Penguin, 1972.

Berlyne, D. E., & Borsa, D. M. Uncertainty and the orientation reaction. *Perception & Psychophysics*, 1968, **3**, 77–79.

Berlyne, D. E., Carey, S. T., Lazare, S. A., Parlow, J., & Tiberius, R. Effects of prior guessing on intentional and incidental paired-associate learning. *Journal of Verbal Learning and Verbal Behavior*, 1968, **7**, 750–759.

Berlyne, D. E., & Crozier, J. B. Effects of complexity and prechoice stimulation on exploratory choice. *Perception & Psychophysics*, 1971, **10**, 242–246.

Berlyne, D. E., & Normore, L. Effects of prior uncertainty on incidental free recall. *Journal of Experimental Psychology*, 1972, **96**, 43–48.

Bexton, W. A., Heron, W., & Scott, T. H. Effects of decreased variation in the sensory environment. *Canadian Journal of Psychology*, 1954, **8**, 70–76.

Broadbent, D. E. *Perception and communication*. London & New York: Pergamon Press, 1958.

Crozier, J. B. Verbal and exploratory responses to sound sequences of varying complexity. Unpublished doctoral dissertation, University of Toronto, 1972.

Day, H. I. Evaluations of subjective complexity, pleasingness and interestingness for a series of random polygons varying in complexity. *Perception & Psychophysics*, 1967, **2**, 281–286.

Hyman, R. Stimulus information as a determinant of reaction time. *Journal of Experimental Psychology*, 1953, **45**, 188–196.

Jones, A. Information deprivation in humans. In B. A. Maher (Ed.), *Progress in experimental personality research*. Vol. 4. New York: Academic Press, 1966.

Karsten, A. Psychische Sättigung. *Psychologische Forschung*, 1928, **10**, 142–254.

Leckart, B. T., Levine, J. R., Goscinski, C., & Brayman, W. Duration of attention: The perceptual deprivation effect. *Perception & Psychophysics*, 1970, **7**, 163–164.

Marcus, S. Two poles of the human language. *Revue Roumaine de Linguistique*, 1970, **15**, 187–198, 309–316.

Miller, G. A. The magic number seven—plus or minus two. *Psychological Review*, 1956, **63**, 81–97.

Nicki, R. M. The reinforcing effect of uncertainty reduction on a human operant. Unpublished doctoral dissertation, University of Toronto, 1968.

Nicki, R. M. The reinforcing effect of uncertainty reduction on a human operant. *Canadian Journal of Psychology*, 1970, **24**, 389–400.

Parlow, J. Effects of prior guessing on immediate recall of incidentally-learned verbal associations. Unpublished doctoral dissertation, University of Toronto, 1970.

Schneirla, T. C. An evolutionary and developmental theory of biphasic processes underlying approach and withdrawal. In M. R. Jones (Ed.), *Nebraska Symposium on Motivation, 1959.* Lincoln: University of Nebraska Press, 1959.

Shannon, C. E. A mathematical theory of communication. *Bell System Technical Journal,* 1948, **27**, 379 – 423, 623 – 656.

3
MEANING, FORCE, AND SYNTACTIC STRUCTURE

J. P. Thorne
University of Edinburgh

Consider the following sentence:

I hate boring students. (1)

Almost certainly you immediately noticed that it is ambiguous. How did you come to this decision? Put like this the question seems strange. All you did was just read the sentence. You certainly did not have to think what you were doing. First you understood it one way, then, suddenly, probably without having to read it a second time, you understood it another way. Just as when looking at an ambiguous drawing you see it first one way and then—as a result of no conscious effort—you see it another. At the moment we can do little more than speculate about the nature of the processes by which we recognize that a sentence like 1 has two meanings.[1] However certain facts relevant to the problem are clear enough. Obviously if you did not know English you would not be able to understand the sentence at all. By the same token your ability to see that it is ambiguous is a consequence of your using your knowledge of English. Let us then change the question. What information about English do you need to have in order to interpret the sentence in two ways?

A rough answer might go as follows. Anyone who knows English knows that (among many others) there are two particular syntactic contexts in which a verb like *hate* can occur. (Other examples of verbs of this kind are *love, detest,* and *worry about.*) The first is illustrated unambiguously by a sentence like

I hate students. (2)

[1]For some experimental evidence see Carey, Mehler, and Bever (1970) and Foss (1970).

Employing the very useful terminology that grammarians have developed over about the last three thousand years for describing the syntactic relationships between words, we can say that in this sentence the noun *students* is the object of the verb *hate* in 1. Then (if we are to make sense of the sentence at all) we must also take *boring* as an adjective going together with *students* to form a noun phrase. This is why the sentence

> I hate the boring students. (3)

is unambiguous. The definite article, *the*, only occurs at the beginning of noun phrases, so *boring* must here be an adjective. Similarly,

> I hate very boring students. (4)

is unambiguous because *very* only occurs in front of adjectives, as in *very pretty*, or adverbs, as in *very quickly*. Since *boring* clearly is not an adverb, then it must be an adjective in the noun phrase *very boring students*, all of which is the object of *hate*.

Thus one reading of Sentence 1 involves taking it as having the same syntactic structure as a sentence like

> I hate ugly students. (5)

We can represent this kind of information about the sentence in the form of a tree diagram, a schematic device commonly employed by modern linguists to reveal the hierarchical form of relationships between words of a sentence.

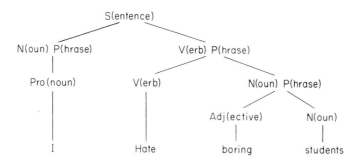

FIG. 3.1.

But now notice that under this reading Sentence 1 has exactly the same meaning as

> I hate students who are boring. (6)

It is, I think, fairly obvious that someone uttering Sentence 6 is, in effect, saying two things. The first is that he hates certain students. The second is that these students are boring. That is to say, Sentence 6 is a ''complex sentence'' made up of two ''simple'' sentences. A correct representation of the structure of this sentence must bring out this fact. It must also bring out the fact that the second sentence forms part of the object of the first, as in the following diagram.

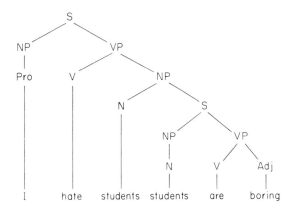

Fɪɢ. 3.2.

Although it is not quite so obvious, a moment's consideration should be enough to convince you that it is also the case that under the reading that we are presently considering, Sentence 1 is made up of two sentences; in fact the same two sentences. This is hardly surprising since, as we have already remarked, Sentence 1 and Sentence 6 have the same meaning. However, this mode of examining sentences helps one to see that for sentences to have the same meaning, not only must the individual words have the same meaning, but these words must relate to each other in the same way. It follows from this that the correct representation of the relationships between the words of Sentence 1 (again, under the reading we are presently considering) and the correct representation of the relationships between the words of Sentence 6 must be identical. If we look again at the representations previously assigned to these sentences it is easy to see that the representation assigned to Sentence 6 is in fact the correct representation for both sentences. For one thing Fig. 2 clearly contains more information than Fig. 1. Of course Fig. 2 relates more directly to Sentence 6 than it does to Sentence 1, which is presumably why it was easier for us to find the right representation for Sentence 6. In Sentence 6 the relationships between the words are more obvious. By comparison, in Sentence 1 those same relationships are obscured.

Let us now turn to the other interpretation of Sentence 1. The most obvious difference is that in this case we take *boring* not as an adjective but as a verb. As evidence for this we can cite the fact that under this reading Sentence 1 is an exact paraphrase of the unambiguous sentence

I hate to bore students.   (7)

We could also cite the fact that a sentence like

I hate meeting students.   (8)

is unambiguous, the reason being that *meeting*, unlike *boring*, can never be an adjective but can only be a verb. Notice that when we take *boring* as a verb in Sentence 1, then we take *students* as the object of this verb rather than of the other verb in the sentence, *hate*. But not only do we know the object of this verb, we also know what its subject is. When we read the sentence in this way we take it that *I*— the speaker—is not only the one who hates, but is also the one who bores students. In fact in sentences of this type (under this way of reading them) the subject of the first verb is always identical to the subject of the second. But in none of these sentences does the subject of the second verb actually occur. It does not have to occur for us to know what it is. Under this reading too, then, Sentence 1 is taken as composed of two sentences. In this case the second sentence forms not just part but the whole of the object of the verb of the first sentence. To show this we need to construct a representation of the sentence of this kind

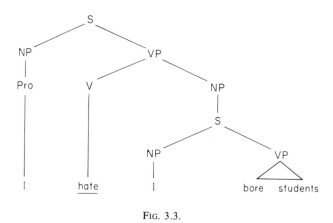

Fig. 3.3.

It is possible that the representations presented of the relationships between the words of Sentence 1 corresponding to two meanings of the sentence are quite wrong. They are certainly incomplete. I have simplified certain points in the analyses and others I have ignored altogether. Even so they serve to bring out three important points about the kind of information a native speaker possesses about the structure of his language. The first point to notice is that to the extent that these representations are correct (i.e., the extent to which the information concerning the structure of these sentences is genuine information) then this must be information possessed by everyone who can understand these sentences. This, of course, is not to say that in order to understand these sentences one must understand the terminology (noun, verb, subject, etc.) used to express this information. Clearly most people do not. Nor is it necessarily the case that those who possess this information — that is, anyone who can speak English — are aware that they possess this information. Clearly most people are not. Notwithstanding these points, and the previous point that we still have very little idea how people actually bring to bear the knowledge that they possess of the structure of their language to understanding sentences in it, it must be the case that they possess knowledge of this kind if they are to understand sentences in it at all.

The second point concerns the fact that a sentence is more than a mere list of words. This point is so obvious that it is easy to forget it. But in order to understand a sentence we must know not only what the individual words mean but also how they are to be related to each other. We arrive at one interpretation for Sentence 1 when we take *boring* and *students* as going together to form a verb phrase. We arrive at another interpretation when we take *boring* as a verb and *students* as its object. Where there are no relationships between the words there is no sentence. The result of rewriting Sentence 1 with the words in the reverse order

Students boring hate I.   (9)

is just a list of words. None of the syntactic relationships into which these words can enter obtains. We can understand each word but nothing more. They do not make up a sentence.

The third point is that what we know about the structure of a sentence cannot always be directly related to what we can actually observe in the sentence. Thus, in order to exhibit fully the relationships holding between the words in Sentence 1, we had to construct one representation containing words over and above those actually occurring in the sentence and another in which, also, some of the words occurred in a different order from that in which they occur in the sentence. In the actual sentences themselves these relationships are expressed in a far less conspicuous form. In fact, as we have seen, the same words in the same order can express two quite different sets of relationships. We also find in English (and probably in all natural languages) the converse of this, that is, cases in which different sentences express the same sets of relationships. Take, for example, active and passive sentences like

John kissed Mary.   (10)

Mary was kissed by John.   (11)

These have exactly the same meaning. Therefore, the relationships between the words in these sentences must be the same in each case, even though the word order is not the same and words occur in Sentence 11 which do not occur in Sentence 10.

The fact that some sentences have more than one meaning and that different sentences can have the same meaning can hardly have failed to strike anyone who pays any attention at all to what he says or to what other people say to him, for it is one of the central facts of language. And yet it has only been in the last few years that these phenomena have received serious attention from linguists. This interest dates from the publication of Noam Chomsky's first book *Syntactic Structures* in 1957. It is a central thesis of the theory of language called "generative grammar" that Chomsky has developed in this and subsequent works that a description of the observable form in which syntactic relationships manifest themselves in a sentence cannot in itself constitute an adequate account of its syntactic structure, and that an adequate account requires this description to be related to an abstract representation of these relationships. Chomsky calls the first the surface structure analysis of the sentence; and the second, the deep structure of the sentence. Thus, for example, the tree-diagram in Fig. 1 is a surface structure analysis of Sentence 1 and the tree-diagram in Fig. 2 is a deep structure analysis of Sentence 1.

For this reason the syntactic component of a generative grammer consists of two parts. The first is a set of rules (called phrase structure rules) that state the conditions that a deep structure must fulfill if it is to be the deep structure of a well-formed sentence. (For example, a tree-diagram in which every node was labelled *NP* could not be the deep structure of a well-formed sentence.) To ensure their completeness the rules are formulated in such a way that following them out in a purely automatic way will generate well-formed deep structures. Hence the term "generative" grammar. The second part consists of rules (called "transformational rules") that map deep structures onto well-formed surface structures. These rules permute or delete elements of deep structures or add elements to them.

A complete account of what a native speaker knows about a sentence in his language would not, of course, be restricted just to a description of its syntactic structure. It would include an account of what it means (its semantic structure) and of how it is pronounced (its phonological structure). Indeed, as I have tried to show, the whole point of formulating the deep syntactic structure of a sentence is to provide the basis for an adequate account of its meaning. A list of the meanings of the individual words it contains does not comprise the meaning of the sentence — because a sentence is more than a mere list of words. In addition to information about the meaning of the individual words, a description of the semantic structure of a sentence must also contain information about the meanings of the ways in which the words relate to each other. For example, the fact that under the second reading of Sentence 1 we take it that the speaker is the source of sensations of boredom in students is a consequence of the fact that we take the first person pronoun *I* as the subject of the verb phrase *bore students*. This is indicated in the deep structure where *I* is shown as the noun phrase associated with this verb phrase but is not shown in surface structure because one of the transformational rules that maps this deep structure onto the surface structure deletes this occurrence of the pronoun. We can therefore think of the semantic structure of a sentence as a projection onto, or an interpretation of, its deep syntactic structure. Similarly we can think of the phonological structure of a sentence as an interpretation of its surface syntactic structure. Just as we cannot stipulate the meaning of a sentence by taking into consideration only the meanings of the individual words it contains, so we cannot stipulate the sound pattern of a sentence by taking into consideration only the sound patterns of the individual words it contains. Again syntactic considerations play a part. For example, the way in which we pronounce the word *convict*, with the major stress either on the first or on the second syllable, depends entirely on whether we take it as a noun or a verb.

A complete grammar—that is, a model of the knowledge that enables us to associate speech sounds with meanings, the knowledge that enables us to speak a language — must incorporate one set of rules for generating deep structures and another set of rules for mapping these onto surface structures, together with a set of phonological rules for interpreting surface structures and a set of semantic rules for interpreting deep structures.[2] However this is to describe a program for research rather than something we already possess, and many problems which are critical for understanding the operation of language remain to be solved.

For example, consider the sentence

Listen carefully.   (12)

It is a good example of a sentence in which an element is, as the traditional grammarians put it, ''understood''; that is, where an element that occurs in the deep structure of the sentence does not occur in its surface structure. How are we to understand the transformation of such deep structures? Anyone who knows English knows that the subject of this sentence is *you*, evidence for this being that an exact paraphrase of the sentence is

You listen carefully.   (13)

But Sentence 13 has two interpretations, depending on whether we take it as an imperative or a declarative sentence. It is, of course, only as an imperative that it can be taken as a paraphrase of Sentence 12. The problem is whether this difference between the two interpretations of Sentence 13 can be explained in terms of its being derived from two different deep structures.

Katz and Postal (1964) propose that the phrase structure rules of the grammar should be written in such a way that the two deep structures assigned to Sentence

---

[2]For a full account of this model see Chomsky (1965).

13 would be of the following kind.

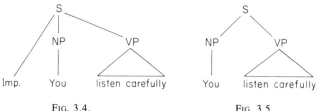

FIG. 3.4.   FIG. 3.5.

It can then be ensured that transformations which take effect only in the production of imperative sentences (such as the deletion of the vocative pronoun subject) will operate only upon deep structures containing the element *Imp*, so that (quite correctly) a sentence like Sentence 12 will receive only one analysis.

But this still leaves us with the problem of the interpretation of *Imp*. Or rather with the problem of whether, strictly speaking, *Imp* has an interpretation. Clearly the way in which the two interpretations of Sentence 13 differ from each other does not exactly parallel the way in which the two interpretations of Sentence 1 differ from each other. But is this to say that the difference between the two interpretations of Sentence 13 should not be described as a difference in meaning? Should we instead explain the difference between the two interpretations making use of a distinction suggested by Austin (1962) and say that under these two readings the sentence has in each case the same meaning but a different force? In which case *Imp* would be taken as relating to the force rather than the meaning of the sentence.

An observation that is clearly relevant to this discussion is that a possible paraphrase of Sentence 12 is

I order you to listen carefully.   (14)

The verb *order* belongs to the class of verbs that Austin calls performative verbs. Other performative verbs are *promise, name, bet, warn*, and *concede*. Austin calls these performative verbs, because to utter sentences like

I promise to come.   (15)

or

I warn you not to laugh.   (16)

is in effect to perform certain kinds of acts which Austin calls "speech acts"—the acts of promising and warning. What makes these sentences count as a promise and a warning is clearly the presence in them of the verbs *promise* and *warn*. This distinguishes these verbs from other verbs in these sentences, *come* and *laugh*, which clearly have no such performative function. But we are overlooking an important grammatical point. Only if the sentences contain these verbs in the first person and in the simple present tense can they be used to perform the acts of promising, warning, etc.

I promised to come.   (17)

is not a promise but a statement, as is

He promises to come.   (18)

While in the case of the sentence

I promise to come whenever she leaves.   (19)

for which there are two readings, it is only under the reading in which *promise* is taken as simple present tense that it is a promise. Under the other reading, in which *promise* is taken as habitual aspect, the sentence is roughly paraphrasable as

I always promise to come whenever she leaves.   (20)

This is a statement. The same, of course, is true of sentences containing the verb *order*. To utter the sentences

I ordered you to listen carefully.   (21)

and

He orders you to listen carefully.   (22)

is not to issue orders but to make statements about orders that have been issued. Similarly Sentence 14 only counts as an order if the verb is taken as being simple present tense. But, of course, it is only under these conditions that it can be taken as a paraphrase of Sentence 12.

This is far from being the only parallel between sentences like 12 and 14. Sentence 12 must have a vocative subject: vocative noun phrases being those which the speaker can use to address those to whom he is speaking, for example, *you, you boys, waiter, John.* For this reason sentences like

The boy listen carefully.   (23)

are not well-formed. Now although the verb *order* can take as its complement a sentence without a vocative subject, for example

I ordered the boy to listen carefully.   (24)

the subject of the complement must be vocative when it functions as a performative verb. If it is possible to regard the sentence

I order the boy to listen carefully.   (25)

as well-formed (which I doubt) then it seems to me that it must be construed as a statement, not an order.

The verb in a sentence like 14 must be tenseless. A sentence like

You listened carefully.   (26)

cannot be taken as an imperative sentence, while sentences like

Listened carefully.   (27)

are always ill-formed. But so too are sentences like

I order you listened carefully.   (28)

Again, whereas there is nothing unusual about imperative sentences having "activity" verbs like *kiss* or *kick*, or in which the predicate is an adjective like *great* or *careful*, imperative sentences in which the verb is a "stative" verb like *know* or *believe* or in which the predicate is a stative adjective like *tall* or *old* are always anomalous. For example

Know that she is late.   (29)

and

Be tall.   (30)

The same is true of sentences like

I order you to know that she is late.   (31)

and

I order you to be tall.   (32)

The fact that the conditions required for the well-formedness of the complements of the performative verb *order* are exactly the same as those for the well-formedness of imperative sentences would seem to constitute strong evidence for the claim that sentences like 12 and 14 are essentially the same sentence, that is, deriving from the same deep structure, the only difference between the two being differences of surface structure resulting from the operation of deletion transformations removing the elements *I order you to*.

On the basis of the premise that the deep structure both of Sentences 14 and 12 is the following:

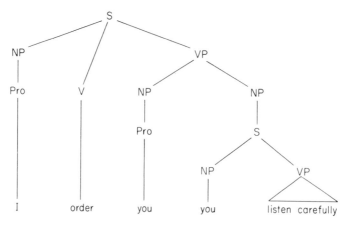

FIG. 3.6.

one would obviously want to argue that the force of the sentence derives entirely from its meaning, irrespective of whether those elements that determine its force appear in its surface structure or not, and that the reason that both Sentence 12 and 14 can be used to issue orders is that they have the same meaning. We must, however, take into consideration the fact that *I order you to listen carefully* represents only one possible interpretation of Sentence 13. Others include *I request you to listen carefully,* and *I implore you to listen carefully.* From the point of view of their meaning it is natural to regard these verbs, together with *order*, as all belonging to the same class. Moreover, notice that the conditions on the well-formedness of the complements that these verbs can take are exactly the same as those that apply in the case of *order*.

I implore the boy to listen carefully. (33)

I entreat you listened carefully. (34)

I request you to know that she is late. (35)

are all ill-formed. And just as *I order you to listen carefully* has the force of an order only when *order* is taken as simple present tense, so *I request you to listen carefully, I entreat you to listen carefully,* etc. have the force of a request and an entreaty, respectively, only when the performative verbs in these sentences are taken as simple present tense. Hence the transformational rule that is required to map the deep structures of the sentence *Listen carefully* and *You listen carefully* can be stated very simply. From any deep structure containing the elements *I verb you S,* where the verb is one of the class of imperative verbs like *order* and *entreat* and is acting as a performative verb (that is, when it is a simple present tense verb), the constituent *I verb you* can be deleted. [3]

If this analysis of imperative sentences is correct then it should be possible to provide corresponding analyses for other sentence types. It is easy enough to see how a case could be made for deriving interrogative sentences from deep structures containing the performative *I ask* (perhaps to be analyzed as *I request you to say*), but the crucial case seems to be declarative sentences. The difference between uttering an imperative sentence and uttering a declarative sentence is not that in the first case one performs a speech act and in the second case one does not, but that different speech acts are performed in each case. Anyone who wants to claim that imperative sentences derive from underlying structures that contain a performative verb must therefore also be prepared to make a case for claiming that declarative sentences derive from underlying structures containing a performative verb.

Linguistic arguments in support of a performative analysis of declarative sentences have recently been advanced by Ross (1970). Among these arguments are the following. Sentences containing first person emphatic reflexive pronouns like

Physicists like myself rarely make mistakes. (36)

---

[3]This discussion of imperatives follows closely that in Lakoff (1968) except that Lakoff argues that the imperative verbs in the deep structure of these sentences are "abstract" verbs.

are well-formed, but the corresponding sentences containing third person emphatic reflexive pronouns are not, for example

Physicists like himself rarely make mistakes.   (37)

However, sentences of this kind do occur as well-formed complements in complex sentences like

Tom claims that physicists like himself rarely make mistakes.   (38)

On the basis of sentences like 38 we might be led to propose that the rule governing the occurrence of emphatic reflexive pronouns is that they must agree in number and gender with the subject of the verb of which the clause in which they occur is the complement. Hence the ungrammaticality of the following through such lack of agreement

Tom claims that physicists like *themselves* rarely make mistakes.   (39)

and

Tom claims that physicists like *herself* rarely make mistakes.   (40)

This would also account for the ungrammaticality of Sentence 37. But it would leave unexplained the grammaticality of Sentence 36. If, however, we were to postulate for these sentences deep structures roughly equivalent to *I tell you that physicists like myself rarely make mistakes* and *I tell you that physicists like himself rarely make mistakes,* then the same rule, stating that an emphatic reflexive pronoun must agree in number and gender with the subject of the verb of that sentence whose complement the pronoun occurs in, will account for the grammaticality of Sentences 36 and 38 and the ungrammaticality of Sentences 37, 39, and 40. If we then amend the rule to read ''an emphatic reflexive pronoun must agree in number and gender with either the subject or the object of the verb of which the clause in which they occur is the complement,'' then we can also account for the grammaticality of

Physicists like yourself rarely make mistakes.   (41)

Ross has an analogous argument based on the evidence provided by sentences like

This paper was written by Anne and myself.   (42)

This paper was written by Anne and himself.   (43)

Tom asserts that this paper was written by Anne and himself.   (44)

I tell you that this paper was written by Anne and myself.   (45)

Here again the hypothesis that declarative sentences, irrespective of whether or not they contain a declarative performative verb in their surface structure, are derived from underlying structures containing such a verb enables us to explain the grammaticality of Sentences 42, 44, and 45 and the ungrammaticality of Sentence 43 by the same rule concerning reflexive pronouns.

Another argument that could be adduced in support of this analysis of declarative sentences (though it is not one that Ross uses) concerns certain adverbs such as *frankly, honestly,* and *incidentally.* Traditionally this group of adverbs have been described either as manner adverbs, i.e., ordinary adverbs denoting the manner of action of the verb, in sentences like

She spoke to him quite frankly.   (46)

or as sentential adverbs, i.e., adverbs which in some way modify the entire sentence, in sentences like

Frankly, I don't care.   (47)

This description of the adverb in Sentence 47, implying as it does the analysis

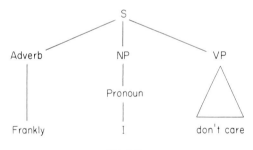

FIG. 3.7.

is not very illuminating, since it is difficult to see from this description what it is that the adverb is modifying. If, on the other hand, we adopt Ross's hypothesis we are able to supply a far more satisfactory explanation of the function of *frankly* in this sentence, since we can take it as a manner adverbial here too, in this case modifying the declarative performative verb which is present in the deep structure but not in the surface structure. The deep structure of Sentence 47 would now be:

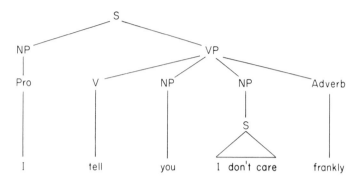

Fig. 3.8.

Additional support for this analysis of declarative sentences comes from its having the further, and unexpected, advantage of providing what seems to be an important insight into the grammar of nonrestrictive relative clauses. The brief discussion of relative clauses above failed to mention the important point that relative clauses are of two kinds, traditionally called restrictive and nonrestrictive. The two constructions are usually not distinguishable in ordinary speech, but in careful speech nonrestrictive relative clauses can be marked by pauses before and after the relative clause and are usually reflected orthographically by the insertion of commas in these positions. Thus

The girl who he liked left.   (48)

is usually read as a restrictive relative clause while

The girl, who he liked, left.   (49)

is usually read as a nonrestrictive relative clause. The easiest way (significantly, as we shall see) of distinguishing restrictive and nonrestrictive relative clauses is in terms of their different uses. Restrictive relative clauses are used to identify individuals. Nonrestrictive relative clauses are used to supply additional information about individuals. This provides at least part of the explanation of why usually only nonrestrictive relative clauses can be attached to a proper name as in

Sebastian, who voted for Lloyd George, was a liberal.   (50)

Here the relative clause has to be taken as nonrestrictive, the use of a proper name usually being sufficient in itself to identify an individual. Only where the use of a proper name is not sufficient to identify an individual can a restrictive relative clause be attached to it, as in

The Sebastian who I know lives in Baltimore.   (51)

This description of the use of nonrestrictive relative clauses as being to supply additional information about individuals fits in well with the fact that sentences containing nonrestrictive relative clauses can always be paraphrased by sentences in which the two clauses are conjoined by *and*. Thus, for example, Sentence 50 has the paraphrase

Sebastian was a liberal, and he voted for Lloyd George.   (52)

Also, and more strikingly in view of the way in which the second clause is embedded within the first, it can be paraphrased

Sebastian, and he voted for Lloyd George, was a liberal.   (53)

These observations form part of an explanation of why it is that nonrestrictive relative clauses cannot be attached to noun phrases containing quantifiers like *any* and *no*; for example

Any girls, who I liked, left.   (54)

and

No girls, who I liked, left.   (55)

For notice that the same restrictions apply in sentences in which these clauses are conjoined by *and*,

Any girls left, and I liked them.   (56)

No girls left, and I liked them.   (57)

At this point it is important to notice that sentences containing two clauses conjoined by *and* are in fact of two quite different types. One type is exemplified by paraphrases for nonrestrictive relative clauses like Sentence 52, and the other type is exemplified by

Sebastian was a liberal and he voted for Lloyd George.   (58)

As in the case of the comparison between restrictive and nonrestrictive relative clauses, the superficial difference between these two kinds of sentences is only very slight, and again it is usually marked only in careful speech, the difference being the occurrence of a pause before the conjunction *and,* and is marked orthographically by a comma. These two types of conjoining are further distinguished by the fact that in the second case we are very likely to drop the pronoun in the second clause as in

Sebastian was a liberal and voted for Lloyd George.   (59)

Indeed, when we leave it in, the sentence seems rather stilted. This is not the case with Sentence 52. Rather than omitting the pronoun in the second clause we are more likely to stress it. This last point provides us with an important clue as to the difference between these sentences. For notice that Sentences 58 and 59 carry the implication that Sebastian's voting for Lloyd George was a normal consequence of his being a liberal. On the other hand Sentence 52, particularly when the pronoun is stressed, carries the implication that Sebastian's voting for Lloyd George was not a normal consequence of his being a liberal. I would suggest this is because in the first case Sebastian's being a liberal and his voting for Lloyd George form part of the same assertion, whereas in the second they form two separate assertions. That is, in uttering Sentences 58 and 59 the speaker asserts that Sebastian was a liberal and voted for Lloyd George; in uttering Sentence 52 he first asserts that Sebastian was a liberal and then asserts that he voted for Lloyd George.

On the basis of the arguments advanced above one would expect these differences to be reflected in the deep syntactic structure of these sentences. One would expect the deep structure of Sentences 58 and 59 to contain one performative verb as in

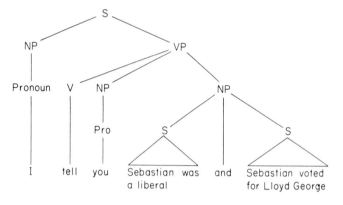

FIG. 3.9.

and the deep structure of Sentence 52 to contain two performative verbs as in

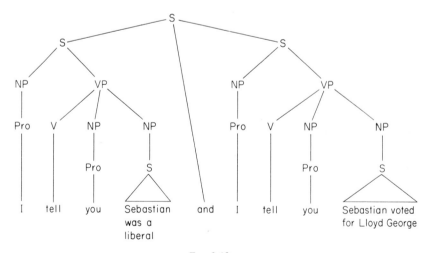

FIG. 3.10.

One way in which one could argue in support of these analyses is as follows. It was pointed out above that the difference between these two kinds of conjoining is only marked in careful speech. In cases where there is no pause made before the conjunction it is usually impossible to tell in which of the two possible ways the utterance is to be taken. However in the case of the sentence

Sebastian was a liberal and incidentally he voted for Lloyd George.   (60)

even when no pause is made before the conjunction (though I would maintain that this would be a very unnatural way of saying this sentence), there seems to be no doubt that it must be taken as comprising two assertions rather than one. Given the representations of the deep structures of the two kinds of conjunctive sentences proposed above, it is possible to provide a syntactic explanation for this fact. Notice first that in both cases it was postulated that the first clause is the complement of a declarative performative verb. (This follows directly from Ross's hypothesis.) In order to explain why only one interpretation is possible in the case of Sentence 60 one must show why in this case the second clause cannot also form part of the complement of the same declarative performative verb. The reason, of course, is the presence of the adverb *incidentally*. *Incidentally* cannot be taken as modifying any of the verbs which occur in the surface structure of the sentence. It was argued above that in this case it must be taken as modifying a performative verb associated with the first clause. By contrast, in a sentence like

I tell you Sebastian voted for Lloyd George, and incidentally, he used to be a liberal.   (61)

there is no question of the adverb modifying the performative verb at the beginning of the sentence. We must, therefore, postulate a second performative verb associated with this second clause. Thus Sentence 60, a sentence where, it has been suggested, the speaker makes two assertions not one, is also a sentence which purely syntactic considerations lead us to analyze as one in which two performative verbs are conjoined.

Exactly the same kind of arguments can be used to show that nonrestrictive relative clauses derive from structures in which two performative verbs are conjoined (that is from deep structures of the type illustrated in *Fig. 10* not *Fig. 9*).

It was pointed out above that restrictive and nonrestrictive relative clauses are differentiated only in careful speech. Hence we can regard a sentence like

The girl who he admired left the room blushing.   (62)

as ambiguous: That is, we can interpret the relative clause either as restrictive or nonrestrictive. But in the sentence

The girl who frankly he admired left the room blushing.   (63)

the relative clause can only be taken as nonrestrictive. It seems quite impossible (except as a result of quite unnaturally taking *frankly* as modifying *admired*) to force an interpretation on the sentence in which the relative clause is read as restrictive. Here again the key fact seems to be that in the position in which it occurs in the sentence *frankly* must be taken as modifying a performative verb associated in the deep structure with the relative clause. Thus the case in which the relative clause has to be taken as nonrestrictive is also the case in which syntactic arguments lead us to postulate an additional performative verb associated with it. On the other hand, notice that if the adverb occurs in a position in which it can naturally be taken as modifying one of the verbs that occurs in the surface structure of the sentence, as in

> The girl who he frankly admired left the room blushing.   (64)

then the relative clause can be taken as either restrictive or nonrestrictive. It is difficult to see how this could be accounted for on the basis of any other hypothesis concerning the structure of sentences containing nonrestrictive relative clauses.

Further support for this hypothesis comes from the fact that sentences like

> No girl who frankly he admired was ever chosen.   (65)

are not well-formed. Only restrictive relative clauses, it was pointed out above, can be attached to sentences whose subjects contain quantifiers like *no* and *any*, but the presence of the adverb here forces us to take the relative clause as nonrestrictive. On the other hand, when it occurs in a position in which it can be taken as modifying a surface structure verb as in

> No girl who he frankly admired was ever chosen.   (66)

then the sentence is well-formed. For the same reason a sentence like

> The girl frankly he admired left the room blushing.   (67)

is not well-formed. The relative pronoun, *who*, can be omitted from a restrictive relative clause but not from a nonrestrictive relative clause. Hence the sentence

> The girl he admired left the room blushing.   (68)

is unambiguous. But in Sentence 67 at the same time that the absence of the relative pronoun indicates that the relative clause is restrictive, the presence of the adverb *frankly* at the beginning of the relative clause indicates that it is nonrestrictive. As a result, the sentence cannot be interpreted.

Finally there is the evidence supplied by the fact that sentences like

> Tom claimed that the paper which was written by Anne and himself was stolen.   (69)

and

> Albert says that the kind of mistakes which physicists like himself make are rarely fatal.   (70)

appear well-formed if the relative clauses are taken as restrictive but not if they are taken as nonrestrictive. Remember that the rule concerning emphatic reflexive pronouns is that they must agree in number and gender with either the subject or object of the verb of which the clause in which they occur is the complement. This condition is fulfilled when the relative clauses are taken as restrictive, in which case they form part of the complement of the verbs *claimed* and *says* whose subjects are *Tom* and *Albert*, respectively. The hypothesis that nonrestrictive relative clauses are always the complement of *I tell you* would explain why this condition cannot be fulfilled if these clauses are taken as nonrestrictive, for the pronoun *himself* fails to agree with the subject *I*. Notice in this connection that, as one would expect, the sentence

> Tom claimed that the paper was stolen, and it was written by Anne and himself.   (71)

is not well-formed as opposed to

> Tom claimed that the paper was stolen and that it was written by Anne and himself.   (72)

The hypothesis that sentences containing nonrestrictive relative clauses have deep structures in which two performative verbs are conjoined helps to explain many facts concerning the grammar of these sentences.[4] In addition it can be seen as providing an explanation of why they are used in the way they are. The use of nonrestrictive relative clauses was characterized above as being to supply additional information about an individual. The point can now be made more precisely. In uttering a sentence like 50 (as in uttering Sentence 52, which we analyzed as having the same deep structure) the speaker is making two assertions. The main clause is used to make one assertion about an individual; the nonrestrictive relative clause is used to make an additional assertion about the same individual.[5] But it could be claimed that this is predictable from the deep structure of the sentence. Put more generally, the hypothesis is that the sentence has the use that it has because it has the meaning that it has.

Throughout this discussion I have tended to minimize, if not to abandon altogether, the distinction between the meaning of a sentence and its force by trying as far as possible to account for the force of a sentence in terms of its meaning. This has involved postulating performative verbs in the deep structure of sentences that have no such verbs in their surface structure. I have tried to show that this can be justified by arguments relating solely to questions of syntactic structure. It should however be emphasized that these arguments cannot be

---

[4]Notice also that Sentence 53 — where the second conjunct has been moved to a position within the first conjunct, the characteristic position for the nonrestrictive relative clause — must be read as two assertions. See also the discussions in Staal (1970) and Thorne (1972).

[5]There is another type of sentence containing a nonrestrictive relative clause exemplified by sentences like *The picnic had to be cancelled, which was a pity*. But the analysis of these sentences does not differ in essentials from that of these discussed above. Notice that the sentence just cited has the paraphrase *The picnic had to be cancelled, and that was a pity*.

regarded as conclusive. It might well be that the whole enterprise is doomed to failure. Not only might it be the case that the distinction between meaning and force is irreducible, it might also be the case that the force of a sentence cannot in any way be related to its deep syntactic structure and that the imperative and declarative force of simple imperative and declarative sentences is determined entirely in relation to certain surface structure characteristics. At the moment perhaps all that it is safe to conclude is that in their search for abstract representations of the meanings of sentences linguists cannot afford to lose sight of the obvious fact that sentences are representations of utterances and that utterances are used by human beings to communicate with each other.

REFERENCES

Austin, J. L. *How to do things with words.* Oxford: Oxford University Press, 1962.

Carey, P., Mehler, J. & Bever, T. When do we compute all interpretations of an ambiguous sentence? In G. B. Flores d'Arcais & W. J. M. Levelt (Eds.), *Advances in psycholinguistics.* Amsterdam: North Holland, 1970.

Chomsky, N. *Syntactic structures.* The Hague: Mouton, 1957.

Chomsky, N. *Aspects of the theory of syntax.* Cambridge, Mass.: MIT Press, 1965.

Foss, D. J. Some effects of ambiguity upon sentence comprehension. *Journal of Verbal Learning and Verbal Behaviour*, 1970, **9**, 699–706.

Katz, J., & Postal, P. *An integrated theory of linguistic descriptions.* Cambridge, Mass.: MIT Press, 1964.

Lakoff, R. *Abstract syntax and latin complementation.* Cambridge, Mass.: MIT Press, 1968.

Ross, J. R. On declarative sentences. In R. Jacobs & P. Rosenbaum (Eds.), *Readings in English transformational grammar.* Waltham, Mass.: Ginn, 1970.

Staal, J. F. Performative and token reflexives. *Linguistic Inquiry,* 1970, **1**, 373–381.

Thorne, J. P. On non-restrictive relative clauses. *Linguistic Inquiry,* 1972, **3**, 552–556.

4

TOWARDS A PSYCHOLOGICAL
THEORY OF THE MEANING
OF SENTENCES[1]

James Deese
University of Virginia

The function of language is to communicate ideas. Put another way, language makes it possible for the results of one human being's intellectual activity to be, however imperfectly accomplished, the common property of all. No culture is possible without an externalization of thought through a language of some sort. Man's thought is chiefly externalized in his psychologically based languages. It can be argued that human cultural achievement is less directly the consequence of high intelligence than it is the consequence of the invention or development of such phonologically realized languages. Language, communication, and ideas cannot be identified with each other. Human languages express ideas, but not all languages do so. The languages of animals do not, so far as we know. They are composed of signals, not symbols. Signals arouse particular reactions in other organisms, usually, but not exclusively, other organisms of the same species. These signals are not designed to evoke ideas in those to whom they are aimed. They merely create actions, and the actions are inevitable and sometimes uniquely produced upon the occasion of a particular signal. Symbols, on the other hand, need not elicit any *particular* reaction, though they may be received and operated upon by the individual to whom they are aimed. The difference between signal and symbol is critical to an understanding of the nature of human language, though not all students of language, particularly psychologists who are concerned with language, would agree. Sometimes ideas can be ideas about actions of particular kinds, and perhaps in these cases the distinction between signal and symbol is an

[1]This paper was prepared with support provided from Public Health Service Research Grant MH–23957–02 from the National Institute of Mental Health.

empty one. However, it is not empty in the general case. The purpose of this chapter is to make that general case — to define and defend the notion that human languages express ideas.

By now nearly everyone agrees that human languages achieve their function, however those functions may be viewed, by virtue of their rule-determined structure. No matter whether we consider language to be signal or symbol — to arouse reactions or communicate ideas — we agree that human languages achieve their purpose because speakers of them share an implicit knowledge of the rules governing their use. In this respect, human languages differ from all animal languages about which we have any knowledge. Animal communication does not depend upon an implicit knowledge of a set of general rules which govern all individual acts of communication. Rather, each response is aroused by a signal, the meaning of which bears nothing but an arbitrary relation to the meaning of any other possible signal. In the jargon of the computer scientist, animal languages are list languages. Items in the list may resemble one another both physically and in meaning — an animal's distress signal may closely resemble its warning signal — but the animal cannot invent some new signal by invoking some aspect of the set of rules that governs the whole of its language. In short, for a new meaning, a new signal must be added; it cannot be brought into being by combining, in some hitherto unused way, elements already available. Human languages, however, possess a high degree of internal structure, and that structure is associated with both the structure of ideas and the structure of our world. In general, when we talk about the grammar of human languages, we refer to the form of their internal structures. When we speak of the association between languages and ideas, or that between languages and the structure of the world, we are talking about meaning or aspects of semantics. This is an important distinction, and it implies that meaning or semantics is only partly linguistic in nature. It can never be divorced from the structure of ideas or the structure of the world, as that world is perceived by human observers.

Discussion of recent discoveries in linguistics has made most of us familiar with sophisticated and highly developed uses of words such as *symbol, meaning, grammar,* and *syntax.* However, the notion of *idea* has tended to disuse. It has a less definite status in modern psychological, linguistic, and even philosophical studies of language than do those other terms. Where it occurs at all, it is likely to be in the context of accounts of the views of the British empiricists, or of their nineteenth century successors in German and English idealism. In psychology, philosophy, and linguistics there is one contemporary point of view which tells us to dispense with the notion of idea in giving an account of language and its relation to knowing and intellectual activity in general. That point of view is perhaps strongest in psychology, where it is, by far, the dominant attitude.

Students of psychology will recognize this attitude as that of behaviorism. The whole notion of talking about psychological events as mental came under a cloud some 60 years ago or so. The prejudice that psychological events are purely physical is a very old one, of course, but the pursuit of empirical or experimental problems in psychology from that point of view first became important with the spread of the ideas of Pavlov and the development, in America, of the behavioristic revolution by John B. Watson (1913). It was Watson's goal to sweep away the whole dusty apparatus of introspective psychology and thus make psychology, at one and the same time, scientific and useful. Watson pointed out that ideas could not be observed or measured in any of the usual senses in which measurement or observation is employed in science. What is worse, the concept of idea was associated with the view that the whole of the subject matter of psychology was the nature of conscious experience. Ideas were supposed to be the elements of conscious experience in the tradition that dominated late 19th century psychological theory.

This notion of ideas is a very limited one, though it has a long and distinguished philosophical history. In the main, the late nineteenth century experimental psychologists identified ideas with images, and, indeed, the claim by members of the Würzburg school that they had discovered evidence for intellectual activity without images led to the most celebrated psychological controversy of the time, an unresolvable controversy that undoubtedly helped prepare the way for the ready acceptance of behaviorism. Not many modern psychologists are willing to defend an identification of ideas with images, though even the behaviorists have come to search for a substitute for both. The most common substitute has been that of the *mediating response*. The mediating response has no unique identifying qualities of its own. It is merely the result of supposing that nonobservable responses have all of the properties (conditionability, etc.) of overt ones. Thus mediating responses are like the classical notion of the idea only in that they are not observable. To someone who takes the mediationist position, language is a kind of signaling device for the elicitation of responses, albeit responses that may not be observable and may, indeed, have the status of "hypothetical constructs."[2] Some important contemporary behavioral theorists, notably B. F. Skinner, ignore the concept of mediating responses (and, indeed, unobservables altogether), but these theorists share the view of the mediational theorists that languages are signals which elicit responses. Meaning in either case is reduced to a relationship modeled after that holding between the conditioned and unconditioned stimuli in conditioning theory. In language, it is the relationship between the linguistic sign and its referent.

This view discourages the notion that there is any structure to language except that apparent in its surface — in the sounds made, the words spoken, and the sentences composed. It was precisely on this point that a generation of American linguists agreed with the behavioristic psychologists. They hoped to be able to discover the rules governing the use of linguistic elements simply by examining

---

[2]For a discussion of whether or not the notion of mediation is an empty one, see the exchange in Fodor (1965) and Osgood (1966).

what people produced in the way of language. The philosophy of science and the metaphysics behind this effort in linguistics owed much to the behaviorists. Grace De Laguna and John B. Watson were directly responsible for many of the attitudes expressed in the most famous American book on linguistics written in the 1930s, Leonard Bloomfield's *Language* (1933). Bloomfield, in turn, was responsible for shaping the views of the "structuralists" who dominated American linguistic theory in the forties and fifties.

In short, there was a convergence of opinion within psychology and linguistics towards the view that the notion of ideas in the mind was totally unnecessary to the successful study of the psychology of language, or to the study of meaning. Certain philosophers also concurred in this view. By now, however, nearly everyone is aware that a counterrevolution originated within American linguistics. Most linguists, many psychologists, and even a few philosophers have been persuaded by Noam Chomsky,[3] the principal figure associated with this counter-revolution, to the view that the most profound regularities in the structure of language never appear in the surface at all (Chomsky, 1968). The most important relations within sentences are in what Chomsky termed the deep structure of sentences. Deep structures never appear in actual spoken sentences or in verbal behavior of any kind, or in conscious experience, for that matter. Deep structures, then, are unobservables. To the extent that they are supposed to reflect psychological events, they function as ideas of a sort. In short, Chomsky has made it possible to once again talk about ideas, but the notion of idea that is implied by linguistic theory is importantly different from the notion of ideas to be found in eighteenth and nineteenth century associationist philosophy. The ideas of modern linguistic theory are, first of all, highly specialized in that they are purely linguistic. They never touch upon the problem of what motivates sentences in the first place, and thus they really do not correspond to a revival of the notion of idea as something apart from, preliminary to, and necessary to some particular act of language. The linguistic concept of deep structure does not, in itself, constitute a revival of the notion of idea, but it has prepared the way by providing a conceptual structure and by making it respectable, indeed obligatory, to talk about mental events in the analysis of language.

I believe that now is the time to reintroduce the concept of idea as something prior to and necessary for the production of language as well as providing for an explanation of other products of human intellectual activity. If for no other reason, we need the notion of idea out of respect for the view that sometimes we do know what we want to say before we say it. The symbolic function of language is in the relation it bears both to ideas and to the structure of events in the world. The relation between ideas and events in the world is the subject matter, within

---

[3]There has always been a minority position, both in linguistics and in psychology. For a defense of the proposition that psychologists actually anticipated modern generative grammar, see Blumenthal (1970).

psychology, of perception. The psychological aspects of the relations between ideas and language have only been investigated in a desultory way, in contrast to the long tradition in the study of perception. I have always thought that a great deal of the popularity of the writings of the late Benjamin Lee Whorf (e.g., 1956) was simply because he shamelessly dealt with this question. In order to know about meaning and communication we need the study of perception, but we also need a more systematic study of how ideas are related to language.

In order to bring this complicated and difficult topic within the confines of a short essay, I must brush some important and interesting questions aside. Included in my disclaimer are all serious references to the problems of epistemology—that is, to the problems of knowing. I shall simply assert that our knowledge of the external world is dictated by those organizational properties of perception and thought that are apart from and independent of the influence of languge. In short, I do not believe that thought and perception depend in any essential way upon language. Quite the reverse, the form and structure of human languages are reflections of the universal character of the underlying characteristics of thought and perception. I believe that it was the most essential message of the famous book by Ogden and Richards, *The Meaning of Meaning* (1921), that idea and referent were independent of language. It is interesting to note, in this connection, that this book, with its bald implication of mentalism, passed through innumerable editions during the behavioristic era, with but little influence upon psychology.

The structure of thought, in its relation to language, is categorical. That is to say, thought is always in the form of and limited by the characteristic of one of a (presumably) small number of categories. Both the expression of thought in language and our conception of the world are limited by the forms of the categories of thought. This notion is by no means new, of course, having been introduced by Kant. I have refrained from applying the adjective Kantian to describe the categories only to avoid an identification with Kant's particular list of categories and with their philosophical context. Our entire subjective apprehension of the world is determined by the structure of these categories. To the extent that certain abstractions embodied in mathematical and, to a lesser extent, physical theory do not correspond to any of the categories, we cannot properly be said to understand those abstractions. My concern here, however, is less with the apprehension of the world than with the influence of the categorical structure of thought upon language and upon the forms which the rules of language take. By considering this relation, we can make sensible and perhaps even answerable such questions as ''How much do people really communicate with each other through language?'' ''What does it really mean to say that someone understands something?'' or ''Of what does understanding consist?''

My purpose here is not to state in detail a theory of the categorical structure of thought, but to show how it is possible to relate categorical structures in thought to categorical structures in language. In order to do this I must make some assumptions about the way in which sentences are produced, and this, in turn, calls upon a particular linguistic theory. I have adopted the main thrust of Chomsky's linguistic theory as presented in *Aspects of the Theory of Syntax* (1965) (taking into account some later modifications) as a convenient framework upon which to project the categories of thought. The principle, however, remains the same no matter which particular theory of language is adopted, so long as that theory is categorical in nature.

The principles governing the relation between language and thought should be the same whether one is concerned with the reception of language or with its production. However, for purposes of presenting an account of this relation, it is easier to present the argument from the point of view of the production of language rather than the reception and understanding of it. For one thing, it makes explicit the assumption that people, in general, can know what they want to say before they begin to generate the linguistic device that expresses what they want to say. This is not to say that a person is fully or even partially conscious of what it is he wants to cast into linguistic form before he begins to do so, but he must have in mind some general schematic notion which provides the core of the eventual sentence. The question of conscious awareness is irrelevant to the matter at hand, and it has often been invoked to obscure the basic nature of the question.

Accepting that the function of language is the communication of ideas implies that the principles governing the relation between language and thought are the same, whether we consider the problem of encoding ideas into language or the problem of understanding — that of encoding linguistic sequences into ideas. I have been arguing for some years now (see, e.g., Deese, 1967) that the correspondence between the ideas possessed by two individuals who are in communication on a common topic is rather poor, a condition which we ordinarily do not notice because we seldom make explicit attempts to validate a communicated idea against the original. When we do, as in the case of giving directions to someone about how to do something, we are suddenly made aware of the discrepancy that exists between "the same" idea in the minds of two different people. Ordinary situations demand that we place only the loosest of interpretations upon some linguistic utterance we hear. This is an important aspect of the relation between language and thought to which I wish to return later in this chapter.

Nearly all contemporary linguistic theories concern themselves with the nature of the sentence. The lesson should be clear. At least at one level, ideas should correspond with something underlying the structure of sentences. Contemporary linguists describe sentences as being generated in some hierarchical fashion rather than in some linear sequence. We speak sentences from left to right, so to speak, but linguistic theory cannot consider them as being generated this way, and it would seem almost certainly to be the case that we do not generate sentences from left to right in our heads. In hierarchical descriptions, the most general schematic characteristics are more basic than the specific characteristics. Thus, the grammatical and semantic structures of large segments of a sentence—a phrase for example —are more linguistically basic than those limited to just a portion of the sentence

— a single word, for example. It is convenient, but not necessary, to consider a sentence as derived from ideas in a series of steps which begin with the most general schematic characteristics of a sentence and then which go on to the specification of particular parts of the sentence. This is simply a convenience of exposition, not a theoretical necessity, however. In fact, we might well expect that a great deal of what psychologists have come to call parallel processing[4] goes on in transforming ideas into sentences, and we might further expect that feedback from the selection of specific elements might serve to alter the selection at the higher or more general level. The point is, however, that a hierarchical organization of sentence structure implies levels, and there is, therefore, more than one locus at which ideas might be mapped onto sentence structures. Let us consider two levels. One is at the very beginning, at which locus the general schema of the sentence is determined. Other, less general ideas may be introduced into the formation of sentences at the loci at which specific lexical items (words) are chosen.

If we accept this scheme, the concept of ideas has at least two components, one which is like a proposition and is mapped onto the most general sentence schema, and the other is a specific component which is mapped onto the selection of words. The latter component corresponds more with traditional treatments of ideas, but in fact, most traditional usage does not clearly differentiate between these possibilities. When, for example, ideas were equated with images, it was not always specified as to whether the image is of a specific thing (a complex idea in Locke's terms) or of some specific thing or things in relation with one another or with an action. It is a commonplace observation that visual images nearly always carry more specific features than are called for by the conceptual definition of the name of the image. Thus, most people, when asked to imagine a horse, will imagine a brown one (a few individuals prefer white, black, or even piebald). What is more, the horse is usually seen in some specific orientation, and, further, may be engaged in some action, such as jumping a fence. Thus, it is at best a half-truth to identify the images associated with specific concepts entirely with the lexical characteristics said to define that concept. It is essential, however, to suppose that the propositional component of ideas and their conceptual components (those corresponding to lexical entries) can, in theory, be independent.

Every English sentence produced, then, is the result of some transformations imposed upon a basic linguistic structure. That structure, in turn, is associated with one or more underlying ideas. The association must be in a one-to-one fashion if ambiguities are not to result. The fact that ambiguity is commonplace in ordinary language suggests that such one-to-one correspondence does not always occur. The base linguistic structure itself will consist of one or more elements corresponding to phrase markers in syntactic theory together with whatever

---

[4]An example of parallel processing at a different level is that of a student trying to understand a lecture while at the same time taking notes on it. Here, too, the processes are somewhat independent, but feedback from the writing of the notes could alter the understanding of the words heard.

elements mark the presuppositions or contextual features inherent in the original idea. These must be ordered with respect to one another in some intrinsic way. For present purposes, a phrase marker may be said to be composed of abstract syntactic structures characterizing such essential linguistic forms as active sentences having direct objects, predicate adjective constructions, sentences with indirect objects, etc. Each sentence type has as its base some particular phrase marker. Thus, the phrase marker Det — Noun — Copula — Adjective would provide the structural basis for the sentence "The sky is blue" (as well as, in a more complicated derivation, for the sentence "Is the sky blue?"). The phrase marker Det — Noun — Verb — Det — Noun provides the structural basis for the sentence "The judge fined the defendant."

The actual surface sentence that results will be based upon the selection of one or more of these phrase markers, picked so as to correspond with the underlying categorical proposition. Note the strong implication that the number of possible categorical propositions is likewise limited. Also, on the assumption that the categorical propositions are psychologically universal, each language must contain underlying phrase markers which may be paired through the underlying idea, with corresponding phrase markers in other languages. The pairing of *surface sentences* may be difficult to accomplish with certainty because of different transformation complexities and because each categorical proposition may contain a presupposition which requires the selection of one particular phrase marker that may be quite similar or indeed superficially identical to another. Thus, the sentence "The new theory errs" and "The theory that errs is new" may be said, at one level of analysis, to assert the same propositions. Yet they are based upon different underlying phrase markers, and I am asserting here that the selection of one way as opposed to another way of saying "the same thing" will be the result of some presupposition or contextual information contained in the original idea.

Note that the surface sentence "The new theory errs" has as its base two propositions (together with the necessary presuppositions). One basic proposition asserts "the theory errs," while the other asserts "the theory is new." I have chosen this example because, among other things, it is not immediately convincing. It is not intuitively convincing because we want to think of a simple sentence, such as "the new theory errs," as being unitary and not being composed of separate ideas or propositions. However, the categorical notion of semantics makes it necessary that such a sentence be composed of at least two underlying propositions. Fortunately, such a view is also consonant with several major theories of grammatical structure.

Each underlying idea, then, can be stated in the form of a proposition, and it is associated with a base phrase marker, together with necessary presuppositions and other contextual features, and these phrase markers are combined and transformed to produce sentences. The transformations themselves are influenced by aspects of the underlying ideas, but that is a complicated issue, and I shall ignore it here. The essential principle is that each base phrase marker in language is associated with some particular meaning.

Consider the following sentences:

John sleeps.

John hits Bill.

John sends Harry to Bill.

These sentences talk about different situations. The third sentence talks about John, Harry, and Bill, while the first sentence talks only about John. However, this difference is less fundamental than the difference among the forms of the propositions implied by the sentences. The propositional meaning of these sentences is independent of the particular persons and the particular actions named. Thus, the first sentence might have as its propositional base something that could be expressed as "X is in state of Y" or "X engages in activity Y." The basic proposition behind the second sentence might be characterized as "X acts in some manner Y, upon concept Z," or alternatively, "X does something Y, to Z." It is possible that these alternatives merely reflect different propositions associated with base phrase markers that differ by having components of them marked by different syntactic or relational features. In the theory of grammar, it is possible to consider all simple declarative sentences with a direct object as alike, or alternatively, it is possible to distinguish among such sentences depending upon certain features of the nouns and verbs (whether, for example, the nouns refer to animate concepts or not). In short, it is possible to consider the nature of the base phrase marker to be dependent upon certain of the semantic features characteristic of the categorical forms in the sentences. Such a supposition, however, leads to difficulties in linguistic theory (it is very difficult to say, with any convincing theoretical justification, which semantic features should be of syntactic relevance), and it also leads to psychological difficulties in that it serves to erase the very distinction between the propositional component of the underlying idea and the categorical content of the elements which give the specific meaning to the idea.

How many different kinds of propositions are there? That is difficult to say. For one thing, it depends upon whether one regards the base phrase markers (or the equivalent) necessary for a given language as exhausting all cognitive possibilities. For my part, I am inclined to the view that there are universal propositions and that they are such because they are determined by the universal nature of our innate perceptual and intellectual processes. It follows that all languages provide means for expressing these. However, there are certainly radical differences among languages in the way in which the underlying propositions can be expressed. Perhaps, as Whorf (1957) pointed out, the structure of English, with its clear division into nouns that name things and verbs that name actions, makes it much easier for an English-speaking person to think of objects and actions as distinct entities than it would be for a Hopi speaker. In Whorf's analysis of Hopi, the structure of that language is such that the conception of object and action are more nearly one. In Chinese, nouns and verbs (verbs also include predicate adjectives) are less conceptually marked than they are marked purely linguistically (by a particle attached to the verb or adjective).

There must surely be differences in the surface expression of underlying ideas as determined by the rules of different languages. In communicating the meaning of any given proposition, a speaker must filter or color his proposition by the structure of the language he speaks. It is not certain, as our self-conscious analysis of English would lead us to suppose, that object and action are clearly separatable in the "primordial idea."

There are a whole set of profound questions centering around the nature of the propositional components of the underlying idea. For example, I have been concerned as to whether the category of cause and effect, which I believe to be a cognitive and perceptual universal, resides in the propositional or the conceptual aspect of the underlying idea. My original view (Deese, 1969) was that cause and effect was a conceptual category; however, it now seems far more natural to conceive of it as a propositional category, depending, as it does, upon the relation among concepts. Some linguistic relativists have argued that the Western notion of causation stems from the noun-verb-noun structure of Indo-European declarative sentences possessing direct objects. These theorists, including Whorf, have asserted that other languages do not have such a structure and therefore do not have our ideas about cause and effect. The work of certain students of perception, particularly Michotte (1954), suggests, however, that immediate and direct perceptions of causation are inherent in certain visual configurations. Therefore, I am inclined to the view that the conception of cause and effect is a universal one arising out of our perceptual experience with objects. Such, I believe, has been the message Piaget has conveyed in a number of different writings.[5]

But our ideas are more than general propositions. They are propositions which relate particular concepts. We not only know what we want to say before we say it, but we also know what it is we want to say it about. Thus, meaning has another level. For convenience we may say that meaning also enters at the level of words, though that can only be said to be an approximation, for meaning does not enter into all words (such as "the" and "to"), and some words are compounds of different meanings or some root meaning together with an affix that identifies some other meaning attached to it. However, for very rough purposes we may identify the elements that carry the information which tells us what propositions are about as corresponding to the entries we find in ordinary dictionaries.

The meaning of these elements is also categorical. The categorical component of the meaning of individual words carries the form of the meaning. The full meaning is given by the experiential content, in memory or perception, associated at any given occasion with that form. Categories include class membership (hierarchical structures), feature specification, spatial relations (including magnitude), group membership, and probably a host of rather particular categories that

---

[5] Piaget's ideas on this topic are scattered in so many places that the best reference is Flavell (1963).

arise from the nature of human social relations (ownership, kinship, etc.). Ordinary dictionary definitions generally offer combinations of categories. For example the dictionary on my desk offers the following definition of an orange (noun): "The nearly globose fruit, botanically a berry, of an evergreen rutaceous tree of several varieties [*Webster's,* 1956, p. 1030]." Globose specifies a feature, and its accompanying adverb modifies the magnitude of that feature. Fruit (or berry) defines a class relation, and several varieties specifies group membership. Thus, the dictionary definition offers a number of ways of thinking about the concept in question. When we think about the concept *orange* in some particular context, we will not think about all these. We may, indeed, have in mind something not really given by the defining characteristic at all. We may have in mind a nondefining feature (the color of the ripe fruit, for example).

The speaker of any sentence does not provide definitions of the words he uses to compose the sentence, of course, and we can only infer from the context what categorical structure generated his sentence. Such inferences are made by hearers, and the frequent need to make such inferences is one more aspect of the extreme looseness of communication in ordinary language. The inference made by the hearer may miss the mark by a wide margin. Fortunately, such a failure in communication is often of no practical importance, for the scanty information in the sentence is embedded in a rich perceptual context. For example, if I say to the grocer, "Give me a dozen oranges," it doesn't make much difference how his conception of oranges differs from mine. I might just as well have said, while pointing, "Give me a dozen of these." In such concrete situations the referential aspect of language is all-important, and the conceptual structure that gives rise to the linguistic segment in question is relatively of trivial importance. Perhaps someone might be interested in knowing what motivated me to ask for oranges, but unless that person were adminstering me the Stanford-Binet intelligence test, he would be unlikely to be interested in my conception of the word *orange.*

Abstract concepts present a more difficult case, however. There is no single or collective referent for such concepts. Their definitions derive from properties separated from various concrete situations and events. Therefore, their categorical structure is a much more significant part of their total meaning. That structure can often be determined by the form of the proposition itself. For example, if I say, "Linguistics is like mathematics," the form of the proposition (generally called analogy) implies a feature specification of both linguistics and mathematics (they are alike in some respects). My hearer is not likely to err in supposing that I am thinking that linguistics and mathematics have features in common (though both he and I may be totally unable to articulate what they are, even though we "understand" the proposition). Other propositions, of course, offer no clue as to the conceptual structure of the words they contain. If I say, "Peace is necessary for progress," you will have no real clue as to the categorical structure of the three concepts in that sentence. You may infer that I intend *peace* to be in contrast to *war* and thus be in feature specification (a contrast necessarily implies a feature analysis), but you could be wrong. I could mean "internal harmony under a rule of law." We all know about these kinds of examples. I point them out in this context to show that there exists not only the possibility of ambiguity in concrete referent but also ambiguity in conceptual category. The often commented-upon greater degree of ambiguity of abstractions, in ordinary language, is the result, I think, of the greater significance of conceptual category in their meaning. If a statement is sufficiently abstract, its entire meaning may come from the category underlying the propositional form of the statement. The individual words in some sentences are so devoid of content that what is communicated by the sentence could be put in the fleshless form of symbolic logic or some other abstract calculus with no loss of meaning. Despite the precision that would be achieved, such a statement would be utterly ambiguous in reference.

Once again it is necessary to raise the question of the universality of such conceptual categories. Here I feel a little more certain about the universality of conceptual categories in the lexicon than I do about the universality of the underlying propositional forms. The lexical categories I have mentioned — class membership, feature specification, spatial relations, magnitude, grouping, all occur in vastly different kinds of languages. However, I am not certain how far to extend the list of universals. Casegrande and Hale (1967) have made a categorical analysis of the definitions given by an informant for an American Indian language, Papago. They discovered fourteen categories in this informant's definitions. These included those given above, but there were also others, perhaps some of which cannot be reduced to my smaller list.

The observations of Casegrande and Hale serve to remind us, however, that there are culturally specific aspects of semantics, and, furthermore, it appears that these culturally specific aspects of semantics are the result of the characteristic assignment of familiar concepts to different conceptual categories. For example, we (meaning speakers of English) most commonly regard the nose as part of the face. That is to say, it belongs in a hierarchical tree of "parts of the body." In Papago, the nose is primarily conceived of by its relative spatial location — it is that which is between the eyes and the mouth. Such conceptual differences must permeate the relations among different languages and make up a considerable portion of the argument for linguistic relativity.

The past generation has seen the invention of an extraordinary range of devices for determining the relations of meaning among words. Their development was based largely upon the behaviorist premise that words' meanings were fundamentally responses which could be empirically measured. The Semantic Differential, invented by C. E. Osgood (1952), is perhaps the best known. The Semantic Differential asks us to judge the extent to which *mother* or *linguistic philosophy* is judged to be *good* or *bad, hot* or *cold, active* or *passive*. Its great virtue and at the same time defect is that the set of adjectives which it uses to define a concept for us is very limited. In the original version of the Semantic Differential there was an attempt to find the most common adjectives we use to describe things. It turns out that these are mainly affective in nature — we most commonly want to describe how things affect us emotionally, apparently. Free associations have also been used to determine relations of meaning among words. These are remarkably free from linguistic constraints, and so, unlike the Semantic Differential, they reveal how we regard things conceptually in a more general way. The trouble is that the conceptual categories are all jumbled together in associations, and there is no rational way to disentangle them.

More recently, psychosemantic investigations have turned to the use of multidimensional scaling and sorting techniques. These are sophisticated mathematical techniques for revealing the patterns of meaningful relations among words. They are a little more orderly than the association techniques, but they too suffer from the fact that they often work at cross-purposes with the particular conceptual category the person, whose data they analyze, had in mind. The fact is that there are many techniques for studying the meaning of words. Some techniques, such as free association, are more general. Others fit a particular conceptual category. For example, spatial relations are peculiarly appropriate for multidimensional scaling, because multidimensional scaling can reveal a kind of spatial map of the meaning of words. The familiar color wheel (the names of the important colors arranged in a circle with complementary pairs opposite one another) is an example. The mathematics of multidimensional scaling applied to the question of how similar pairs of colors are judged to be will produce just such a wheel. However, a hierarchical relation, such as that among parts of the body, will be grossly distorted by the application of multidimensional scaling to how people judge words in the hierarchy. In short, there are methods that are particularly appropriate to particular conceptual categories. However, there is a real question about how much we learn by studying the relationships of meaning among familiar words, for the most we can do is to confirm, by explicit and quantitative means, what we know intuitively.[6]

There are many reasons for insisting that the categorical structure of propositions and the categorical structure of lexical elements are separate, though it is not certain that they do not interact in the process of producing and understanding sentences. One can, using the basic notions presented here, produce several different models of how sentences are produced and understood, the specifications of which will differ according to whether we allow these two components of ideas to interact and whether or not we allow information from the linguistic portion (say, a partially composed sentence) to feed back to the ideational component. However, this all has nothing in it to contradict the notion that we require meaning both at the sentential level and at the level of words. The fact that we can characterize the meaning of individual words, independent of any syntactic context, has always been a stumbling block to semantic analysis, because it has always

---

[6]For an account of the varieties of devices used to explore the subjective lexicon, see Fillenbaum and Rapoport (1971).

been apparent, despite our efforts to the contrary, that one cannot come to the meaning of a sentence simply by concatenating the meaning of the individual dictionary entries. Meaning enters into language at least at two levels, and this fact makes the dual conception of the structure of ideas.

In summary: I have argued that there are forms of meaning determined by the structure of ideas. These structures must be universal, for they are determined by the biological substrate of the human mind. Human experience is endlessly variable, but that inconceivably variable experience must be confined within the structure of human ideas in order to have meaning. One can imagine a man in an environment that is totally alien to anything that human experience has had yet to cope with, but the perception of that environment and our judgments (that is to say, our intellectual processes) about that experience will be within the comfortable and familiar confines of the forms of experience and, hence, will be readily expressible in the forms of meaning in ordinary language.

REFERENCES

Bloomfield, L. *Language*. New York: Holt, Rinehart & Winston, 1933.

Blumenthal, A. L. *Language and psychology*. New York: Wiley, 1970.

Casegrande, J. B., & Hale, K. L. Semantic relationships in Papago folk definitions. *Studies in Southwestern Linguistics*. The Hague: Mouton, 1967.

Chomsky, N. *Aspects of the theory of syntax*. Cambridge, Mass.: MIT Press, 1965.

Chomsky, N. *Language and mind*. New York: Harcourt, Brace & World, 1968.

Deese, J. Meaning and change of meaning. *American Psychologist*, 1967, **22**, 641*–651.

Deese, J. Conceptual categories in the study of content. In Gerbner, G. (ed.), *Communication and content*. New York: Wiley, 1969.

Fillenbaum, S., & Rapoport, A. *Structures in the subjective lexicon*. New York: Academic Press, 1971.

Flavell, J. H. *The developmental psychology of Jean Piaget*. Princeton: Van Nostrand, 1963.

Fodor, J. A. Could meaning be an r_m? *Journal of Verbal Learning and Verbal Behavior*, 1965, **4**, 73–81.

Michotte, A. *Le Perception de la Causalité*. (2nd ed.) Louvain: Publication Universitaires de Louvain, 1954.

Ogden, C. K., & Richards, I. A. *The meaning of meaning*. New York: Harcourt, Brace, 1921.

Osgood, C. E. The nature and measurement of meaning. *Psychological Bulletin*, 1952, **49**, 197–237.

Osgood, C. E. Meaning cannot be an r_m? *Journal of Verbal Learning and Verbal Behavior*, 1966, **5**, 402–407.

Watson, J. B. Psychology as the behaviorist views it. *Psychological Review*, 1913, **20**, 158–177.

Webster's new world dictionary of the American language. (College Ed.) New York: World Publishing, 1956.

Whorf, B. L. *Language, thought and reality*. Cambridge, Mass.: MIT Press, 1956.

5
SOME PUZZLES ABOUT MEANING

Max Black
Cornell University

The basic question which I would like to raise is, What is Meaning? Or, if you prefer it, What are Meanings? in the plural. Or, to put it somewhat more pompously, I should like to become clearer about the nature of meaning.

This way of stating the problem implies that I am somewhat muddled about the subject, which is certainly the case. On the other hand, I am in excellent company, since many thinkers of the highest ability, with Aristotle at their head, have tried unsuccessfully to answer the question. It is rather extraordinary that their answers should be so varied and, indeed, mutually incompatible. So we can be sure of one thing, that nearly all of them are wrong. Probably, at most one of them is close to the truth, and the chances are, on general principles, that none of them is. On the other hand, the question itself is obviously of prime practical, as well as theoretical, importance. We are constantly faced, in private life and in public affairs, with questions of the form, What does he mean? What does he really mean? What are we to make of that statement? and so on. Sometimes one's very survival depends upon a good answer. One could cite many anecdotes to illustrate this: We have all heard of the famous Charge of the Light Brigade. That extraordinary episode resulted from a misinterpretation of a message: a simple direction was misunderstood, and so the famous Light Brigade thought they had to charge *at* the guns and went to their deaths.

In New York not long ago, I saw a sign that read, "The No-Embarrassment Barber Shop," and to this day I don't know what that meant. I need not supply further examples. It is clear that problems of interpretation, of grasping meaning, constantly arise. Furthermore, our skill in handling these tasks will be influenced, for better or worse, by the theories, whether elaborate or rudimentary, that we have at the back of our minds.

One embarrassment is that no good theory is available; and behind that is the more disturbing fact that we lack a good methodology, so that nobody really knows how to look for the answer.

Let us begin with some elementary reflections about the type of question that we are asking. The question, I remind you, is the deceptively simple one, What is meaning?

Let us take, by way of analogy, the question, What is electricity? Now there you might suppose that answers are readily available—and indeed they are; one learns in elementary courses in physics, or from a textbook, just what electricity is. But a philosopher, or indeed an inquisitive child, may not be satisfied with those answers. You might tell a child the kind of thing that you find in a good textbook of electricity, and at the end of it the child might reasonably say, "Well, I know what electricity does—it lights lamps and gives you shocks and so on—but what really *does* all this? What is this thing called electricity, which is responsible for all of those effects?" The point here is that this is no longer a scientific question. A scientist is satisfied when he can tell you what electricity does. If you now raise questions of the form, Well, is it a sort of spirit? Is it perhaps a kind of fluid? Is it a substance? or Is it perhaps just a fiction, invented only to make phenomena easier to describe? these questions, whether you regard them as legitimate or not, are not, strictly speaking, scientific. They are typically philosophical questions. For something which, from a certain standpoint, is perfectly familiar, has, from another perspective, become mysterious.

One possible definition of a philosopher might well be that he is somebody who is apt to find the familiar mysterious. There is a peculiar kind of philosophical puzzlement which arises when something with which we are quite familiar suddenly appears, not only mysterious, but in a certain sense, inconceivable.

To take an example close to our topic: There is nothing extraordinary about talking to somebody else and understanding what is being said. But if you have the idea, which is natural enough, that the other person's thoughts and feelings are impenetrably hidden from you, that he is somewhere — how shall we say it — inside his body, or behind his face, then the idea of the gap between yourself and him can, from a philosophical point of view, seem extraordinarily strange and mysterious. How is it possible that another mind, which manifests itself to me only as an appearance, should be able to be in communication with me?

Take another example: We are accustomed to making statements about the future, and I can say with reasonable confidence that I shall be leaving Rhode Island tomorrow. But—the future does not exist yet; and some people even think that it is not yet determined. How can I, here and now, make true statements about the future, when there is this logical gap between now and what is yet to come?

Those of you who have taken philosophical courses will be familiar with this kind of point; anybody to whom such trains of thought seem perverse is, perhaps happily, immune from philosophical wonder and puzzlement. But the existence of philosophical perplexity is a fact; that nearly all people at a certain age suffer from it is another fact; and that some people never recover is still another. Tolstoy, in one of his autobiographical sketches, says that as a young man he was so caught up in some of these philosophical perplexities, especially after reading Bishop Berkeley, that at one point he found himself doing the following absurd thing: jumping around very fast, in the hope, perhaps, of finding a void behind him, before he had time to reconstruct it. That, perhaps, verges upon the pathological.

Well, let us now consider what the main philosophical puzzles are in connection with meaning. One that we might mention arises from the extraordinary disparity between certain linguistic means and their nonlinguistic consequences. You may be asked a question in a certain situation, having to choose between the physically trifling sounds "yes" and "no," and a great deal may turn on whether you make the one sound or the other. People have been killed by hearing the word "yes." A man asks whether his son died in the accident; on hearing "yes," he has a stroke and dies. That already looks extraordinary; it seems fantastic that a puff of wind, something which, considered as a physical act, is trivial, should have such massive consequences. And throughout the history of mankind, people have been extraordinarily impressed by what has been called the magic of words. This has been inflated in mythology and religion to the superstition that if you can find the right sound, the right puff of wind, then you can have control over spirits, other men, or nature.

Closely related is the point that very slight differences in the sound can make the difference between the meaningful and the nonsensical. For example, let us take two sounds which are very close: first, the sound of "pin," which you all understand; and, now with a slight change, "pon," which nobody understands. (According to the large Oxford Dictionary, there is no such word in the English language.) It is not a matter of your being ignorant, but of there being a meaning attaching to one sound and not to the other.

Sometimes such slight differences can have monstrous consequences. There was, in the fourth century after the birth of Christ, a famous theological controversy that turned upon the following two Greek words: "homoousian" and "homoiousian," meaning roughly "of the same substance" and "of like substance," respectively. The question at issue was, whether the Son was of the same substance as the Father, or simply of an analogous, or like, substance. Many people lost their lives because they chose to say "homoousian" rather than "homoiousian" or *vice versa*. So much depended upon an insignificant vowel. Or compare the difference, say, between "killing" a person and "calling" him.

How is it possible that such almost imperceptible differences should make all that difference? How is it that certain sounds can be meaningful and others be meaningless when, physically speaking, there seems almost nothing to choose between them?

What is the commonsense answer? In the pin-pon case it might be that, after all, there are things called ''pins'' and there are no such things as ''pons.'' I hope you can see at once that this answer, which is one that you might get from a layman, really cannot satisfy us.

In the first place, what does it mean to say that there are things that are called ''pins''? Isn't that really a trivial transformation of the original question? If ''pins'' means what it does mean, then perhaps in the intended sense, there *must* be things called ''pins.'' So, introducing the word ''called'' does not really help us much. In the second place, we said that there are no things called ''pons''; well, how do we know? Perhaps there are. Perhaps there are ''pons'' around in the world, and we just haven't heard about them. And in the third, but not the last, place, there are many meaningful words and expressions to which no real things correspond. Consider the word ''unicorn,'' or the expression ''completely honest President of the United States.'' These have meaning: a *question* can be raised about the existence of unicorns even by those who don't believe in their existence. So our first formula, that a word has meaning if it stands for things in the world, is unacceptable.

Now, for a moment, let us jump to another kind of case, which may seem a little easier to handle. Consider the case of a personal name — and why don't we take, switching countries, ''Pompidou.'' Of course, here we have a proper name and not a general one, but still the name is somehow or other meaningful. What would common sense say about this? How is it that ''Pompideau'' (you will notice I have made a slight change in the sound), for all we know, has no meaning? Here again, the commonsense formula, that there *is* somebody called ''Pompidou,'' seems unsatisfactory because it is unclear what ''called'' means. No doubt you can find the name in the Paris telephone directory. But that looks inessential. *Must* a man have his name in the telephone directory? You might say, ''Well, if you were to meet him and say, 'Pompidou,' he would look at you or reply or do *something*.'' But how do you know that he wouldn't do the same if you said ''Pompideau''? Especially if you were an American.

There seems to be a sort of gap; over here is the sound (the name), and there, at a conceptual distance, is the person. But if that gap is there, how is it that the name ''attaches'' to the person?

Let us imagine, in the manner of science fiction, that in some other constellation, people have been worried by this philosophical difficulty. So they have decided to eliminate the gap. As soon as a child is born in their world, they simply tattoo a name indelibly onto the skin; and now there is no gap. But now a terrestrial philosopher arrives by rocket and asks the same tiresome question: How do you people understand the connection between the name and the person? They answer, ''Look at the tattoo.'' But then he says, ''Why should that name, tattooed on that skin, be *his* name and not some other person's?'' There is nothing that guarantees that if I carry a name around, that's my name. Suppose I choose to tattoo ''Pompidou'' on my skin. Does that make ''Pompidou'' my name? Or suppose I just say, as I do now, ''My name is Pompidou'' and repeat that formula with boring frequency. Has it become my name; and if not, why not?

I have been giving you some glimpses, as simply as I can, of how some fundamental questions of philosophical semantics arise. By this time, we should be entitled to suspect that the meaning of a word cannot be some objective correlate — the *bearer* of a proper name, or something less obvious in the case of a general name. Yet the idea that there must be an "objective correlate" that *is* the meaning dies hard. And it can arise in all sorts of connections.

Let me tell you, now, about some of the types of theories that have been proposed. All of these theories, though some may sound rather extraordinary, have been elaborately defended, sometimes for centuries. All have certain advantages and corresponding weaknesses.

In connection with the case of a personal name, it is tempting to suppose that the thing itself — in this case, the man himself — is what is meant. For when I say "Pompidou," if I am using the word correctly, I am trying to refer to that very man.

This has sometimes been called, in the philosophical literature, the "bearer" theory. The basic idea is that the man meant is the bearer of the name and that the meaning of a name is the actual person or thing. There are real, actual things in the world; and, in some way or other yet to be explained, words are attached to, or correlated with, those things, and those very things are the meanings.

This is somewhat paradoxical, but paradox may have to be accepted, no matter what view you take. It would follow, for example, that you can eat meanings. If I point to something and say, I want *that* ice cream, and get it, then when I eat it, I am literally eating the meaning. And by the time I have eaten it up, that meaning has been destroyed, and so I can't talk about it anymore. So that if my wife asks me, "Did you enjoy that ice cream?" I say, "I can't tell you." She retorts, "Why not?" until she realizes that I am talking like a philosopher and shuts up. In general, one of the obvious difficulties of the "bearer" theory, as we have already seen, is that it seems to preclude talking about the nonexistent or the merely possible. But one of the obvious and enormous advantages of language, or of symbolism generally, is that it enables us to talk about what has not happened, but might. Or what did happen, and no longer exists. It is very hard to square a "bearer" theory with the existence of history or with the possibility of prophecy.

A different kind of theory, having a certain formal resemblance, but otherwise very different in character, is that some meaningful items in the vocabulary stand for corresponding abstract entities. For example, if I use a word like "red," then there is something called "redness," and a certain abstract property that can be manifested in any number of places, and the word "red" (or the word "redness") is a name for that abstract entity. You notice that this theory would have to be modified to fit the case of personal names, but even there one could make a case for saying that a person is an abstraction — that what actually *happens* in reality is an instantaneous condition, a time-slice, and when we speak of Pompidou or Nixon, we are speaking of an abstraction. Some of you will know that the General Semanticists have insisted on this, and have said with some plausibility that if you talk about Nixon *in 1958* you must not confuse him with Nixon *in 1973*. So that if you ignore the date, you are employing an abstraction, and a questionable one. A case can be made for saying that persons, as well as institutions, books, theories, are all abstractions and that when we use language, we typically talk in terms of abstractions.

The link between the two theories is that they both take names as paradigms of words having meaning. Ryle (1968) once invented a quaint label for this kind of theory, viz., " 'Fido'-Fido theory" (the name "Fido" conceived as standing for the dog Fido). The "bearer" theory and the abstract entity theory are examples, since in both cases the meaning of the name is thought of as something correlated with the name itself, though in one case you have a nominalistic type of theory with particular, individual things as the meanings, while in the other you have a "realistic" theory.

Other thinkers have thought that any theory of this character suffers from a fatal weakness. The objection is, roughly speaking, that the meaning of terms must reside in human beings, not in objects external to them. Meaning is a human product; there is no natural correlation between the word "Fido" and the dog of that name. If there is a connection, it is something created by human beings. So meaning is located in human intentions or purposes and so, ultimately, in the human mind. This point of view, as old as Aristotle, has been reaffirmed by thousands of philosophers, psychologists, and linguists. We might call it a "mentalistic" type of theory.

One important variety is based on the idea that meaning is a matter of having a distinctive image. A physicalistic variant is based on the idea that there is some lasting pattern or structure, in the brain, or in the central nervous system — anyway, in the body — which *is* the meaning. Some writers have talked of a so-called "engram," a sort of trace in the brain supposedly produced by appropriate external stimuli.

The basic idea, then, is that the meaning of any word, say that of any example I have already used, depends upon something about the individual speaker concerned, or about groups of speakers who have similar neurological or psychological structures.

A fine example of this approach can be found in Ferdinand de Saussure's famous book, *Course in General Linguistics* (1959), that has exerted so much influence on generations of linguists. There you will find a schematic diagram, locating the speaker's meaning in his mind, as the starting point for a process of translation into a physical message and eventual translation back into a corresponding meaning in the hearer's mind. (For present purposes, it does not matter whether the meaning is supposed to be located in a mind or in a brain.) Essentially the same conception is to be found in the writings about language, still well worth reading, of the great philosopher John Locke (1894). This type of view continues to be very popular: there is something about it that strikes the layman as obviously right.

The root idea, then, is that meaning is, roughly speaking, located in the head or in the mind. In communication, we get a transformation of the initial mental or neurological event into a physical process, followed by reception by the hearer and a corresponding de-translation. Whether the hearer understands correctly then depends upon something happening in his mind or brain.

Many years ago I argued publicly with Bertrand Russell about the nature of meaning. He said at the time — but of course he often changed his mind with fantastic rapidity — that every meaningful word had its corresponding mental image. And I said, "So if I now say to you, speaking as fast as I possibly can, 'Almost certainly you're in error,' you think that with every word that I said, each one of which had a meaning that you understood, there was a corresponding image." And he replied, emphatically, "There *has* to be." That's a mark of one kind of serious philosopher. Having found an answer that satisfies him, he will legislate that it *must* be right, no matter what. If you can't notice the images, then, by God, or Something, they must be unconscious or passing too fast for you to observe them. Of course, physiologists will sometimes say the same sort of thing. There *must* be a process in the brain (what else could it be?), and if we haven't observed these processes, they must be there all the same.

I would like you to see that nothing compels us to accept any such theory. Let us take the image theory first. There is, as all of us know, considerable doubt as to whether imagery is sufficiently prevalent to do the job. My introspective reports are of no interest to anybody who isn't a friend or a relative, and of precious little interest to them; but for what it is worth, I believe that I have very little imagery. As I am talking to you, I can hear the sound of my voice, but that's all. I am not aware of any imagery — and if you insist that I *must* be having unconscious imagery, that's your privilege — for what it is worth.

However, we can bypass this dispute in the following way: Let us assume (what certainly should not be done, except for the sake of argument) that the imagery is there. Let us also concede that there may be a special situation in which somebody produces distinct and articulated imagery when we tell him: "The time is four o'clock."

I might say, in passing, that William James thought that even words like "the" had corresponding images. If you read his *Principles of Psychology* (1950, Ch. 9), you will find interesting passages about the imagery which is supposed to go with words like "and," "if," and "but"; he thought there was an "and" feeling, an "if" feeling, and so on. I am going to grant all of this for the sake of argument (though I don't believe it). I cannot conceive what it would be like to have a "the"-feeling, but if somebody is going to claim that he has a distinctive image that goes with "the," I will accept his word. Similarly for the other words in our sentence: perhaps "time" induces some kind of flowing feeling. "Is" looks problematic, but let us be generous and assign an image to it as well. And so on. So there was, we suppose, a train of distinctive imagery.

Now, the crucial question is: Supposing that the hearer we have imagined really does have that train of imagery, how does he know what those images mean? Let us suppose, so long as we are being fanciful, that we have some extraordinary device by means of which we can verify the existence of this train of images, even re-induce them in somebody else. So that when I sit in front of this machine, and the operator presses the buttons, I get a train of images just like the images that the hearer had. *Now* do I now know what he meant? Why should I?

Take a more trivial case, say, that of any color word, such as "red." It could happen, by some kind of freakish mechanism, that when you said "red," I always had a green image. Would that mean that I couldn't understand what "red" meant? Well, of course not, since I could always make the appropriate correction. But the fact is, I would not need to make any correction. Whether I have the green image in my head or not has nothing to do with understanding what you say; all that matters is that when I see something which is properly called red, I recognize it and use the right word. What goes on in my mind may be subjectively important, but does not determine the semantics of the word. And the same conclusion applies in general. To put it another way, the existence of images simply pushes the whole problem one stage further back, since we are still faced with the problem of explaining what the supposed images mean.

Philosophers from Aristotle to the present have thought that there was some kind of primitive language, *Ursprache,* composed of images, and even having a distinctive grammar. But if there is a language of images, then that language itself must have meaning. One might ask for the meaning of the images, and the meaning might be misinterpreted.

You can conceive of a child being taught by somebody who believed this theory, and upon being told, "The time is four o'clock," showing by his actions that he thought it was time for breakfast. But when you check on the imagery (if that even makes sense), you find that the imagery is right — only when the image that we associate with "four o'clock" occurs in the child it means "breakfast," not four o'clock. So you have got essentially the same problem. How does the image mean? By this strategy you only move from something relatively observable, the linguistic phenomenon, to something merely postulated, a mysterious and inaccessible surrogate.

I can make a similar point about the physicalistic theory that identifies meaning with some supposed "engram" or brain trace. Again, a fantastic hypothesis will help us to understand the issues.

To the best of my knowledge, nobody has ever seen an engram, nor is there any hope, in the foreseeable future, of finding a distinctive neurological structure that corresponds, let us say, to the word "red." But once again, let us take a leap into some fantastic future in which we can directly observe people's brains. So we say "red," while the brain-viewing machine observes the hearer's cerebrum and central nervous system. To make things a little easier for us, let us suppose that the machine shows a particularly active system of neurons arranged in *this* pattern:

RED

Very convenient!

So somebody says, "Aha! Now, at last, after 2,000 years of inconclusive debate, you can *see* the meaning: there it is, right there in his brain." Is there anything wrong with that argument? (At this point, somebody will inevitably suggest that "r-e-d" does after all spell "red.") Well, how do we know that "r-e-d" *means* red? There may well be some language—if not, we can invent one—in which "r-e-d" means green.

Or put it this way: suppose we look at his brain, see the r-e-d constellation, and are convinced that he must know the meaning. But in order to check up, we now show him all sorts of color samples with very strong positive and negative inducements to answer sincerely and correctly. Thus if he recognizes the red card, he gets a thousand dollars right away; but if he doesn't, he gets whipped a thousand times. (And he's not a masochist, either.) So we show him the *green* card—he has every inducement, is panting and sweating in his eagerness—and says, "That's red!" A thousand lashes! (And all the time the constellation is glittering in his head.) So what are we going to say? That he *must* understand the word, because the meaning is right in his head? Of course, that's absurd. Any person who still retained some common sense, after being exposed to higher education, would say that if that is what the theory implies, then, so much the worse for the theory. It is perfectly clear that the man who cannot properly discriminate between colors, in cases where he has every inducement to do so, cannot understand the use of the word, and whatever is going on in his brain is irrelevant.

So we pass on, by a natural transition, to theories that identify meaning with behavior. Given the train of thought I have just presented, it is tempting to think that grasp of meaning must, surely, be a matter of what the person *does* and can do. Then, if it should turn out that we also find some supplementary physiological or mental criteria, so much the better. But when we talk about a person's meaning something, what we really have in mind is some kind of behavior.

Well, that sounds promising; but the question is, What behavior? What behavior shows that somebody really understands the word? In the case of color terms, one might think of plausible test situations. You get somebody to discriminate between colors. But please notice that *that* simple test is already somewhat more complicated than it might seem. If I find an unsophisticated person and have a supply of color samples on hand, I still have to *talk* to him in order to get him to take the test. Try doing it without saying anything. Turn up somewhere in the middle of Africa, with a whole lot of color samples, and a word from the local vocabulary—let's suppose it to be "ujgi." Now, in the cause of methodological purity you are not going to talk to these people: you are just going to do this particular experiment, which is to find out whether "ujgi" means "red." What *do* you do? If you merely say "ujgi" while shuffling the color samples, they will probably think you are crazy. It is essential, even for this simple experiment, that the person you are experimenting with understands what you are doing, and understanding presupposes communication, and communication presupposes mastery, via language, of a number of abstract ideas.

Consider a familiar utterance such as "I am trying to get you to sort these colors." Now, if the hearer can understand that, you can perform differential experiments on whether, say, "shocking pink" means anything to him, and if so, what, and so on. This sort of experiment, I want to suggest, has to be conducted against a background that presupposes rather sophisticated linguistic skills. And conversely, where such skills cannot be confidently assumed, as, say, in the case of very young children, the corresponding behavioral tests become almost impossible to perform. Any young parent will testify, without recourse to any recondite observation, that it is hard to know whether a child understands a word, because there is no simple behavioral test.

I should like, finally, to mention one more type of theory which might perhaps be called, somewhat provocatively, the "No Meaning" theory.

Stated very crudely, the basic idea of this type of theory is that the question we started from, formulated as, What *is* the meaning of a word, an expression, or a sentence? is already misleading, because it suggests there is something to be looked for. And the various types of theories that I have been sketching all accept that suggestion. Various theorists have identified meaning with the man who bears a name, or some abstract entity to which the label is attached, or part of the mental stream, or neurological traces; and these answers, if they were right, would all presuppose that meaning was something separately identifiable. Now the "No Meaning" type of theory attacks that presupposition as a fundamental mistake. Belief that meaning is some kind of entity is, indeed, a special case of a more general mistake, of confusion about what some philosophers call "logical grammar." It is very often the case that presuppositions about what a word refers to are erroneously based on the parallel uses of that word and words of very different kinds of meaning in the same grammatical classes of sentence. Thus "meaning" and "length" are used in very nearly identical linguistic ways and are therefore erroneously assumed to be similar in the logical class of event they refer to.

Many writers have said that the structure of language seems, in some ways, almost deliberately misleading. Take a child and say that a certain place on the map is North Ithaca and another place South Ithaca. If this child is either rather stupid or some sort of precocious philosophical genius, he may say, "Okay, I know where North Ithaca is, and I know where South Ithaca is, but where's *just* Ithaca?" And you reply, "Right here—all of this is Ithaca." But now comes the flash of genius or imbecility: The child insists on knowing also where "*just* North" is. Now, if you should point in the right direction, you might seriously mislead the child, because he might think that just as there is a place here called Ithaca, so up there, somewhere, there is something called North. And if he has that idea, and has any talent for philosophy, he might even tell you that it is very strange that two different places—North and Ithaca—should both be in some mysterious way right *here*. Please notice that the easy way out, of saying "Well, North is only a direction" is no answer at all, because this child, if he really is a prodigy, can say, "Well, what's a direction?" And how are we to answer *that*?

This is a crude and manufactured example of how the structure of ordinary language can confuse thought. There are more impressive examples. I shall mention only one, connected with that fascinating and confusing word, infinity. There are people who think of infinity as if it were some definite place. A talented man who taught me mathematics long ago thought about infinity in that way, and I can still remember a favorite slogan of his, that infinity was "a place where things happen that don't." He would explain his idea in this way (and please remember that he was quite serious): Take a curve that has asymptotes, say, a rectangular hyperbola. Now, if you go up a rising branch in the direction of the *y*-axis, then, of course, you always remain at a distance from that axis: the distance gets smaller and smaller the further you go up (for that's partly what we mean by the curve being asymptotic); but no matter how far you go, there will always be a gap. But, when you "get to infinity," he suggested, something happens that doesn't; namely, there will be contact. And in fact, this rising branch of the curve will turn up down below, infinitely far down. Because where there's a continuous curve, the crossover happens at infinity, and infinity is down here as well as up there — it's one and the same place. Obviously this talented teacher loved this confusing idea — and you can see how well he taught, because I can still remember that particular lesson. Other people have been known to talk this way about infinity, as if it were some place a very, very long way away. Thus it is sometimes said that parallel lines always stay the same distance apart, until you get to infinity, or more precisely, the point of infinity associated with all those parallel lines, and at infinity they intersect. This case of a confusion in logical grammar can be cleared up by pointing out that infinity is not a place beyond the finite, that the adjective "*in*finite" and the noun "infinity" are used in special ways. (Notice, for example, that we have no noun "finity"—and for good reason.) There is no time, unfortunately, to pursue this further.

Now, the basic idea behind the "No Meaning" approach is that the term "meaning" functions somewhat like "infinity" in this respect. Put crudely and rather misleadingly, there is no such thing as *the* meaning of a term, or *the* meaning of an expression, or *the* meaning of a sentence. And any search for the meaning is doomed to failure at the start: it is as pointless and self-defeating as the search for some *place* called "infinity." You could scour the universe and you would never find infinity, not for lack of technical skill, but because there is a logical confusion behind the effort. Similarly, the "No Meaning" approach claims that there is logical confusion in looking for anything that *is* the meaning. Please notice that this kind of view by no means implies that the word "meaning" is meaningless, any more than the remarks I made about "infinity" imply that mathematicians or physicists, who talk about infinity, with proper precautions, are talking nonsense.

If I say the limit of $1/2^n$ as n goes to infinity is zero, that use of infinity is perfectly respectable. And I can use the mathematical symbol for infinity and understand it, without supposing that there is some number which is denoted by the infinity mark. Similarly, when I say that "nephelococcygian" (a word that *is* in the dictionary) means, roughly, "cloud-cuckoolandish" or "visionary," I have succeeded *in telling you what it means*. So there is no doubt at all that meaning exists and can be communicated.

Well, what then can the "No Meaning" approach say positively? Something of this sort: that the word "meaning" has basically a relational function, expressing a connection *between symbols*. That is the crucial point; it need not be a relation between a word and something nonverbal, but may be regarded as a relation between symbols. I am not suggesting this as the whole story, but this is at least a highly salient feature of the approach. So when I say, "nephelococcygian" means, say, "visionary," I am saying—very roughly, of course—that where you would otherwise have used the word "visionary," now you can say "nephelococcygian" instead. I am therefore offering a sort of equation of synonymy. And this approach can be made to fit, with some stretching, even the so-called "ostensive" type of case—where I define by pointing to something. If somebody doesn't know what a file folder is, and I say, "That's a file folder," it looks as if I am setting up a connection between the thing itself and something verbal. But it might be held that even here we encounter a kind of synonymy. For the learner must be able to recognize *what* I call a "file folder" by means of some other description. This is controversial, however.

At any rate, this is the general pattern, and you may gather, from the way that I have been talking, that I am more inclined to this relational type of view than to any of the others that I have been discussing. It has all sorts of difficulties but also has a number of inviting possibilities.

I have time only to hint at some of the implications. One is that statements of meaning belong to a sophisticated self-referential level of languge. One might get along without the word "meaning" at all, if communication were fairly smooth, which is not always the case. There is a primary level of language where you learn words for people, events, animals, states of mind, and so on. It is only when communication becomes problematic or defective that we need words like "meaning" in order to resolve our difficulties. This is connected with the point I have already made, that in order even to understand a question about meaning, you must already possess many basic linguistic skills. The pattern I am recommending, therefore, looks somewhat like this: There is a basic linguistic level at which we talk about nonverbal things, and there is another, so-called "metalinguistic" level, at which we use language to talk *about* language. "Meaning" belongs to this "higher" level. Questions about meaning are, roughly speaking, questions about the functioning of language. They are to be answered by showing how parts of the language can replace one another.

What I have just said is all very crude and raises all manner of provoking questions.[1] But that, after all, was my purpose in presenting such a view of meaning.

REFERENCES

Black, M. *The labyrinth of language*. New York: New American Library, 1969.

de Saussure, F. *Course in general linguistics*. New York: Philosophical Library, 1959.

James, W. *Principles of psychology*. New York: Dover, 1950.

Locke, J. Of words. In A. C. Fraser (Ed.), *An essay concerning human understanding* Book III. Oxford: Clarendon Press, 1894.

Ryle, G. The theory of meaning. In M. Black (Ed.), *The importance of language*. Ithaca, N.Y.: Cornell University Press, 1968.

[1]One such question that will occur to many readers is that of how one can decide whether what someone has said really means anything or whether it is nonsense. Often, non-sense utterances appear to have meaning because they are cast in a form whose logic is similar to a class of utterances that are meaningful. An example of this class of mistake was presented on page 85; i.e., the belief that meaning is an entity, arising because the word "meaning" is used in types of sentences which also use nouns that identify entities. A treatment of this important question will be found in the author's *Labyrinth of Language* (1969, pp. 105 – 110 and 181 – 187).

6
LINGUISTIC RELATIVITY

Eleanor Rosch
University of California at Berkeley

Are we "trapped" by our language into holding a particular "world view?" Can we never really understand or communicate with speakers of a language quite different from own because each language has molded the thought of its people into mutually incomprehensible world views? Can we never get "beyond" language to experience the world "directly"? Such issues develop from an extreme form of a position sometimes known as "the Whorfian hypothesis," after the early twentieth century linguist Benjamin Lee Whorf, and called, more generally, the hypothesis of "linguistic relativity."

According to linguistic relativity, it is naive to think that when we learn a "foreign" language, we simply learn a new vocabulary to name the same objects and a new grammar to express the same relations between objects as exist in our own language. Rather, "the background linguistic system . . . of each language is not merely a reproducing instrument for voicing ideas but rather is itself the shaper of ideas . . . . We dissect nature along lines laid down by our native language. The categories and types that we isolate from the world of phenomena we do not find there because they stare every observer in the face; on the contrary, the world is presented in a kaleidoscopic flux of impressions which has to be organized by our minds—and this means . . . by the linguistic system in our minds [Whorf, 1956, pp. 212–213]."

When many of us first came in contact with the Whorfian hypothesis, it seemed not only true but profoundly true. We felt we could look inward and see our comprehension of the world molded by language just as we could "watch" as our

¹The writing of this chapter was supported by a grant to the author (under her former name, Eleanor Rosch Heider) from the Summer Faculty Fellowship Program, University of California, Berkeley.

personalities were irrevocably shaped by society and upbringing. But profound and ineffable truths are not, in that form, subject to scientific investigation. Is linguistic relativity an empirical "theory"? If so, it must be possible to derive from it concrete statements about specific relations of actual languages to the thought of the people that speak them; and these statements must be of a type which can be judged true or false by comparing them to facts about those actual languages and thoughts.

There are a number of important distinctions within the Whorfian position which lead to differing empirical implications. Relatively "weak" or "strong" claims may be asserted about the role of language in thought: at the weak extreme is the simple claim that both languages and thoughts are *different* in different language communities, while the strong version is that language differences necessarily *cause* (are necessary and sufficient conditions for) thought differences. The stronger claim is sometimes called Linguistic Determinism to distinguish it from the less specific Linguistic Relativity. Perhaps even more important, operationally, are distinctions among the aspects (or units) of language considered as potential influencers of thought. Are we focusing on overt or covert units in language? On basic grammatical divisions? On grammatical form classes in general? On classifications and references inherent in language vocabularies? We will consider these possibilities in turn.

COVERT LINGUISTIC CLASSIFICATIONS

Language as Metaphysics

The strongest and most inclusive form of the Whorfian hypothesis (and the only form, perhaps, that Whorf would today recognize) is that each language both embodies and imposes upon the culture a particular world view. Nature is, in reality, a kaleidoscopic continuum, but the units which form the basis of the grammar of each language serve both to classify reality into corresponding units and to define the fundamental nature of those units. Thus, in English and other "Standard Average European" tongues, the basic units of reality are objects (nouns), composed of substance and form, and actions (verbs) — both of which exist in an objective, three-dimensional space (expressed by such linguistic devices as locatives) and a "kinetic one-dimensional uniformly and perpetually flowing time [Whorf, 1956, p. 59]" (expressed by forms such as tense). In the Hopi language, however, things and actions are not distinguished; rather, they are both Events, differentiated only according to duration. Even to say that about Hopi may be misleading, for rather than substance, motion, space, and time, Hopi grammar divides the universe by two great "principles," "Manifested" (Objective) and "Unmanifest" (Subjective). "Manifested" comprises all that is or has been accessible to the senses, while "Unmanifest" (Subjective) includes, as one group, all that we call future and all that we call mental, including that which is perceived as future-potential-mental in the "heart" of men, animals, plants, inanimate objects, and the Cosmos. The metaphysics implicit in the grammar of Standard Average European makes it sensible to analyze sentences, and thus reality, into agents, actions, and the objects, instruments, and results of actions; but such constructions, Whorf argues, are gross distortions when used as units of analysis for various American Indian languages. In support of his contentions, Whorf provides a variety of translations of statements in various Indian languages into English to show how unlike ours are the thought processes of speakers of those languages. Thus, in Apache, "It is a dripping spring" is expressed by "As water, or springs, whiteness moves downward." In Shawnee, "cleaning gun with a ramrod" is "direct a hollow moving dry spot by movement of tool."

The Whorfian hypothesis is, at the least, intriguing: what is it like to live in a mental world in which there are no things or actions but only events, where there are no agents and acts, no separate space and time? Can we ever hope to communicate with people who have such a world view? At the most, the Whorfian view challenges our most fundamental beliefs. Are commonsense distinctions (such as that between object and action) which appear to us to be "given" unequivocally by our senses, actually an illusion fostered by the grammar of English? Is Newtonian physics not a necessary first step in the development of physical theory, but merely a metaphor derived from the grammatical units of Standard Average European? Are the basic concepts of linguistics perhaps the only means by which we may hope to surmount the limitations of our own language and become able to analyze differences between languages, or are these concepts themselves only reifications of the grammar of our own language family?

• Upon what evidence are such sweeping claims based? As a linguist, Whorf found the grammar of several American Indian languages to differ from English grammar to such an extent that literal translations between those languages and English made no sense. The literal translations, given above, of "a dripping spring" and "cleaning a gun with a ramrod" do, indeed, appear to be products of a very alien mode of thought. Of course, it is also true that all languages have somewhat different grammars, even the languages which Whorf calls "Standard Average European." However, notice that when we learn French, we are taught to translate "Comment allez vous?" not literally as "How go you?" but as the standard English greeting to which it corresponds, "How are you?" And if a student translates "le chat gris" as "the cat gray," he is told he has made an error; in English, modifiers come before the noun, not after, and the correct rendition of the phrase in English is "the gray cat." Let us, however, try to take a Whorfian view of French and suppose that the order of noun and modifier is indicative of a difference in metaphysics. The French language, we may assert, defines the basic units of nature not as substantive things but as pervasive attributes such as colors, shapes, and sizes. What we see as a thing-with-attributes, the Frenchman sees as a specific local perturbation of a general Attribute; thus what we call a cat with a particular color is, in French, a particular modification of the general color manifold—some "cat gray" as opposed, perhaps, to some "fog gray." Why should such interpretations seem absurd for French but not Hopi? Is it that we have other evidence for concluding that Frenchmen are not that different from ourselves? If there were a sovereign Hopi nation to the south of the United States, might we today be learning in our classrooms not to make errors of literal translation in Hopi?

The argument for language as implicit metaphysics is circular. It is circular because the only evidence that we have for the metaphysics is the grammar, yet we are clearly unwilling to interpret every grammatical difference between languages as metaphysical. The circularity applies just as well to the weaker form of linguistic relativity as to the stronger deterministic hypothesis. The seriousness of the circularity becomes apparent when we consider how it might be eliminated. Can we go out and gather independent evidence for thought differences? What should we look for? The problem appears to be conceptual rather than empirical. What would it "look like" if a language community had a particular implicit metaphysics? We can recognize *explicit* metaphysics and differences between them; for example, Aristotle's metaphysics was different from Hegel's, and the Upanishads contain a different metaphysics from the New Testament. If the Hopi made explicit metaphysical statements ("the Cosmos consists of four mutually antagonistic Substances," etc.), we could contrast those statements with the explicit statements of like kind made by other communities. But an implicit metaphysics? After all, the Hopi act in the physical world much like anyone else; they walk through space, bump into solid objects, and keep track of time in planting and harvesting. How are we to know that they conceive of these abstractions in a manner uniquely corresponding to and/or determined by their language?

In summary: the most dramatic form of the Whorfian hypothesis—the assertion that each language embodies and imposes upon the culture an implicit metaphysics — does not, in that form, appear to be an empirical statement. If it must be interpreted as meaning only that languages differ, then it is true but trivial. If it is to mean more than that, we find that we have no idea what the state of the world would "look like" if the hypothesis were true, or, correspondingly, if it were false. The rest of this chapter discusses successive attempts to reinterpret the Whorfian view into claims which are sufficiently specific that we can understand their meaning and test whether they are true or false.

Grammatical Form Class

The words (actually, the morphemes, or units of meaning) of any language can be divided into classes of grammatical equivalents on the basis of the positions which they can occupy in word sequences (such as sentences). The most basic units of grammar, which Whorf claimed formed the basis of the metaphysics of a language, are none other than the most general form classes of the language — in English the parts of speech such as nouns, verbs, adjectives, and adverbs. Many form classes are more limited in scope than the basic "parts of speech": gender defines classes of nouns in French; English nouns are either "mass" (occur in the position "Some X") or "count" (occur in the position "An X"); and in Navajo, verbs of handling take a different form depending on the nature of the objects handled. Obviously, form classes are not the same in all languages.

As long as form classes are considered only "structural" (defined only by position of occurrence in sentences), they do not suggest important cognitive differences between speakers of different languages. However, Whorf and others have stressed that form classes also have semantic (meaning) correlates. Thus, nouns are seen as substances; verbs as actions; mass nouns as indefinite, uncontained, flowing masses of matter; count nouns as singular, self-contained objects; gender as masculine, feminine, and neuter; and Navajo verb stem classifiers as shape types (round, long, granular, etc.). Generally, the members of a linguistic community are unconscious of the semantics of form class. For example, even in a relatively grammatically self-conscious society like ours, most people have never spontaneously noticed the distinction between mass and count nouns, nor ever thought about which English verbs can or cannot take the prefix "un-." Whorf speaks of the semantic correlates of form classes (he calls them "cryptotypes") as the "covert categories," the "underlying concepts" of the language. In fact, it is the pervasive, covert influence of cryptotypes on thought which may be one relatively concrete interpretation of what it might mean for grammar to influence metaphysics.

The semantic interpretation of form class has not gone unchallenged. Descriptive linguistics considers the relation between structurally defined form classes and their semantic correlates highly dubious (cf. Fries, 1952). Semantic definitions of form class are always unclear or overextended; not all nouns are substances (e.g., "space") nor all verbs active (e.g., "hold"); mass nouns can come in discrete units ("some bread"), and count nouns can refer to fluid masses ("a martini"); masculine and feminine gender forms are used for innumerable genderless objects; and specific Navajo shape classifiers are used for abstractions ("news" takes the round classifier).

There is, however, undoubtedly a *partial* correlation between some form classes and some semantics. It would be to the advantage of individuals learning a language to be aware (at some level) of these partial correlations. Roger Brown (1958) has shown that even 4-year-old children can use structural syntactic cues for guessing the semantic referent of form classes. Brown showed the children pictures in which an action, a discrete object, and an unbounded flowing mass were depicted, introducing the picture either with "This is a picture of latting" or "of a latt" or "of some latt." The 4-year-olds easily identified the object by means of the form-class cue. A similar experiment was performed on the form-class gender by Ervin (1959). Italian speakers living in Boston were read nonsense syllables formed with Italian gender. When subjects were asked to rate the syllables on a series of adjective scales (called the semantic differential—cf. Osgood, Suci, &

Tannenbaum, 1957), they rated the masculine gender syllables more similar to their ratings for "man" than "woman" and vice versa. Such experiments demonstrate that we can make use of what semantic information there is in form classes when we are learning and applying words. They do not, however, prove that speakers of languages with different sets of form classes take different views of the semantic nature of the world. After all, discrete solid objects and unbounded fluids, and male and female organisms, have quite different physical properties which all peoples might well be required to take equal account of whether or not their grammar makes such distinctions.

If we wished to test whether semantic aspects of form class do affect thought, what kinds of correlates or effects on thought might we look for? In fact, there has been little systematic consideration and little research concerning this issue. One possibility is that there is a "metaphorical generalization" of the meaning from members of the form class to which it literally applies to members to which it does not apply literally at all. Thus, the French may really think of and treat tables as feminine, and the Navajo may consider news to be round. Whorf himself suggests this kind of interpretation when he claims that we read action into all words that are verbs, and, since all English sentences contain verbs, into every statement. "We therefore read action into every sentence, even into 'I hold it' . . . . We think of it (i.e., holding) and even see it as an action because language formulates it in the same way as it formulates more numerous expressions, like 'I strike it,' which deals with movements and changes ⌊Whorf, 1956, p. 243⌋." But *do* we read action into all verbs? How can we tell? One test would be to go to the natural logic of language use itself; if action is being "read into" verbs like "hold," they should be capable of occurring modified by action adverbs just as do "true" action verbs. The actual state of such verbs is described by the philosopher Max Black: "a man may strike slowly, jerkily, energetically, and so on. Now if somebody were to attach these adverbs to the verb 'to hold' that would be sufficient indication that he was 'reading action' into the verb. I suppose a child might say he was holding his hat slowly, and the poet is allowed a similar license; but otherwise the conceptual confusion is too gross to occur ⌊Black, 1959, pp. 252–253⌋."

Are there *any* cases in which the partially correlated semantics of a form class are extended to other words that happen to be in that class? Is there a systematic way of studying such extensions so that we might conclude that it never happens? These intriguing questions remain entirely open to future investigation, and the interested student might well try using his intuition as a speaker of his own language to consider them.

Even if the semantic partial correlates of form class do not extend beyond the clear-cut cases, they may have effects on thought—one obvious possibility is that they continually draw the attention of speakers of the language to those aspects of the world which are the basis for the (even partial) form-class semantic distinctions. Such an effect would be most likely demonstrable in the case of a form class which was sufficiently salient linguistically and sufficiently correlated with a clear-cut semantic for it to be reasonable to expect speakers of the language to be influenced by habitual use of the class. Navajo shape classifiers appear to be just such a case. Use of verb stems which indicate shape in Navajo is obligatory linguistically, and such stems are very high frequency items in the language. For all objects that actually have a shape, the classifiers are used consistently — even English speakers new to the system perceive the classifiers to refer predictably to shape types. Most importantly, the classifier used for an object is not an invariable attribute of the object (as is generally the case with gender) but varies with the actual shape of the object at the time of reference. Thus, a rolled-up rug will take a different classifier from the same rug when it is lying flat (S. Ervin-Tripp, personal communication, 1972). It is reasonable to suppose that Navajo speakers are continually noticing shape when speaking and, thus, would be more likely to notice shape and to use shape as a basis of classification than speakers of a language which does not incorporate obligatory grammatical shape distinctions.

A test for this hypothesis was devised by Carroll and Casagrande (1958). Subjects were presented with a reference object and two other objects, each one resembling the standard by a different attribute. For example, the standard might be a red circle and the other objects a red square and a blue circle. Subjects were asked to choose which of the two objects was most like the standard. A variety of objects were used, incorporating all combinations of the attributes form, color, and size. The basic hypothesis was that Navajo speakers would prefer to classify by form rather than by the other equally correct attributes. Three groups of children were tested: Navajo children whose dominant language was Navajo; Navajo children for whom English was the dominant language; and monolingual English speakers. As predicted, the Navajo-dominant Navajo preferred to classify on the basis of form; however, so did the English-speaking Boston children. English-dominant Navajo, on the other hand, preferred color. These results are not unequivocal. They have been treated both as evidence against the Whorfian view — because English speakers, whose grammar does not call attention to form, preferred form classifications just as much as the Navajo-dominant Navajo — and as evidence in support of Whorf — because the English-dominant Navajo, whose culture and early environment, but not language, were the most similar to that of the Navajo-dominant Navajo, preferred color and not form. The reader might pause and consider what arguments might be offered on each side.

In fact, the results are probably even more difficult to interpret than has been supposed. Since the time of Carroll and Casagrande's experiments, a great many tests of color-form preference in classification have been performed on a variety of populations, and a consistent but, to the present author, incomprehensible pattern of results has emerged. Around the world, the younger the subject and/or the less Western schooling he has received, the more likely he is to use color as the basis of classification in the kind of "triads" test used by Carroll and Casagrande (see Serpell, 1969, for a review of studies). However, it is just young children and non-Western peoples who appear to be the populations least likely to classify by color in more naturalistic contexts. It is the technologically less advanced cultures which appear to have smaller color vocabularies and less cultural concern with color distinctions and coordinations (see Berlin & Kay, 1969, and the latter part of the present chapter). Young children in Western cultures only come to use color terms correctly and consistently at about the age when they begin to prefer form classification in the color-form preference triads (Heider, 1971; Istomina, 1963). Further evidence comes from a study of the published diaries of the language development of individual children (usually kept by fond linguist parents). Clark (1973) has examined all of the diary examples of young children's overgeneralizations of words—that is, of cases where a child applies a newly learned word to a variety of things to which that word does not actually apply in the adult language (e.g., calling all animals "dogs" or all men "daddy"). Clark was interested in finding out the attributes by which children generalize meaning. What is relevant to the present issue is that, in all of the diary literature, there is not one single instance reported in which a child seemed to overgeneralize a word on the basis of color! So classifying by color or form on the triad type of test may well be the result of factors very specific to operations and cognitions in that test situation and may not reflect any tendency to use either attribute as the basis of classification in any other context.

Navajo shape-classifying verb stems appeared to be a case ideally suited to a demonstration of the effect of grammatical form class on attention. However, preference for form over color in a triad-classification task may involve too crude a hypothesis or may be too task-specific to test the issue. The interested reader might try to think of a more reasonable test. Does anything in the literature on perception, memory, learning, problem solving, or other human cognitive functions suggest such a test? Unfortunately, at present, the evidence concerning the effects of form class on attention remains equivocal.

If the semantics of form class provide the cryptotypes — the underlying categorization of reality — for speakers of a language, then at the very least, at some cognitive level, speakers of the language should code form classes as categories. Overt semantic categories have been shown to have several reliable effects on human memory—do categories consisting of form classes have similar effects?

One such effect occurs in the kind of experiment called "free recall." A subject is read a list of ordinary words and then attempts to recall the words in any order he wishes. The list may consist of random, unrelated words, or it may contain a number of words from the same semantic categories (for example, flowers, animals, musical instruments). When subjects receive a "categorized" word list, they remember more words than in uncategorized lists, and they tend to recall those words in "clusters" from the same category — even when the input list contained the words in random order. If grammatical classes are "meaningful" cognitive categories, shouldn't they also provide a basis for clustering and improved recall? Cofer and Bruce (1965) presented lists in which words could be categorized into the form classes nouns, verbs, and adjectives, but were otherwise unrelated. They found no effects of the categories on either accuracy or clustering in recall. (See Cofer, 1965, for a discussion of some of the complex issues involved in recall of categorized lists.)

A second effect of semantic categories on memory arises in the type of task in which subjects must try to remember an item (such as a number, word, or nonsense syllable) for short periods of time while performing an interfering task, such as counting backwards. In such experiments, ability to remember becomes rapidly poorer with each succeeding item, generally attributed to interference from preceding items. If all of the items up to some point have belonged to one semantic class and the experimenter switches suddenly to another class (e.g., switches from letters of the alphabet to numbers, from animals to plants, or from words with a "good" connotation to words with a "bad" connotation), subjects regain their ability to remember the items. However, switching from one grammatical class to another (e.g., from verbs to adjectives) has no such effects (Wickens, 1970). So, at least in these memory tasks, grammatical class seems to be more like a dead metaphor than like a psychologically real classification of reality. [2]

We began this section with the notion that the semantic correlates of grammatical form class might provide those basic classifications of reality which are the covert metaphysics embodied and perpetuated by language. However, we have been unable to verify the specific meanings which such a claim might have. Members of grammatical classes which do not share the "semantic meaning of the class" also do not seem to be treated metaphorically as though they did share it by other uses in the language itself. The one attempt to test the hypothesis that speakers of a language are led to pay particular attention to attributes of the environment coded in obligatory form classes in the language was rendered difficult to interpret by a variety of factors. Finally, there is some evidence that form classes do not seem to be coded as cognitive categories at all—at least, they do not have the properties that other meaningful semantic categories do. However, it should be apparent from the preceding sections that the evidence now available is anything but systematic.

Most actual research directed toward the Whorfian hypothesis has not addressed itself to grammar at all, but has dealt with the relatively concrete and overt classifications made by language vocabulary. It is to that topic which we turn next.

OVERT LANGUAGE CLASSIFICATIONS: VOCABULARY

According to Whorf, language affects thought basically by means of the kinds of classifications it "lays upon" reality. Whorf focused on classifications of a

---

[2] There are tasks in the human learning and memory literature in which grammatical class does not have an effect; however, these are all tasks in which predicted differences are derived from and easily explained by the formal syntax of grammatical class—that is, from privileges of occurrence in strings of words.

general and abstract nature—the covert "metaphysics" and "cryptotypes" embedded in language. However, we have seen the difficulty of demonstrating that classifications on that level are actually related to meaningful cognitive units. There is another level of language, however, in which semantic classifications are quite overt, the level of the lexicon (vocabulary). If the same Hopi word refers to what English codes with the three words "airplane," "insect," "aviator," or if the language of the Eskimo uses three words to refer to that thing coded by the one English word "snow," these are overt semantic differences in the way the world is "cut up" and coded.

In fact, it is not unreasonable to suppose that there are concrete and identifiable aspects of the lexical code that affect identifiable and measurable aspects of thought. Earlier in this book, the background for a clear-cut empirical demonstration of just such a case was presented. Berlyne (this volume) defined the concept of "information" and discussed human limitations in the capacity to process and retain information. How much information can be retained, however, is dependent on the way in which it has been "coded." Normally, for example, only about seven digits can be remembered, even for very brief periods (Miller, 1956). However, if a string of 0 and 1 digits is recoded by a subject into octal (a system by which groups of three digits are "named" by a single number), he can remember almost three times as many. Here is a prototypical case in which a classificatory aspect of vocabulary (the number of digits named by a single number in a particular code) can be shown directly related to an aspect of cognition (amount of information stored in memory).

Octal is an "artificial" code developed for particular purposes within our culture. The Whorfian hypothesis on the level of the lexicon might be considered to contain an additional assertion, namely that *natural* languages as they are spoken by the world's speakers contain differences in codes (analogous, perhaps, to recoding groups of digits into octal) which affect cognitive processes such as perception, classification, and memory.

The bulk of the empirical work on linguistic relativity has involved language at the lexical level, and the rest of this chapter will be concerned with work at this level. It is well, therefore, at this point to pause and consider how such a hypothesis about natural languages can (and cannot) be tested. In the previous sections, we saw in operation various problems concerned with testing Whorfian views; at this point, let us look systematically at the relevant methodological issues.

A Discussion of Method

Many facts which have been offered in support of the effects of language on thought (at all levels of language) have been only descriptions of differences between cultures. To avoid such confusions, it is necessary to bear in mind the important distinction between the *content* of a language or culture and the thought *processes* of members of the culture. Of course, cultures differ in content; we would probably not call them different cultures if they did not. A rice farmer in the Phillipines and a college student in America live quite different lives, and presumably the *content* of their thoughts, knowledge, and memory mirror those differences in experience. But from knowing that, we cannot automatically assume that members of the two cultures *operate* on that content in different ways. It is probable, for example, that they forget their experiences according to the same laws of decay or interference in memory regardless of what it is that they are forgetting.

There is, of course, a sense in which any lexical difference between languages implies a difference in the content of thought of the speakers. In learning to use a term, speakers must learn the class of things to which the term refers; thus knowledge of and reference to that class of objects is part of the content of the speaker's thought. In this sense, the weaker form of linguistic relativity (that there are differences in thought in different linguistic communities) is necessarily true. The really interesting hypothesis at the lexical level, however, is the stronger deterministic claim that lexical differences themselves affect thought processes in some manner.

It is tempting, when making claims supporting the Whorfian hypothesis at any level of language, to rely primarily on content differences. They are often very striking differences; if a language has only two color terms or thousands of elaborate distinctions and classifications for skin diseases, surely that must affect the way in which these domains are dealt with by the cognitive manipulations of the speakers. To illustrate how misleading a direct inference from lexical content can be, we may recall the even more striking differences between the Hopi grammatical classifications of things on the basis of duration and the English division into substances and actions. The evidence concerning that distinction left us in grave doubt about whether nouns and verbs are meaningful semantic cognitive categories for English speakers at all.

Most "demonstrations" of the Whorfian hypothesis have done more than simply point to differences between the content of languages; they have, in addition, identified aspects of the culture of the speakers which covary with language. Such evidence is not entirely adequate either, however, for two reasons. In the first place, covariation does not determine the direction of causality. On the simplest level, cultures are very likely to have names for physical objects which exist in their culture and not to have names for objects outside of their experience. Where television sets exist, there are words to refer to them. However, it would be difficult to argue that the objects are caused by the words. The same reasoning probably holds in the case of institutions and other, more abstract, entities and their names. In the second place, covariation between cultural content and language content neither proves the further existence of covarying cognitive processes nor would it determine the direction of causality even were such covariation to be demonstrated. Thus, if Eskimos were shown both to have more names for snow than Americans and to remember different types of snow better than Americans, both might simply be due to the fact that there is more snow in the Arctic and to Eskimos having more active experience with it than Americans; it would not have been proved that the greater number of words per se affected the memory.

The preceding argument has stressed the point that cognitive processes must be measured independently of, and not simply deduced from, linguistic or cultural content. However, this raises a second major problem of method: How are we to define and measure cognitive processes cross-culturally? Too often such measurement is based on a psychometric "deficit" model. Hypotheses are stated in terms of "how well" entire cultures perform on a particular test. For example, a hypothesis might state that "members of traditional cultures cannot think creatively" or that "the more words a language has for colors, the better speakers can remember colors." The investigator might administer a test of "creative thinking" to Americans (not a traditional culture) and to the Yemenites (a traditional culture), or might administer a color memory test to Americans (many color terms) and to the Dani (few color terms). When the Yemenites performed poorly on the creativity test and the Dani poorly on the color memory test, the investigator would conclude that his causal hypothesis was supported. However, it should be obvious that innumerable other factors besides those in which the investigator is explicitly interested vary between "us" and "them." Motivations, cultural meaningfulness of the materials, general familiarity with, or even previous explicit training with, the kind of task used are some obvious examples. In fact, any preliterate culture will probably perform "less well" than a Western culture given almost any Western "test." But if Dani can be expected to perform below Americans in *any* memory test, how may we conclude that it was the number of color terms which determined their poor performance in the color memory test? In short, positive results are assured the investigator who frames hypotheses such that a single Western and single non-Western culture are compared, with a prediction in the direction of the non-Western culture giving poorer performance than the Western — but such results will be uninterpretable.

Are there ways out of the impasse? One trend has been to try to invent tasks which are as culturally relevant in content and form of administration to a particular preliterate culture as Western tests are to Western cultures. This excellent idea has, however, given rise to a special sort of circular "dialectic." The format of the research is typically this: Stage 1 — an investigator demonstrates that the people of "Culture X" fail to exhibit some ability (for example, "abstract thinking") on a standard Western test. Stage 2 — the same or a different investigator manipulates the content and context of the test until he has demonstrated that, under the right circumstances (for example, if asked to reason about animal husbandry in their own culture rather than about colored geometric forms), the people of Culture X do exhibit "abstract thinking." The Stage 2 demonstration may be beautiful in its ingenuity; however, the two stages tend simply to cancel each other and make little contribution to our understanding of basic human thought processes. It ought to go without saying that all tasks in cross-cultural research should be as appropriate for the people taking them as possible and, indeed, some level of appropriateness is essential if any meaningful data are to be collected at all. However, culturally meaningful tasks do not of themselves produce well-conceived research; why should hypotheses be framed in terms of differences in absolute level of performance between "us" and "them" at all?

A second approach to the problem uses a model based on epidemiological methods in the health sciences. If traditionalism were proposed to be related to creative thought, *many* different cultures which differed in degree of traditionalism might be studied, as might groups within the same culture which differed in degree of traditionalism. Cultures and groups to be compared would ideally be chosen so as to hold constant various other factors which might influence creative thought. (For a more detailed discussion of the epidemiological model, see LeVine, 1970; and for an interesting example of its use, see Segall, Campbell, & Herskovitz, 1966). Unfortunately, owing to practical considerations, the epidemiological method has seldom been applied to the study of cognitive factors.

Perhaps the simplest and most direct way of circumventing the problem of measuring cognitive variables cross-culturally, is to abandon research designs whose emphasis is on "main effects" of culture per se. Hypotheses can be formed, not in terms of absolute differences between cultures, but in terms of interactions between variables within and between cultures. Take, for example, the hypothesis that the number of color terms affects color memory. Instead of comparing speakers of two languages one of which has more color terms than the other, we might search for cases where it is possible to compare relative performance for different areas of the color space for languages which differed in the relative number of terms they had for these areas. Perhaps one language has many terms for blue and green colors but few terms for the yellow-brown color area, another language just the opposite. Our prediction could then be that speakers of the first language would show relatively better memory for the blue-green than for the yellow-brown area; whereas, speakers of the second language would be relatively more proficient with yellow-brown colors than with blue-green. With research so designed, it would not matter how well either culture remembered color terms in total. Such an approach may be a key to meaningful comparisons, even between quite different cultures.

To return to the Whorfian hypothesis: it should by now be apparent that many factors are necessary in order to have a real test of the effect of a natural language lexicon on thought. *(a)* We must have at least two natural languages whose lexicons differ with respect to some domain of discourse — if languages are not different, there is no point in the investigation.[3] *(b)* The domain must be one which

---

[3] An anthropologist's report of the existence, nonexistence, or denotation of semantic categories in the language of a culture he has studied is usually accepted at face value. Although we will follow that practice here, it should be realized that there are additional methodological problems with traditional field techniques for studying language. For a discussion, see Heider (1972b).

can be measured by the investigator independently of the way it is encoded by the languages of concern (for example, color may be measured in independent physical units such as wavelength)—if that is not the case (as, for example, in such domains as feelings or values), there is no objective way of describing how it is that the two languages differ. *(c)* The domain must not itself differ grossly between the cultures whose languages differ — if it does, then it may be differences in experience with the domain, and not language, which are affecting thought. *(d)* We must be able to obtain measures of specific aspects of cognition — such as perception, memory, or classification — having to do with the domain which are independent of, rather than simply assumed from, the language. *(e)* We must have a cross-culturally meaningful measure of differences in the selected aspects of cognition — preferably we should be able to state the hypotheses in terms of an interaction between the linguistic and cognitive variables, rather than in terms of overall differences between speakers of the languages.

One domain only has appeared to researchers to be ideal for such research— color. Color is a continuous physical variable which can easily be designated by objective measures which are independent of the color terms in any given language (for example, wavelength). Many reports in the anthropological literature have described differences in color terminologies between languages — that is, differences in the way in which color terms appear to classify the physically invariant color space. The physical aspects of color, the domain of colors as such, is the same in every part of the world—although, of course, the colors most frequently viewed may differ ecologically. Color discrimination, memory, and classification can be readily measured independently of color names, rather than simply inferred from the color terminology of the culture. And, finally, colors lend themselves readily to hypotheses stated in terms of interactions—as has already been illustrated by the preceding examples.

It may seem a long way from the initial introduction of linguistic relativity as an assertion about differences in "world view" to a study of the possible cognitive effects of differences in color terms. The transition was made necessary by the requirement that assertions be made in the form of empirically testable hypotheses. Much of the remainder of this chapter will trace the history of language-cognition research in the domain of colors, the primary domain in which such research has been carried out.

Color

Color is perceived when the human visual system interprets certain aspects of the physical properties of light. Sensory psychologists describe color with a solid using three psychological dimensions: hue (roughly, the dominant wavelength of the light), brightness (loosely speaking, an intensity dimension), and saturation (the apparent degree of dominance of the dominant wavelength, the "purity" of the light).[4] The color solid is divisible into literally millions of perceptually just noticeable differences. There is no evidence that human populations differ in the physiology of the visual system, nor that there are any cultures which differ in actual ability of their members to perceive and discriminate colors (Lenneberg, 1967). In fact, there is evidence that the old world primates, whose color physiology is similar to that of humans, are not different from humans in color perception and discrimination (De Valois & Jacobs, 1968). There are far fewer color names in any language than there are discriminable colors, and fewer still commonly used color names. Thus, it appears that cultural differences are to be found on the level of categorization rather than perception of color.

A seminal study in the effects of language on cognition was performed by Brown and Lenneberg (1954). Brown and Lenneberg reasoned that cultures, perhaps because of differing color ''ecologies,'' should differ with respect to the areas of the color space to which they paid the most attention. ''Culturally important'' colors should tend to be referred to often in speech and, thus, their names should become highly ''available'' to members of the culture. ''Availability'' of a name should have three measurable attributes: as Zipf (1935) has shown, words used frequently tend to evolve into shorter words (for example, automobile becomes auto or car); thus, the length of color words should be an index of their availability. Secondly, a more available word should be one which a speaker can produce rapidly when asked to name the thing to which the word refers. Finally, words frequently used in communication should come to have meanings widely agreed upon by speakers of the language. These three indices of availability are *linguistic* measures; for a measure of cognition, Brown and Lenneberg chose recognition memory, the ability of subjects to recognize a previously viewed color from among an array of colors. The hypothesis relating the linguistic and cognitive variables was similar to the case, described previously, of the effectiveness of octal as a code for digits; names which are more available should be more efficient codes for colors (you can hang on to them better in memory)—thus, people should be able to retain them longer.

Brown and Lenneberg's actual experiment was in two stages. They first had a sample of English-speaking American undergraduates name a sample of colored chips. Because the three linguistic measures were found to correlate highly (the same chips tended to be given short, rapid, agreed-upon names), the measures were combined into a composite measure which Brown and Lenneberg named ''codability.'' Other subjects performed a memory task; they were shown either one or four colors, waited a predetermined length of time during which the colors were not visible, and then attempted to pick out which color(s) they had seen from an array of many colors. The hypothesis was that the more codable colors would

----

[4]Color plates illustrating what these dimensions actually look like are printed in many standard introductory psychology text books—for example, in Ruch's *Psychology and Life* (6th Edition) and in Hilgard, Atkinson, & Bower's *Introduction to Psychology* (5th Edition).

also be the best remembered. That is exactly the result which was obtained. Furthermore, the advantage of the more codable colors increased as the number of colors and the length of time they had to be remembered increased. This study is the classic demonstration of an effect of language on memory.[5]

The Brown and Lenneberg study used only speakers of a single language. However, its logic can easily be extended to a cross-cultural comparison. Which particular colors are most codable would be expected to vary between languages, but the lawful relationship between memory and codability should remain true— those colors which are most codable should be better remembered by speakers of that language than the less codable colors. That this would be the case seemed so obviously true that it was not tested for many years. Is it obvious?

The first, almost trivial requirement for testing the Whorfian hypothesis which we listed previously was that there be at least two natural languages whose terminologies with respect to some domain were different. The anthropological literature contains many reports of such differences in color names—for example, cultures which have only one word to describe the colors which English distinguishes as "green" and "blue," or cultures whose word for "orange" includes much of what we would classify as "red." From this kind of evidence, it appeared that languages could arbitrarily cut up the color space into quite different categories. Recently, two anthropologists have challenged this assumption.

Berlin and Kay (1969) first looked at the reported diversity of color names linguistically, and claimed that there were actually a very limited number of basic —as opposed to secondary—color terms in any language. "Basic" was defined by a list of linguistic criteria: for example, that a term be composed of only a single unit of meaning ("red" as opposed to "dark red"), and that it name only color and not objects ("purple" as opposed to "wine"). Using these criteria, Berlin and Kay reported that no language contained more than 11 basic color names: three achromatic (in English, "black," "white," and "gray") and eight chromatic (in English, "red," "yellow," "green," "blue," "pink," "orange," "brown," and "purple").

Berlin and Kay next asked speakers of different languages to identify the colors to which the basic color names in their language referred. Their initial group of subjects were 20 foreign students whose native language was not English. Subjects saw a two-dimensional array of colored chips—all of the hues at all levels of brightness (all at maximum saturation) available in the Munsell Book of Color (Munsell Color Company, 1966). The students performed two tasks: (a) they traced the boundaries of each of their native language's basic color terms, and (b) they pointed to the chip which was the *best example* of each basic term. As might

---

[5]In fact, another variable, "communication accuracy," was found to correlate with memory more generally than codability (Lantz & Stefflre, 1964; Stefflre, Castillo Vales, & Morely, 1966). However, because this line of research is more relevant to the relation between interpersonal and intrapersonal communication than it is to the relation between a linguistic domain and the nonlinguistic domain which it encodes (Lenneberg, 1967), it will not be pursued further here.

have been expected from the anthropological literature, there was a great deal of variation in the placement of boundaries of the terms. There was not, however, *reliable* variation. Speakers of the same language disagreed with each other in placement of the boundaries as much as did speakers of different languages; and the same person, when asked to map boundaries a second time, was likely to map them quite differently from the way he had at first. It is, thus, likely that even anthropological reports of differences in the boundaries of color terms are confounded by this unreliability. Surprisingly, in spite of this variation, the choice of best examples of the terms was quite similar for the speakers of the 20 different languages. Berlin and Kay called the points in the color space where choices of best examples of basic terms clustered "focal points," and argued that the previous anthropological emphasis on cross-cultural differences in color names was derived from looking at boundaries of color names rather than at color-name focal points.

Brown and Lenneberg's results had been interpreted as a demonstration of the effect of codability on memory. However, Berlin and Kay's focal points suggested a disturbing alternative. Suppose that there are areas of the color space which are perceptually more "salient" to all peoples and that these areas both become more codable and can be better remembered as the direct result of their salience? The present author (Heider, 1972c) tested this possibility. If codability is the result of salience, the same colors should be the most codable in all languages; specifically, focal colors should be universally more codable than nonfocal colors. A focal color representing each of the eight basic chromatic terms was chosen from the center of each of the best-example clusters produced by Berlin and Kay's subjects; nonfocal colors were chosen from the "internominal" areas of the color space, areas which were never picked as the best example of any basic color name.[6] The chips were mounted on cards and shown, one at a time, in scrambled order, individually, to 23 people whose native language was not English. A subject's task was to write down what he would call each color in his language. The results of the study were clear: the focal colors were given shorter names and named more rapidly than were the nonfocal colors. Thus, in 23 diverse langues, drawn from seven of the major language families of the world, it was the same colors that were most codable.

There was a second part to the hypothesis. If memory were the direct result of salience rather than of codability, focal colors should be better remembered than nonfocal, even by speakers of a language in which these colors were not more codable. Berlin and Kay's claim about the number of basic color terms was

---

[6]These may not actually be the "best" chips to represent focal and nonfocal colors. Neither Berlin and Kay's linguistics nor their research methods are above reproach (cf. Hickerson, 1971). Berlin and Kay may have included some colors in their basic name list which should be considered secondary names, or may have assigned secondary status to legitimate basic terms; or they may have systematically skewed the location of their best-example clusters by the use of bilinguals as subjects. All such "errors" would only contribute to "noise" in the present author's research design and make it more difficult to demonstrate significant differences between focal and nonfocal colors.

that there were never more than, but could be fewer than, 11 terms; in fact, they argued that color terms entered languages in a specific evolutionary order. The Dani of West Irian (Indonesian New Guinea) are a stone-age, agricultural people who have a basically two-term color language (K. G. Heider, 1970; Heider, 1972b; Heider & Olivier, 1972). Color systems of that character have been reported for other cultures as well and form Stage I, the first and simplest stage, of Berlin and Kay's proposed evolutionary ordering of color systems. For Dani, the eight chromatic focal chips were not more codable than the internominal chips (established by having 40 Dani name all of the color chips in the Berlin and Kay array). Would Dani, nevertheless, better remember the focal colors? To find out, Heider (1972c) administered, to a sample of Dani and a sample of Americans, a color memory test very similar to Brown and Lenneberg's. Subjects were shown focal and nonfocal colors, individually in random order, for 5 seconds, and after a 30-second wait, were asked to recognize the color they had seen from an array of many colors. The mean number correctly recognized by people of each culture for each kind of chip is shown in Table 1. The main results were clear: Dani, as well as Americans, recognized the focal colors better than the nonfocal.

This study also illustrates a point about method which was emphasized earlier. A striking aspect of Table 1 is that Dani memory performance as a whole was poorer than American. If the hypothesis had been in terms of absolute differences between cultures, we would have noted that Dani both had fewer color terms and poorer memory for colors than Americans, and might have claimed that linguistic relativity was thereby supported. However, it must be remembered that the Dani are a preliterate people, living in face-to-face communities, probably without need for or training in techniques for coping with the kind of overloads of information which this unfamiliar memory test required. All of those extraneous factors undoubtedly affected Dani memory performance as a whole. Our hypothesis, however, concerned differential memory for different types of color within culture and, therefore, was not negated by general cultural differences in "test taking."

Color initially appeared to be an ideal domain in which to demonstrate the effects of lexical differences on thought; instead, it now appears to be a domain particularly suited to an examination of the influence of underlying perceptual

TABLE 1

Accuracy of Color Memory:
Mean Number of Correctly Recognized Colors

	Stimulus colors	
Culture	Focal	Internominal
U.S.	5.25	3.22
Dani	2.05	.47

factors on the formation and reference of linguistic categories. Certain colors appear to be universally salient. There are also universals in some aspects of color naming. How (by what mechanism) might the saliency be related to the naming? What we are asking for is an account of the development (both in the sense of individual learning and the evolution of languages) of color names which will specify the precise nature of the role played by focal colors in that development.

Such an account is related to issues more general than that of linguistic relativity alone. Learning theories in psychology tend to be designed primarily to account for connections formed between initially arbitrary stimuli and responses. The concepts learned in typical concept-formation tasks (cf. Bourne, 1968; Bruner, Goodnow, & Austin, 1956) are also arbitrary; what a subject learns when he learns such a concept is a clear-cut rule, usually stated in terms of combinations of the discrete attributes of artificial stimuli, which define the boundaries of member-ship in the experimenter-determined "positive subset" (for example, "anything which is square and has two borders around it" is a member of the "concept"). Color categories, however, appear to be concepts with a very different kind of structure.

Rosch (1973) proposed the following account of the development of color names: there are perceptually salient colors which more readily attract attention (even of young children — Heider, 1971) and are more easily remembered than other colors. When category names are learned, they tend to become attached first to the salient stimuli (only later generalizing to other, physically similar, in-stances), and by this means these "natural prototype" colors become the foci of organization for categories. How can this account be tested? In the first place, it implies that it is easier to learn names for focal than for nonfocal colors. That is, not only should focal colors be more easily retained than nonfocal in recognition over short intervals (as has already been demonstrated), but they should also be more readily remembered in conjunction with names in long-term memory. In the second place, since a color category is learned first as a single named focal color and second as that focal color plus other physically similar colors, color categories in which focal colors are physically central stimuli ("central" in terms of some physical attribute, such as wavelength) should be easier to learn than categories structured in some other manner (for example, focal colors physically peripheral, or internominal colors central, and no focal colors at all).

A test of these hypotheses obviously could not be performed with subjects who already knew a set of basic chromatic color terms provided by their language. This brings us to another important possible method for cross-cultural research which has seldom been applied — a learning paradigm. Many cultures lack codes (or a full elaboration of codes) for some domain. If an investigator has theories about that domain, instead of framing his hypotheses in terms of deficits in performance resulting from the lack of codes (with attendant problems in interpreting absolute differences between cultures), he can frame hypotheses in terms of *learning* the codes for that domain. Codes can then be taught — the input stimuli precisely specified and controlled within the context of the experiment in accordance with the relevant hypotheses. Since the variations are within culture, any general difficulty which the people may have with the learning task per se will not influence the conclusions. The Dani, with their two-term color language, provided an ideal opportunity to teach color names.

Three basic types of color category were taught. In Type 1, the physically central (i.e., of intermediate value in wavelength or brightness) chip of each category was the focal color, and the flanking chips were drawn from the periphery of that basic name area. In Type 2, central chips lay in the internominal areas between Berlin and Kay's best-example clusters; flanking chips, thus, tended to be drawn from the basic color name areas on either side. Since two different basic color name chips were included in the same Type 2 categories, these categories "violated" the presumed natural organization of the color space. Type 3 categories were located in the same spaces as Type 1; however, instead of occupying a central position, the focal color was now to one side or the other of the three-chip category.

Subjects learned the color names as a paired-associate task, a standard learning task in which subjects learn to give a specific response to each of a list of stimuli. In the present case, colors were the stimuli, and the same Dani word was the correct response for the three colors in a category. Finding suitable "names" for the colors at first seemed a serious obstacle to the study since Dani would not learn nonsense words, even those constructed according to the rules of the Dani language. Here is an example of a case in which it was necessary to make the task culturally meaningful if it was to be performed at all. Eventually, it was found that there was a set of kin groups called *sibs* (something like clans) whose names were all well known to the Dani and which the Dani could readily learn as names for the color categories. (*Sibs* did not have particular colors associated with them in Dani culture.) The task was described to each subject as learning a new language which the experimenter would teach him. The subject was told the "names" for all of the color chips, then presented with each chip and required to respond with a name. Chips were shown in a different random order each run, five runs a day, with feedback after each response, until the criterion of one perfect run was achieved.

The results of the learning supported Rosch's account of the role of focal colors in the learning of color names. In the first place, the focal colors were learned with fewer errors than other colors, even when they were peripheral members of the categories. In the second place, the Type 1 categories in which focal colors were physically central were learned as a set faster than either of the other types. The Type 2 categories, which violated the presumed natural organization of the color space, were the most difficult of all to learn. Thus, the idea of perceptually salient focal colors as "natural prototypes" (rather like Platonic forms) for the development and learning of color names was supported.

We have been speaking of focal colors as "perceptually" salient. Is this just a metaphor, or is there an actual mechanism of color vision which could be responsible for the salience? The answer is "both." There is a theory of color perception (Hering, 1964) supported by both psychophysical and physiological data (De Valois & Jacobs, 1968; Hering, 1964), which claims that the primary colors red, green, yellow, and blue correspond to physiologically "unique hues." To get some notion of the meaning of unique hues, imagine that there are two "opponent" color-coding systems in the primate nervous system (in actual fact, in the lateral geniculate), each of which can respond positively or negatively. One system is responsive to red and green wavelengths of light, the other to yellow and blue wavelengths. Think of the probabilities of stimulation of each system distributed over wavelengths. There will be four points (particular wavelengths) at which one system responds uniquely; that is, a point at which the yellow-blue system is neutral and the red-green system positive, a point at which yellow-blue is neutral and red-green negative, and points at which red-green is neutral and yellow-blue positive and negative.

Do the wavelengths of the proposed four unique hue points correspond to "focal" colors? They cannot correspond exactly because physiological and psychophysical visual research tends to be performed with monochromatic light (radiant light of a single wavelength), whereas Munsell chips are "broadband" light (reflected light containing many wavelengths). However, the dominant wavelength of each Munsell chip has been calculated (Munsell Color Company, 1970). It is, in fact, the case that the dominant wavelengths of focal red, yellow, green, and blue correspond reasonably well to the proposed unique hue points. Evidence of an even more direct match of focal yellow, green, and blue to unique hue points (red was not tested) is provided in McDaniel (1972). While unique hue points are not presently an unchallenged physiological theory, and while the theory fails to account for the other four proposed basic chromatic color terms (pink, orange, brown, and purple), it does lend considerable concreteness to the supposition that focal colors are physiologically, rather than mysteriously, salient.

At this point, the reader may well feel a sense of discontent. We appear to have concluded that color terminology is entirely universal. But what of color term boundaries, and what of the degree of elaboration of secondary color terms? If color terms make no difference to perception, cognitive processes, communication, or life, why should languages have any color terms at all, much less differences in terms?

What are color terms used for? One theory is that we have them in order to communicate about objects which are the same except for color. All of the cultures which have fewer than the full complement of 11 basic terms are also technologically not at an industrial level. According to this theory, color terms only become necessary for communication when manufactured objects can be produced in multitudes, and coloring agents are available for imparting different colors to the otherwise identical objects. A paradigmatic situation for using color terms in this context would be to say "Bring me the orange bowl," thereby specifying which of several, otherwise indistinguishable, bowls was desired.

But why should anyone want to specify the "orange bowl?" Think about the contexts in which you actually pay attention to subtle differences in color. They are probably activities such as deciding what articles of clothing to wear simultaneously, decorating houses, landscaping gardens, and producing and appreciating works of art.

There is one study which bears on this point. Greenfield and Childs (1971) studied the effect of knowing how to weave certain patterns in cloth upon pattern conception among the Zinancantecos of Chiapas, Mexico. The patterns consisted of simple groups of red and white threads. Subjects were asked to "copy" the pattern by placing sticks into a frame. They were given their choice of various widths and colors of sticks. While some subjects used only the red and white sticks to copy the red and white patterns, others freely substituted pink for white and orange for red. A separate test determined that all subjects could discriminate the differences between red, orange, pink, and white sticks equally well. The important point for our argument is that it tended to be subjects who named the red, pink, orange, and white sticks with different names who adhered strictly to the red and white sticks for copying the patterns; subjects who used only a single term for white and pink and a single term for red and orange were the ones who tended to make the substitutions. It may well be that it is in little understood domains such as aesthetic judgment that the use of color terms will be found to "make a difference." (Of course, the Zinancantecos who used differentiating terms may have done so because they were the more sensitive to aesthetic differences). What difference terms do make can now be explored against our background of knowledge of what is universal in color.

We began with the idea of color as the ideal domain in which to demonstrate the effects of the lexicon of a language on cognition, thereby supporting a position of linguistic determinism. Instead, we have found that basic color terminology appears to be universal and that perceptually salient focal colors appear to form natural prototypes for the development of color terms. Contrary to initial ideas, the color space appears to be a prime example of the influence of underlying perceptual-cognitive factors on linguistic categories.

Other Natural Categories

Is color the only domain structured into "natural categories"? It seems unlikely. Color may, in fact, provide a better model for the nature of human categorizing than do the artificial concepts used by psychologists in concept-formation research. In the first place, there are other domains in which perceptually salient natural prototypes appear to determine categories; geometric forms and facial expression of emotion are cases in point. In the second place, categories not based on biologically "given" prototypes may also obey psychological laws for the perception and segmentation of experience, thereby yielding naturally structured categories.

That there is something particularly "well formed" about certain forms, such as circles and squares, was long ago proposed by the Gestalt psychologists. Rosch

(1973) tested the hypothesis that such forms act as natural prototypes in the formation of form categories just as focal colors do for color categories. The Dani also do not have a terminology for two-dimensional geometric forms, and some pilot studies showed that they neither possessed usable circumlocutions for referring to forms in a communication task nor did they tend to sort forms by form type. Thus, it was reasonable to teach Dani form concepts just as they had been taught color concepts. The logic of the form-learning experiment was the same as that of the color learning. Circle, square, and equilateral triangle were taken as the presumed natural prototypes of three form categories. In the "naturally structured" categories, these "good forms" were physically central to a set of distortions (such as gaps in the form or lines changed to curves). In other categories, a distorted form was the central member, the good forms peripheral. The results mirrored those for color. The good forms themselves were learned faster than the distorted forms, and the sets of forms in which the good forms were central were learned faster than sets in which they were peripheral. Furthermore, for the forms (though not for the colors), Dani were willing, at the conclusion of learning, to point to which stimulus they considered the best example of the name they had just learned. The good forms tended to be designated as the best examples even when they were actually peripheral to the set; it was as though subjects were trying to structure the categories around the good forms even when the actual sets were structured otherwise.

Facial expressions of emotion are a surprising addition to the class of natural categories. Not only were they once not considered universal; but there was considerable doubt that, even within one culture, emotion could be judged better than chance from the human face (Bruner & Tagiuri, 1954). As had been the case with colors, such judgments seemed to stem from the unsystematic employment of miscellaneous facial expressions in judgment experiments. Ekman (1972) claimed that there are six basic human emotions (happiness, sadness, anger, fear, surprise, and disgust) and that each is associated with a quite limited range of facial muscle movements constituting a pure expression of that emotion; other expressions tend to be blends of emotions, or ambiguous or nonemotional expressions which could not be expected to receive reliable judgments. When Ekman put together sets of pictures of pure expressions of the proposed basic emotions, he found that these pictures were judged correctly by Americans, Japanese, Brazilians, Chileans, and Argentinians. Furthermore, two preliterate New Guinea groups with minimal contact with Caucasian facial expression, the Fore and the Dani, were able to distinguish which of the expressions was meant on the basis of stories embodying the appropriate emotion. Like color, universality was discovered in facial expressions of emotion only when an investigator thought to ask, not about all possible stimuli, but about the prototypes (best examples) of categories. As is the case for color terms, there appears to be a residual function of emotion names themselves. In a communication task in which one subject attempted to communicate verbally to another which one of a set of pictures of faces was intended, Americans performed far better with pictures of the pure emotions than with ambiguous expressions; Dani, however, who lack a set of emotion terms, showed no difference in performance between the two types of pictures (E. Rosch, unpublished data, 1973).

It is unreasonable to expect that humans come equipped with natural prototypes in all domains. Dogs, vegetables, and volkswagens, for example, are probably culturally relative. Yet such categories may also possess an "internal structure" which renders them more similar to color than to artificial categories. That is, the color, form, and emotional expression categories were composed of a "core meaning" (the clearest cases, best examples) of the category, "surrounded" by other category members of decreasing similarity to the core meaning. Think about the common semantic category "dog." Which is a better example of your idea or image of what that word means (which is doggier?): a German Shepard or a Dachshund? Rosch (1973) had college students rate members of a number of semantic categories as to their prototypicality and found high agreement in judgment between subjects. Evidence has since been obtained, in a variety of tasks, that such categories seem to be "stored mentally," not as a list of logical criteria for category membership, but rather seem to be coded in a "shorthand" form consisting of a fairly concrete representation of the prototype (for further explanation, see Heider, 1972a, and Rosch, 1973).

If internal structure and prototypes, whether "given" or learned, are important aspects in the learning and processing of semantic categories, the fact has implications for cross-cultural research. Present anthropological linguistic techniques (for example, componential analysis) tend to emphasize discovery of the minimal and most elegant, logical criteria needed to determine membership in, and distinctions between, classes. Analysis of the best-example prototypes of categories may provide us with a new, psychologically real, and fruitful basis for comparison of categories across cultures.

Even completely aside from internal structure, given any collection of stimuli or cultural environment, it is unreasonable to expect that categories will be formed randomly. For example, there are undoubtedly psychological rules for perceiving "clusters" of stimuli and "gaps" between stimuli. Such factors as frequency of particular objects, order of encounter with the objects, "density" of nonidentical but similar stimuli, and the extent to which objects in one "cluster" are distinctively different from objects in other "clusters" are examples of the kinds of factors which might determine psychological grouping. Of course, categories of all types probably not only have labels, but also have some rationale which makes them not purely arbitrary but rather natural categories.

CONCLUSIONS

We began with the notion of linguistic relativity defined in terms of insurmountable differences in the world view of cultures brought about by differences in natural languages. Because of the variety of requirements for specificity and cross-cultural controls in testing such assertions, we were reduced to the far less sweeping claim that color names affect some aspects of thought. However, we discovered that colors appeared to be a domain suited to demonstrate just the opposite of linguistic relativity, namely, the effect of the human perceptual system in determining linguistic categories. Very similar evidence exists in the domains of geometric form and emotion categories. Furthermore, psychological principles of categorization may apply to the formation of all categories, even in culturally relative domains.

At present, the Whorfian hypothesis not only does not appear to be empirically true in any major respect, but it no longer even seems profoundly and ineffably true. Why has it been so difficult to demonstrate effects of language on thought? Whorf referred to language as an instrument which "dissects" and categorizes "nature." In the first part of the chapter, we saw that it has not been established that the categorizations provided by the grammar of the language actually correspond to meaningful cognitive units. From the latter part of the chapter, we can now see that for the vocabulary of language, in and of itself, to be a molder of thought, lexical dissections and categorizations of nature would have to be almost accidentally formed, rather as though some Johnny Appleseed had scattered named categories capriciously over the earth. In fact, the "effects" of most lexical linguistic categories are probably inseparable from the effects of the factors which led initially to the formation and structuring of just those categories rather than some others. It would seem a far richer task for future research to investigate the entire complex of how languages, cultures, and individuals come, in the first place, to "dissect," "categorize," and "name" nature in the various ways that they do.

REFERENCES

Berlin, B., & Kay, P. *Basic color terms: Their universality and evolution.* Berkeley: University of California Press, 1969.

Black, M. Linguistic relativity: The views of Benjamin Lee Whorf. *Philosophical Review,* 1959, **68**, 228–238.

Bourne, L. E. *Human conceptual behavior.* Boston: Allyn & Bacon, 1968.

Brown, R. W., & Lenneberg, E. H. A study in language and cognition. *Journal of Abnormal and Social Psychology,* 1954, **49**, 454–462.

Brown, R. W. *Words and things.* New York: Free Press, 1958.

Bruner, J. S., Goodnow, J. J., & Austin, G. A. *A study of thinking.* New York: Wiley, 1956.

Bruner, J. S., & Tagiuri, R. The perception of people. In G. Lindzey (Ed.), *Handbook of social psychology.* Vol. 2. Cambridge: Addison-Wesley, 1954.

Carroll, J. B., & Casagrande, J. B. The function of language classifications in behavior. In E. E. Maccoby, T. M. Newcomb, & E. L. Hartley (Eds.), *Readings in social psychology.* (3rd ed.) New York: Holt, Rinehart & Winston, 1958.

Clark, E. V. What's in a word? On the child's acquisition of semantics in his first language. In T. E. Moore (Ed.), *Cognitive development and the acquisition of language,* New York: Academic Press, 1973.

Cofer, C. N. On some factors in the organizational characteristics of free recall. *American Psychologist,* 1965, **20**, 261 – 272.

Cofer, C. N., & Bruce, D. R. Form-class as the basis for clustering in the recall of nonassociated words. *Journal of Verbal Learning and Verbal Beahvior,* 1965, **4**, 386 – 389.

De Valois, R. L., & Jacobs, G. H. Primate color vision. *Science,* 1968, **162**, 533 – 540.

Ekman, P. Universals and cultural differences in facial expressions of emotion. In J. Cole (Ed.), *Nebraska Symposium on Motivation.* Lincoln: University of Nebraska Press, 1972.

Ervin, S. The connotations of gender. *Word,* 1962, **18**, 248 – 261.

Fries, C. C. *The structure of English: An introduction to the construction of English sentences.* New York: Harcourt, Brace, 1952.

Greenfield, P. M., & Childs, C. Weaving skill, color terms, and pattern representation among the Zinacantecos of Southern Mexico: A developmental study. Unpublished manuscript, Center for Cognitive Studies, Harvard University, 1971.

Heider, E. R. "Focal" color areas and the development of color names. *Developmental Psychology,* 1971, **4**, 447 – 455.

Heider, E. R. Nature of the mental code for natural categories. Paper presented at the meeting of the Psychonomics Society, St. Louis, November 1972. (a)

Heider, E. R. Probabilities, sampling, and ethnographic method: The case of Dani color names. *Man,* 1972, **7**, 448 – 466. (b)

Heider, E. R. Universals in color naming and memory. *Journal of Experimental Psychology,* 1972, **93**, 10 – 20. (c)

Heider, E. R., & Olivier, D. C. The structure of the color space in naming and memory for two languages. *Cognitive Psychology,* 1972, **3**, 337 – 354.

Heider, K. G. *The Dugum Dani: A Papuan culture in the Highlands of West New Guinea.* Chicago: Aldine, 1970.

Hering, E. *Outlines of a theory of the light sense.* Trans. by L. M. Hurvich & D. Jameson. Cambridge: Harvard University Press, 1964.

Hickerson, N. P. Review of "Basic color terms: Their universality and evolution." *International Journal of American Linguistics,* 1971, **37**, 257 – 270.

Istomina, Z. M. Perception and naming of color in early childhood. *Soviet Psychology and Psychiatry,* 1963, **1**, 37 – 46.

Lantz, D., & Stefflre, V. Language and cognition revisited. *Journal of Abnormal and Social Psychology,* 1964, **69**, 472 – 481.

Lenneberg, E. H. *Biological foundations of language.* New York: Wiley, 1967.

LeVine, R. A. Cross-cultural study in child psychology. In P. H. Mussen (Ed.), *Carmichael's manual of child psychology.* (3rd ed.) New York: Wiley, 1970.

McDaniel, C. K. Hue perception and hue naming. Unpublished honors thesis, Harvard College, April 1972.

Miller, G. A. The magical number seven, plus or minus two. *Psychological Review,* 1956, **63**, 81 – 97.

Munsell Color Company. *The Munsell book of color: Glossy finish collection.* Baltimore: Munsell Color Company, 1966.

Munsell Color Company. *Dominant wavelength and excitation purity for designated Munsell color notation.* Baltimore: Munsell Color Company, 1970.

Osgood, C. E., Suci, G. J., & Tannenbaum, P. H. *The measurement of meaning.* Urbana: University of Illinois Press, 1957.

Rosch, E. On the internal structure of perceptual and semantic categories. In T. E. Moore (Ed.), *Cognitive development and the acquisition of language.* New York: Academic Press, 1973.

Rosch, E. Verbal and nonverbal communication of the same array: Effects of code, culture, and class. Unpublished manuscript, 1973.

Segall, M. H., Campbell, D. T., & Herskovitz, M. J. *The influence of culture on visual perception.* Indianapolis: Bobbs-Merrill, 1966.

Serpell, R. The influence of language, education and culture on attentional preferences between colour and form. *International Journal of Psychology,* 1969, **4**, 183 – 194.

Stefflre, V., Castillo Vales, V., & Morely, L. Language and cognition in Yucatan: A cross cultural replication. *Journal of Personality and Social Psychology,* 1966, **4**, 112 – 115.

Wickens, D. D. Encoding categories of words: An empirical approach to meaning. *Psychological Review,* 1970, **77**, 1 – 15.

Whorf, B. L. *Language, thought and reality: Selected writings of Benjamin Lee Whorf.* (Ed. by J. B. Carroll.) Cambridge, Mass.: MIT Press, 1956.

Zipf, G. K. *The psycho-biology of language.* Boston: Houghton-Mifflin, 1935.

7

THE DEVELOPMENT OF THE HUMAN CHILD'S NATIVE LANGUAGE[1]

Roger Brown[2]
Harvard University

All over the world the first sentences of small children are being painstakingly taped, transcribed, and analyzed as if they were the last sayings of great sages. Which is a surprising fate for the likes of: *That doggie, No more milk,* and *Hit ball.* Reports already made, in progress, or projected for the near future sample development in children from many parts of the United States, England, Scotland, France, and Germany and also development in children learning Luo (central East Africa), Samoan, Finnish, Hebrew, Japanese, Korean, Serbo-Croatian, Swedish, Turkish, Cakchiquel (Mayan-Guatemala), Tzeltal (Mayan-Mexico), American Sign Language in the case of a deaf child, and many others. What accounts for all this activity is a strong motivation to obtain a body of cross-cultural data about the ways in which children's speech gradually changes to conform more closely to the model set for them by the adult community; a corpus that will make it possible to

[1]The ideas presented in this chapter were originally delivered as a Distinguished Scientific Contribution Award Address to the American Psychological Association, which was subsequently published in the *American Psychologist,* 1972, **27,** 56–64. A revision of that paper was specially prepared for this volume by the author and the editor who wish to thank the American Psychological Association for permission to quote large sections of it and also the Harvard University Press for permission to quote several paragraphs from R. Brown, *A First Language: The Early Stages.*

[2]The first five years of the author's work was supported by United States Public Health Service Grant MH–7088 from the National Institute of Mental Health, and the second five years by Grant HD –02908 from the National Institute of Child Health and Development. He is deeply grateful for the generosity of this support and the intelligent flexibility with which both grants have been administered.

compare progressions in various languages and isolate any features in those progressions that are universal. The count you make of the number of studies now available for comparative analysis depends on how much you require in terms of standardized procedure, the full report of data, explicit criteria of acquisition, and so on. Brown (1973), whose methods demand a good deal, finds he can use some 33 reports of 12 languages. Slobin (1971), less interested in proving a small number of generalizations than in setting down a large number of interesting hypotheses suggested by what is known, finds he can use many more studies of some 30 languages from 10 different families. Of course this is still not even a 3% sample of the world's languages, but in a field like psycholinguistics in which "universals" have sometimes been postulated on the basis of one or two languages, 30 languages represents a notable empirical advance. The credit for inspiring this extensive field work on language development belongs chiefly to Dan Slobin at Berkeley whose vision of a universal sequence in the *development* of children's language abilities has inspired research workers everywhere. The quite surprising degree to which results to date support his vision has sustained the researcher when he gets a bit tired of writing down Luo, Samoan, or Finnish equivalents of *That doggie* and *No more milk*.

It has taken some years to accumulate data on a wide variety of languages and even now the variety is largely limited to just the first period of sentence construction, which is called Stage I. Stage I is defined as beginning when the child produces any utterances at all which are made up of more than one word. When that happens the average length of his sentences (a measure called "mean length of utterance" of MLU) will rise above 1.0. The end of Stage I is defined by the attainment of a mean length of utterance of 2.0. When the mean is 2.0 there will be many utterances of one, two, and three words, and a few of four, and an upper limit of about 7 morphemes. The most obvious superficial fact about child sentences is that they grow longer as the child grows older. Leaning on this fact, modern investigators have devised a set of standard rules for calculating MLU, rules partially well motivated and partially arbitrary. Whether the rules are exactly the right ones, and it is already clear that they are not, is almost immaterial because their only function is a temporary one; to render children in different studies initially comparable in terms of some index superior to chronological age. It has been shown (Brown, 1973) that while individual children vary enormously in rate of linguistic development, and so in what they know at a given chronological age, their constructional and semantic knowledge is fairly uniform at a given MLU. It is common in the literature to identify five stages, with those above Stage I defined by increments of .50 to the MLU.

The study of first language development in the preschool years began to be appreciated as a central topic in psycholinguistics in the early 1960s. The initial impetus came fairly directly from Chomsky's *Syntactic Structures* (1957) and, really, from one particular thesis in that book and in transformational, generative grammar generally. The thesis is, to put it simply, that in acquiring a first language one cannot possibly be said simply to acquire a repertoire of sentences, however large that repertoire is imagined to be, but must instead be said to acquire a rule system that makes it possible to generate a literally infinite variety of sentences, most of them never heard from anyone else. And this is something all normal children unquestionably learn to do between the ages of 18 months and 5 years. They do not simply commit to memory the sentences they hear other people speak. They extract from other people's speech a set of rules of construction that enable them to produce indefinitely numerous new sentences which will be correctly understood in their language community. This staggeringly impressive accomplishment has so captured the imagination of present-day students of language development that most of our energies have gone into the study of grammar or the sentence construction process.

In saying that a child acquires construction rules one cannot of course mean that he acquires them in any explicit form; the preschool child cannot tell you any linguistic rules at all. And the chances are that his parents cannot tell you very many either. It is also obvious that parents do not attempt to teach the mother tongue by the formulation of rules of sentence construction. One must suppose that what happens is that the preschool child is able to extract from the speech he hears a set of construction rules, many of them exceedingly abstract, which neither he nor his parents knows in explicit form.

That something of the sort described goes on has always been pretty obvious for languages like Finnish or Russian which have elaborate rules of word formation, or morphology, rules that seem to cause children to make very numerous systematic errors of a kind that parents and casual observers notice. In English, however, morphology is fairly simple, and errors that parents notice are correspondingly less common. Nevertheless they do exist, and it is precisely in these errors that one glimpses from time to time the largely hidden but presumably general process. For example, most American children about 4 years old use the form *hisself* rather than *himself*. How do they come by it? It can be shown that they use it when they have never heard it from anyone else and so presumably they make it up or construct it. Why do they invent something that from the adult point of view is a mistake? To answer that, we must recall the set of words most similar to the reflexive pronoun *himself*. They are such other reflexive pronouns as *myself, yourself,* and *herself*. But all of these others, we see, are constructed by combining the possessive pronoun, *my, your,* or *her* with *self*. The masculine possessive pronoun is *his* and, if the English language were consistent at this point, the reflexive would be *hisself*. As it happens English is not consistent at this point but is rather irregular, as all languages are at some points, and the approved form is *himself*. Children by inventing *hisself* and often insisting on it for quite a period, "iron out" or correct the irregularity of the language. And, incidentally, they reveal to us the fact that what they are learning are general rules of construction — not just words and phrases they hear. Close examination of the speech of children learning English shows that it is often replete with errors of syntax or sentence construction as well as morphology (e.g., *Where Daddy went*). But for some reason, errors of word formation are regularly noticed by parents who are commonly quite unconscious of errors of syntax. And so it happens that even casual observers of languages with a well-developed morphology are aware of the creative construction process whereas casual observers of English find it possible seriously to believe that language learning is simply a process of memorizing what has been heard.

The extraction of finite structure with an infinite generative potential which is furthermore accomplished in large part, though not completely, by the beginning of the school years (see Chomsky, 1969, for certain exceptions; no doubt there are others) and without explicit tuition was not something any learning theory was prepared to explain. And so it appeared that first language acquisition was a major challenge to psychology.

While the first studies of language acquisition by children were inspired by transformational linguistics, they were, nevertheless, not really approved of by the transformational linguists. This was because the studies took the child's spontaneous speech performance, taped and transcribed at home on some regular schedule, for their basic data and undertook to follow the changes in these data with age. At about the same time in the early sixties, three studies of roughly this sort were independently begun: Martin Braine's (1963) at Maryland, Roger Brown's (1963) at Harvard with his associates Ursula Bellugi (now Bellugi-Klima) and Colin Fraser, and Susan Ervin (now Ervin-Tripp) and Wick Miller's (1964) at Berkeley. The attempt to discover constructional knowledge from ''mere performance'' seemed quite hopeless to the MIT linguists (e.g., Chomsky, 1964; Lees, 1964). It was at the opposite extreme from the linguist's own method which was to present candidate-sentences to his own intuition for judgment as grammatical or not. In cases of extreme uncertainty he might also, I suppose, have stepped next door to ask the opinion of a colleague. In retrospect I think they were partly right and partly wrong about our early methods. They were absolutely right in thinking that no sample of spontaneous speech, however large, would alone enable one to write a fully determinate set of construction rules. I learned that over a period of years in which I made the attempt 15 times, for three children at five points of development. There were always, and are always, many things the corpus alone cannot settle. The linguists were wrong in two ways. First, in supposing, that because one cannot learn everything about a child's construction knowledge, one cannot learn anything. One can, in fact, learn quite a lot, and one of the discoveries of the past decade is the variety of ways in which spontaneous running discourse can be ''milked'' for knowledge of linguistic structure; a great deal of the best evidence lies not simply in the child's own sentences but in his exchanges with others during actual discourse. I do not think that tranformational linguists should have ''pronounced'' on all of this with such discouraging confidence since they had never, in fact, tried. The other way in which I think the linguists were wrong was in their gross exaggeration of the degree to which spontaneous speech is ungrammatical, a kind of hodge-podge of false starts, incomplete sentences, and so on. Except for talk at learned conferences adult speech, allowing for some simple rules of editing and ellipsis, seems to be mostly quite grammatical (Labov, 1970). For children and for the speech of parents to children this is even more obviously the case.

The first empirical studies of the 1960s gave rise to various descriptive characterizations of which "telegraphic speech" (Brown & Fraser, 1963) and "Pivot Grammar" (Braine, 1963) are the best known. These two characterizations are descriptions of surface form alone. Telegraphic speech characterized the small child's first sentences as made up exclusively of content words which refer to real events in the world, omitting all functor words whose roles in adult sentences is that of relating content words syntactically. This is roughly correct, but for superficial, almost accidental, reasons, and it fails to predict any details of the child's grammatical productivity. Pivot Grammar is a system that classified the words of children's first sentences into two broad classes, pivot and open, and formulated rules which predicted that a pivot word would occur only in a fixed sequential position, in combination with an open word, never alone or in combination with another pivot word. Open words, on the other hand, were viewed as occurring with either pivot or other open words. While Pivot Grammar does make predictions about children's early grammatical productivity, more recent evidence indicates that the distribution of children's earliest word combinations are not universally like that predicted by its rules. The most serious shortcoming of both characterizations is that, by staying very close to the observable data and not attempting to determine what children *mean* by their first sentences, they cannot be viewed as sufficient characterizations of children's full linguistic knowledge. For this and other reasons, telegraphic speech and Pivot Grammar did not lead anywhere very interesting. But they were unchallenged long enough to get into most introductory psychology textbooks where they will probably survive for a few years even though their numerous inadequacies are now well established.[3] Bloom (1970), Schlesinger (1971), and Bowerman (1970) made the most telling criticisms both theoretical and empirical, and Brown (1973) has put the whole now overwhelmingly negative case together. It seems to be clear enough to workers in this field that telegraphic speech and Pivot Grammar are false leads that we need not even bother to describe them extensively.

Along with their attacks on Pivot Grammar, Bloom (1970) and Schlesinger (1971) made a positive contribution that has turned out to be the second major impetus to the field. For reasons which must seem very strange to the outsider not immersed in the linguistics of the 60's, the first analyses of child sentences in this period were in terms of pure syntax in abstraction from semantics, with no real attention paid to what the children might intend to communicate. Lois Bloom added to her transcriptions of child speech a systematic running account of the

---

[3] An example of this can be found in a recent article in the Satruday Review of Literature in which Pivot Grammar was upheld as the model of a universal children's grammar which "can be described with the rigorous mathematical precision used by Chomsky." (Ed).

nonlinguistic context. And in these contexts, she found evidence that the child intends to express certain meanings with even his earliest sentences, meanings that go beyond the simple naming in succession of various aspects of a complex situation to assert simple propositions and to express or request the existence of simple relations.

Parents, and adults generally, have always been willing to interpret child sentences. Brown and Bellugi in their 1964 article discussed these interpretations which they called "expansions." It quite often happens that a "telegraphic" sentence from a child is immediately followed by a parental interpretation or "gloss." These are intended as confirmations of the truth of what the child is thought to have meant or, if pronounced questioningly, as communication checks asking the child if he meant what the parent said. So, for example, if the child says "Baby Highchair" the mother might say, "Baby is in the highchair." Adult "glosses" stand in a kind of reciprocal relation to the child's imitation of adult sentences. Whereas the child "reduces" the model by omitting functors, the adult "expands" the child's sentence by adding functors. The child's imitations usually preserve contentives in their original order and the adult's expansions do the same. It is as if the adult takes the child to mean at least all that he says by means of contentives and word order. Using the ordered contentives as "givens" the adult builds up the child's utterance into a well-formed simple sentence by adding words. Any telegraphic utterance out of context is susceptible to a variety of interpretations, but since the child's utterance takes place within a context, the adult uses that context to decide on one out of the set of possible expansions. The adult glosses the child's utterance as just that simple sentence which, in view of all the circumstances, the child ought to have said and presumably did mean.

The justification for attributing to very small children the intention to communicate semantic relations comprises a complex and not fully satisfying argument. At its strongest it involves the following sort of experimental procedure. With toys that the child can name available to him he is, on one occasion, asked to "make the truck hit the car," and on another occasion "make the car hit the truck." Both sentences involve the same objects and action but word order in English indicates which object is to be in the role of agent (hitter) and which in the role of object (the thing hit). If the child acts out the two events in ways appropriate to the contrasting word orders, he may be said to understand the difference in the semantic relations involved. Similar kinds of contrasts can be set up for possessives ("Show me the Mommy's baby" versus "Show me the baby's Mommy") and prepositions ("Put the pencil on the matches" versus "Put the matches on the pencil"). The evidence to date, of which there is a fairly considerable amount collected in America and Britain (Bever, Mehler, & Valian, in press; de Villiers & de Villiers, 1973b; Fraser, Bellugi, & Brown, 1963; Lovell & Dixon, 1965), indicates that, by late Stage I, children learning English can do these things correctly (experiments on the prepositions are still in a trial stage). By late Stage I children learning English are also often producing what the nonlinguistic context suggests are intended as relations of possession, location, and agent-action-object. For those cases in English and for languages which do not utilize contrasts between word orders in these ways, the evidence for relational intentions is essentially limited to the nonlinguistic context. It is, of course, the nonlinguistic context that parents use as an aid to figuring out what their children mean when they speak.

It is, I think, worth a paragraph of digression to point out that another experimental method, a method of judgment and correction of word sequence and so a method nearer that of the transformational linguist himself, yields a quite different outcome. De Villiers and de Villiers (1972) asked children to observe a dragon puppet who sometimes spoke correctly with respect to word order (e.g., Drive your car) and sometimes incorrectly (e.g., Cup the fill). A second dragon puppet responded to the first when the first spoke correctly by saying "right" and repeating the sentence. When the first puppet spoke incorrectly the second, tutorial puppet, said "wrong," and corrected the sentence (e.g., Fill the cup). After observing a number of such sequences, the child was invited to play the role of the tutorial puppet and new sentences, correct and incorrect, were supplied. In effect this is a complicated way of asking the child to make judgments of syntactic well-formedness, supplying corrections as necessary. The instruction is not easily given in words but, by role-playing examples, de Villiers and de Villiers found they could get the idea across. While there are many interesting results in their study, the most important is that the children did not make correct word-order judgments over 50% of the time until after what we call Stage V, and only the most advanced child successfully corrected wrong orders over half the time. This small but most important study suggests that construction rules do not emerge simultaneously on the levels of spontaneous use, discriminating response, and judgment. The last of these, the linguist's favorite, is after all not simply a pipeline to competence but a metalinguistic performance of considerable complexity.

In spite of the fact that the justification for attributing semantic intentions of a relational nature to the child when he first begins composing sentences is not fully satisfactory, its practice (often called the method of "rich interpretation" by contrast with the "lean" behavioral interpretation that preceded it) is by now well justified simply because it has helped expose remarkable developmental universals that had formerly gone unremarked. There are now I think three reasonably well-established pre-school developmental series in which constructions and the meanings they express appear in a nearly invariant order.

The first of these, and still the only one to have been shown to have validity for many different languages, concerns Stage I. By definition, Stage I children in any language are going to be producing sentences of one to seven morphemes long with the average steadily increasing across Stage I. What is not true by definition but is true in fact for all the languages so far studied is that the constructions in Stage I are limited semantically to a single rather small set of propositions and relations. Furthermore, elaborations of that set which occur in the course of the Stage are also everywhere the same. Finally, in Stage I, the only syntactic or expressive devices employed are the combination of the semantically related forms under one sentence contour and, where relevant in the model language, correct word order. It is important to recognize that there are many other things that *could* happen in Stage I, many ways of increasing MLU besides those actually utilized in Stage I. In Stage I, MLU goes up because simple two-term relations begin to be combined into three- and four-term relations of the same type but occurring in one sentence. In later stages MLU, always sensitive to increases of knowledge, rises in value for quite different reasons; for instance, originally missing obligatory function forms like inflections for tense and number begin to be supplied. Still later, the embedding of two or more simple sentences within one another begins, and eventually the coordination of simple sentences.

What are the semantic relations that seem universally to be the subject matter of Stage I speech? In brief it may be said that they are relations or propositions concerning the sensorimotor world, and they seem to represent the linguistic expression of the sensorimotor intelligence which the great developmental psychologist, Jean Piaget, has described as the principal acquisition of the first 18 months of life. The Stage I relations also correspond very closely with the set of "cases" which Fillmore (1968) has postulated as the universal semantic deep structure of language. This is surprising since Fillmore did not set out to say anything at all about child speech but simply to provide a universal framework for adult grammar.

In actual fact there is no absolutely fixed list of Stage I relations. A short list of 11 will account for about 75% of Stage I utterances in almost all language samples collected. A longer list of about 18 will come closer to accounting for 100%. What are some of the relations? There is, in the first place, a closed semantic set having to do with reference. These include the Nominative (e.g., *That ball*), expressions of Recurrence (e.g., *More ball*), and expressions of disappearance or Nonexistence (e.g., *All gone ball*). Then there is the Possessive (e.g., *Daddy chair*), two sorts of Locative (e.g., *Book table* and *Go store*) and the Attributive (e.g., *Big house*). Finally there are two-term relations comprising portions of a major sort of declarative sentence: Agent-Action (e.g., *Daddy hit*); Action-Object (e.g., *Hit ball*); and, surprisingly from the point of view of the adult language, Agent-Object (e.g., *Daddy ball*). Less frequent relations which do not appear in all samples but which one would want to add to a longer list include: Patient-State (e.g., *I hear*); Datives of Indirect Object (e.g., *Give Mommy*); Comitatives (e.g., *Walk Mommy*); Instrumentals (e.g., *Sweep broom*) and just a few others. From all these constructions it may be noticed that in English, and in all languages, "obligatory" functional morphemes like inflections, case endings, articles, and prepositions are missing in Stage I. This is, of course, the observation that gave rise to the still roughly accurate descriptive term "telegraphic speech." The function forms are thought to be absent because of some combination of such variables as their slight phonetic substance and minimal stress, their varying but generally considerable grammatical complexity, and the subtlety of the semantic modulations they express (number, time, aspect, specificity of reference, exact spatial relations, etc.).

Stage I speech seems to be almost perfectly restricted to these two-term relations, expressed, at the least, by subordination to a single sentence contour and often by appropriate word order, until the MLU is about 1.50. From there on, complications which lengthen the utterance begin but they are, remarkably enough, complications of just the same two types in all languages so far studied. The first type involves three-term relations, like Agent-Action-Object; Agent-Action-Locative; and Action-Object-Locative which, in effect, combine sequentially two of the simple relations found before an MLU of 1.50 without repeating the term that would appear twice if the two-term relations were simply strung together. In other words, something like Agent-Action-Object (e.g., *Adam hit ball*) is made up *as if* the relations Agent-Action *(Adam hit)* and Action-Object *(Hit ball)* had been strung together in sequence with one redundant occurrence of the Action *(hit)* deleted.

The second type of complication involves the retention of the basic line of the two-term relation with one term, always a noun-phrase "expanding" as a relation in its own right. Thus there is development from such forms as *Sit Chair* (Action-Locative) to *Sit Daddy chair* which is an Action-Locative, such that the Locative is itself expanded as a Possessive. The forms expanded in this kind of construction are, in all languages so far studied, the same three types: expressions of Attribution, Possession, and Recurrence. Near the very end of Stage I there are further complications into four-term relations of exactly the same two types described. All of this, of course, gives a very "biological" impression, almost as if semantic cells of a finite set of types were dividing and combining and then redividing and recombining in ways common to the species.

The remaining two best established invariances of order in preschool language acquisition have not been studied in a variety of languages; they were established from the data of the three unacquainted children in Brown's longitudinal study; the children called, in the literature, Adam, Eve, and Sarah. The full results appear in "Stage II" of Brown (1973) and in Brown and Hanlon (1970). "Stage II" in Brown (1973) focuses on 14 functional morphemes including the English noun and verb inflections, the copula *be*, the progressive auxiliary *be*, the prepositions *in* and *on*, and the articles *a* and *the*. For just these forms in English it is possible to define a criterion of acquisition that is considerably superior to the simple occurrence-or-not used in Stage I and to the semi-arbitrary frequency levels used in the remaining sequence to be described. In very many sentence contexts one or another of the 14 morphemes can be said to be "obligatory" from the point of view of the adult language. Thus in a Nomination sentence accompanied by pointing, such as *That book*, an article is obligatory; in a sentence like *Here two book,* a plural inflection on the noun is obligatory; in *I running* the auxiliary *am* inflected for person, number, and tense is obligatory. It is possible to treat each such sentence frame as a kind of test item in which the obligatory form either appears or is omitted. Brown defined as his criterion of acquisition, presence in 90% of obligatory contexts in 6 consecutive-sampling hours.

There are in the detailed report many surprising and suggestive outcomes. For instance "acquisition" of these forms turns out never to be a sudden all-or-none affair such as categorial linguistic rules might suggest it should be. It is rather a matter of a slowly increasing probability of presence, varying in rate from morpheme to morpheme, but extending in some cases over several years. The most striking single outcome is that for these three children, with spontaneous speech scored in the fashion described, the order in which these morphemes were acquired was almost identical, with rank-order correlations between pairs of children all at about .86. This does not say that acquisition of a morpheme is invariant with respect to chronological age; the variation of rate of development even among three children was tremendous. But the order, that is which construction follows which, is almost constant, and Brown (1973) shows that it is not predicted by morpheme frequency but is well predicted by relative semantic and grammatical complexity. Of course in languages other than English the same universal sequence cannot possibly be found because grammatical and semantic differences are too great to yield commensurable data (as they are not with the fundamental relations or cases of Stage I). However, if the 14 particular morphemes are reconceived as particular conjunctions of perceptual salience and degrees of grammatical and semantic complexity, we may find laws of succession which have cross-linguistic validity (see Slobin, 1971).

Until the spring of 1972, Brown was the only researcher who had coded data in terms of the presence in, or absence from, obligatory contexts of particular morphemes. At that time, Jill and Peter de Villiers (1973a) did the job on a fairly large scale. They made a cross-sectional study (one time) from speech samples of 21 English-speaking American children of ages 16 to 40 months. The de Villiers scored the 14 morphemes Brown scored; they used his coding rules to identify obligatory contexts and they calculated the children's individual MLU values according to his rules. Two different criteria of morpheme acquisition were used in the analyses of the data. Both constitute well-rationalized adaptations to a cross-sectional study of the 90% correct criterion used in Brown's longitudinal study; let us simply call the rank orders of acquisition obtained by these criteria "A" and "B." To compare with the de Villiers' two orders of acquisition, there is a single rank order (C) which Brown obtained by averaging the orders of acquisition of the three children in his study: Adam, Eve, and Sarah.

There are then three rank orders for the same 14 morphemes scored in the same way and using closely similar criteria of acquisition. The degree of invariance is amazing, even to one who expected a substantial similarity. The rank-order correlations were between A and B, .84; between B and C, .78; and between A and C, .87. These values are only very slightly lower than those for the relations of order among Adam, Eve. and Sarah themselves. Thanks to the de Villiers, it has been made clear that we have a developmental phenomenon of substantial generality.

Numerous other outcomes of the de Villiers' study are extremely interesting. The rank-order correlation between age and order B was .68, while that between MLU and the same order was .92, very close to perfect. So MLU was a better predictor than age of morpheme acquisition in their study, as it was in Brown's. In fact, with age partialled out by the use of a Kendall partial-correlation procedure, the original value of .92 for this correlation was only reduced to .85, suggesting that age adds little or nothing to the predictive power of MLU.

The third sequence, demonstrated only for English by Brown and Hanlon (1970), takes advantage of the fact that what are called tag questions are, in English, very complex grammatically though semantically they are rather simple. In many other languages tags are invariant in form (e.g., *n'est-ce pas,* French; *nicht wahr,* German), and so are grammatically simple, but in English the form of the tag, and there are hundreds of forms, varies in a completely determinate way with the structure of the declarative sentence to which it is appended and for which it asks confirmation. Thus,

John will be late, won't he?

Mary can't drive, can she?

And so on. The little question at the end is short enough, as far as superficial length is concerned, to be produced by the end of Stage I. We know, furthermore, that the semantic of the tag, a request for confirmation, lies within the competence of the Stage I child since he occasionally produces such invariant and simple equivalents as *right?* or *huh?* Nevertheless, Brown and Hanlon(1970) have shown that the production of a full range of well-formed tags is not to be found until after Stage V, sometimes several years after. Until that time there are, typically, no well-formed tags at all. What accounts for the long delay? Brown and Hanlon present evidence that it is the complexity of the grammatical knowledge that tags entail.

Consider such a declarative sentence as: His wife can drive. How might one develop from this tag *can't she?* It is in the first place necessary to make a pronoun of the subject. The subject is *his wife,* and so the pronoun must be feminine, third person, and, since it is a subject, the nominative; in fact *she.* Another step is to make the tag negative. In English this is done by adding *not* or the contraction *n't* to the auxiliary verb *can;* hence *can't.* Another step is to make the tag interrogative since it is a question, and in English that is done by a permutation of order, placing the first member auxiliary verb ahead of the subject. Still another step is to delete all of the predicate of the base sentence except the first member of the auxiliary, and that at last yields *can't she?* as a derivative of His wife can drive. While this description reads a little bit like a program simulating the process by which tags are actually produced by human beings, it is not intended as anything of the sort. The point is simply that there seems to be no way at all by which a human could produce the right tag for each declarative without *somehow* utilizing all the grammatical knowledge described. Just how this happens no one knows, but memorization is completely excluded by the fact that while tags themselves are only finitely numerous the child's problem is to fit the one correct tag to each declarative, and declaratives are infinitely numerous.

In English all of the single constructions, and also all of the pairs, which entail the knowledge involved in tag creation themselves exist as independent sentences in their own right; for example, interrogatives, negatives, ellipses, negative-ellipses, and so on. One can, therefore, make an ordering of constructions in terms of complexity of grammatical knowledge (in precise fact only a partial ordering) and ask whether more complex forms are always preceded in child speech by less complex forms. This is what Brown and Hanlon (1970) did for Adam, Eve, and Sarah, and the result was resoundingly affirmative. In this study, then, we have evidence that grammatical complexity as such (when it can be disentangled, as it often cannot, from semantic complexity) is itself a determinant of order of acquisition.

Of course the question about the mother tongue that we should really like answered is: "How is it possible to learn a first language at all?" On that question which ultimately motivates the whole research enterprise I have nothing to offer that is not negative. But perhaps it is worthwhile making these negatives explicit since they are still widely supposed to be affirmatives, and to provide a large part of the answer to the question. What I have to say is not primarily addressed to the question: "How does the child come to talk at all?" since there seem to be fairly obvious utilities in saying a few words in order to express more exactly what he wants, does not want, wonders about, or wishes to share with others. The more exact question on which we have a little information which serves only to make the question more puzzling is: "How does the child come to *improve* upon his language, moving steadily in the direction of the adult model?" It probably seems surprising that there should be any mystery about the forces impelling improvement since it is just this aspect of the process that most people imagine that they understand. Surely the improvement is a response to selection pressures of various kinds; ill-formed or incomplete utterances must be less effective than well-formed, complete utterances in accomplishing the child's intent; parents probably approve of well-formed utterances and disapprove of or correct the ill-formed. These ideas sound sensible and may be correct but the still scant evidence available does not support them.

At the end of Stage I the child's constructions are characterized by, in addition to the things we have mentioned, a seemingly lawless oscillating omission of every sort of major constituent including sometimes subjects, objects, verbs, locatives, and so on. The important point about these oscillating omissions is that they seldom seem to impede communication; the other person, usually the mother, being in the same situation and familiar with the child's stock of knowledge, usually understands, so far as one can judge, even the incomplete utterance. At home, in an action situation, with behavioral evidence of intention generally attendant on the linguistic, the child's utterances are almost redundant. If something is missing, it can be supplied. If word order is wrong, it can be set right.

Thus, as Brown (1973) has suggested, the speech of the Stage I child is well adapted to his purposes, but, as a speaker, he is very *narrowly* adapted. A sentence well adapted to its function is, like a piece in a jigsaw puzzle, just the right size and shape to fit the opening left for it by local conditions and community understandings. The child has to learn to adapt the size and complexity of his sentences to changing situations and interlocutors. We may suppose that when speaking to strangers or of new experiences, he will have to learn to express obligatory constituents if he wants to get his message across. Language development, then, from the first word to the compound sentence would be largely a matter of learning how to put more of what is intended into adequate expressive form. With what useful result? Ultimately with the result of making the utterance more freely "exportable," making it intelligible in a wider variety of situations and to a wider community. In the end it can be written in isolation on a piece of paper and understood by all who speak the language.

In Stage II Brown (1973) found that all of the 14 grammatical morphemes were at first missing, then occasionally present in obligatory contexts, and, after varying and often long periods of time, nearly always present in such contexts. What makes the probability of supplying the requisite morpheme rise with time? It is surprisingly difficult to find cases in which omission results in incomprehension or misunderstanding at home. With respect to the definite and nondefinite articles, it even looks as if listeners almost never really need them, and yet child speakers learn to operate with the exceedingly intricate rules governing their production. Adult Japanese speaking English as a second language do not seem to learn how to operate with the articles as we might expect they would if listeners needed them. Perhaps it is the case that the child automatically does this kind of learning but that adults do not. Second-language learning may be responsive to familiar sorts of learning variables and first-language learning not. The two, often thought to be similar processes, may be profoundly and ineradicably different.

Consider the Stage I child's invariably uninflected generic verbs. In Stage II parents regularly expand these verbs in one of four ways: as imperatives, as past tense forms, as present progressives, or as imminent-intentional futures. It is an interesting fact, of course, that these are just the four inflections of the verb that the child then goes on, first, to learn to express. We had for years thought it possible that expansions or glosses like those described previously might be a major force impelling the child to improve his speech. However, all the evidence available, both naturalistic and experimental (it is summarized in Brown, Cazden, & Bellugi, 1969), offers no support at all for this notion. Cazden, for instance, carried out an experiment (1965) testing for the effect on young children's speech of deliberately interpolated "expansions" (the supplying of obligatory functional morphemes) introduced for a period on every preschool day for three months. She obtained no significant effect whatever. It is possible, I think, that such an experiment done now, with the information Stage II makes available, expanding only by providing morphemes of a complexity for which the child was "ready," rather than as in Cazden's original experiment, expanding in all possible ways, would show an effect. But no such experiment has been done, and so no impelling effect of expansion has yet been demonstrated.

Suppose we look at the facts of the parental glossing of Stage I generic verbs not, as we have done earlier, as a possible tutorial device but rather as Slobin (1971) has done, as evidence that the children already intended the meanings their parents attributed to them. In short, think of the parental glosses as accurate readings of the child's thought. From this point of view he has been correctly understood even though his utterances are incomplete. In that case there is no selection pressure. Why does he learn to say more if what he already knows how to say works quite well?

To these observations of the seeming efficacy of the child's incomplete utterances, at least at home with the family, we should add the results of a study reported in Brown and Hanlon (1970). Here it was not primarily a question of the omission of obligatory forms but of the contrast between ill-formed primitive constructions and well-formed mature versions. For certain constructions, Yes-No questions, tag questions, negatives, and Wh questions, Brown and Hanlon (1970) identified periods when Adam, Eve, and Sarah were producing both primitive and mature versions, sometimes the one, sometimes the other. The question was, did the mature version communicate more successfully than the primitive version? They first identified all instances of primitive and mature versions, and then coded the adults responses for comprehending follow-up, calling comprehending responses "Sequiturs" and uncomprehending or irrelevant responses "Nonsequiturs." They found no evidence whatever of a difference in communicative efficacy, and so once again there was no selection pressure. Why, one asks oneself, should the child learn the complex apparatus of tag questions when right? or huh? seem to do just the same job? Again one notes that adults learning English as a second language often do not learn tag questions, and the possibility again comes to mind that children operate on language in a way that adults do not.

Brown and Hanlon (1970) have done one other study that bears on the search for selection pressures. Once again it was syntactic well-formedness versus ill-formedness that was in question rather than completeness or incompleteness. This time Brown and Hanlon started with two kinds of adult responses to child utterances: "Approval" directed at an antecedent child utterance and "Disapproval" directed at such an antecedent. The question then was, did the two sets of antecedents differ in syntactic correctness? Approving and Disapproving responses are, certainly, very reasonable candidates for the respective roles, "Positive Reinforcer" and "Punishment." They do not, of course, necessarily qualify as such because Reinforcers and Punishments are defined by their effects on performance (Skinner, 1953); they have no necessary, independent, nonfunctional properties. Still, of course, they are often put forward as plausible determinants of performance and are thought, generally, to function as such. In order differentially to affect the child's syntax Approval and Disapproval must, at a minimum, be selectively governed by correct and incorrect syntax. If they should be so governed, further data would still be needed to show that they affect performance. If they are not so governed, they cannot be a selection pressure working for correct speech. Brown and Hanlon found that they are not. In general the parents seemed to pay no attention to bad syntax nor did they even seem to be aware of it. They approved or disapproved an utterance usually on the ground of the truth value of the proposition that the parents supposed the child intended to assert. This is a surprising outcome to most middle-class parents since they are generally under the impression that they do correct the child's speech. From inquiry and observation I find that what parents generally correct is pronunciation, "naughty" words, and regularized irregular allomorphs like *digged* or *goed*. These facts of the child's speech seem to penetrate parental awareness. But syntax — the child saying, for instance, "Why the dog won't eat?" instead of "Why won't the dog eat?" seems to be automatically set right in the parent's mind, with the mistake never registering as such.

In sum, then, we do not presently have evidence that there are external selection pressures of any kind operating on children to impel them to bring their speech into line with adult models. It is, however, entirely possible that such pressures do operate in situations unlike the situations we have sampled, for instance away from home or with strangers. A radically different possibility is that children work out rules for the speech they hear, passing from levels of lesser to greater complexity, simply because the human species is programmed at a certain period in its life to operate in this fashion on linguistic input. Linguistic input would be defined by the universal properties of language. And the period of progressive rule extraction would correspond to Lenneberg's (1967 and elsewhere) proposed "critical period." It may be chiefly adults who learn a new, a second, language in terms of selection pressures. Comparison of the kinds of errors made by adult second-language learners of English with the kinds made by child first-language learners of English should be enlightening.

David Premack, who has directed recent fascinating research on the learning of linguistic paradigms by a chimpanzee (Sarah), once remarked to me that there is no reason to suppose that children at home are trained in language in anything like an optimal way, and that is probably the response he would make to the negative findings from the largely naturalistic research reported earlier. Premack's research with Sarah, and the research of Allan and Beatrice Gardner with the chimpanzee Washoe, provide two surprising research examples of linguistic skills that seem to have been wholly or largely acquired as a result of selection pressures from a reinforcing tutorial program. The surprise lies in the fact that both Sarah and Washoe have learned vastly more, in a linguistic way, than any other nonhuman animal. Comparisons of the achievements of these chimpanzees with the development of human children's linguistic competence should ultimately prove enlightening regarding the nature of the *process* by which the child steadily makes his utterances more like those of his linguistic community. Have these chimps demonstrated a capacity for language? If so, how is this capacity and its development different from those of human children and why do chimps not exhibit it in their natural environments? We are still very far away from anything but the beginning of answers to these provocative questions, but they cannot be approached at all without taking a position on the nature of language.

If one attempts to define language in terms of all the properties appearing in all known languages, then Washoe and Sarah are both disbarred from full linguistic participation. For the very first such property is vocal production and aural reception and the linguistic performance of both chimpanzees is manual rather than vocal, signs with the hands for Washoe and manipulation and placement of plastic tokens on a magnetic board for Sarah. But it is precisely this manual production of signs we believe accounts for the fact that these chimps have accomplished so much more than any of their predecessors. There is good reason to believe that the production of vowels, consonants, and prosodic features is a motor performance to which chimpanzees are not well adapted, and the trainers of Washoe and Sarah felt that previous experiments in the linguistic-chimpanzee tradition might have failed mainly because of a motoric ineptitude that was only incidentally linguistic. Moreover, vocal production cannot be the essence of linguistic capacity, since writing systems and also sign systems used by human communicators are languages. On the other hand, the search for attributes which are *essential* to language raises the difficult question of the grounds on which one makes the distinction between incidental and essential features of language. If we take a view like Chomsky's (1969) that the essential features are *(a)* a set of sound-meaning correspondences which have an infinite range and *(b)* the distinction between the surface and deep structures of sentences, then the delineation of essential features rests on theoretical assumptions that not all linguists are willing to make and also seems to exclude the speech of children in the early stages. An alternative approach focuses on the evolutionary question: "Why is the mode of life of the human species radically unlike that of any other animal species?" The answer seems to rest on the vastly greater importance of cultural as opposed to biological evolution for human life. It is evident that every human being knows very much more, whether true or false, than he could possibly have learned from his own direct experience, and that he has learned a great deal of it by means of linguistic transmission. Of the universal properties of language, those which are essential for this sort of evolution are semanticity (or meaningfulness), productivity (the immense scope of events for which we can construct communications to transmit), and displacement (the possibility of transmitting information from another time and place, the independence that sentences have of their nonlinguistic context). With these criteria in mind we can look at the achievements of Washoe and Sarah and see how close they come to language.

The training of Washoe by Allen and Beatrice Gardner (Gardner & Gardner, 1969) began when she was about one-year old. While not raised in quite the same way as a child, Washoe spent each day in the Gardners' house or fenced yard with at least one person almost always interacting with her by means of the American

Sign Language (ASL), a system which is believed to have most of the properties common to human languages generally. The method used to teach ASL was essentially the naturalistic one; language was steadily beamed at Washoe. At age four she was making semantically appropriate use of 85 different signs and producing sequences of them, which may or may not be sentences, up to five signs long. There is a great deal of evidence, some of it experimental and well controlled, that Washoe's 85 signs were understood by her. And her errors in testing typically fall into semantic clusters; one article of grooming is confused with another, one food with another, etc.

Of course the strings that Washoe *creates* are the most exciting thing, since they suggest a degree of semantic and syntactic productivity. She did not simply respond to the intiative of her trainers, but herself constantly initiated communication. Some of the strings of signs she produced were her own creations, and in many ways they are very much like the first sentences of children. Using our Stage I categories, the Gardners found that 78% of Washoe's two-sign combinations fit the semantic relations expressed by the Stage I child, a striking correspondence. There is an important difference, however, between Washoe's constructions and those of Stage I children in that the former tended eventually to occur in all possible orders with no evident changes of meaning correlated with the changes in order. For English-speaking, Stage I children words are used in just that order appropriate to the semantic relations which the referent circumstances suggest that the child intends to express. If Washoe freely alternates the equivalents of *Cat bite* and *Bite cat*, regardless of the cat's semantic role, then what is there to show that she intends more than a kind of sequence or list of names? But while the consistent use of appropriate word order is evidence *for* the intention of express semantic relations, its absence does not establish the *absence* of such intentions. This is because most of the early child or chimpanzee sequences are produced concurrently with the referent situations so that appropriate word order is not strictly necessary for successful communication. The fact that the Gardners were able to classify 78% of Washoe's combinations in terms of Agent, Location, Patient, Action, and so on shows this to be the case. It is possible, moreover, that a visual input of the sort that Washoe must operate on is simply more difficult to sequence than is the auditory input that children learning a language operate on. A final consideration in favor of Washoe's expressing semantic relations is the fact that she, like humans who use ASL, keeps her hands in the signing area until a ''sentence'' is finished and only then lets them fall into loose fists or to rest on some nearby surface. This is quite analagous to the utterance-segmentation of speech by stress and pitch. If Washoe has a Stage I competence, this is not enough to conclude that she has language in the sense of all its universal properties or its unique properties, but it does seem to be enough of a linguistic capacity to have supported a considerable degree of cultural evolution. The Gardners have not reported on the period beyond the first 36 months, and it is possible that Stage I may not be the limit of Washoe's linguistic abilities. The last word must be the

Gardners' since only they have all the data and the daily direct experience with Washoe.

Premack's (1970a, 1970b, 1971) results with Sarah suggest that the limits of chimpanzee capacity are far beyond anything in Stage I. Sarah is a mature caged chimp who has not been in continual interaction with human beings but has been carefully "shaped" in experimental sessions toward terminal accomplishments by the Skinnerian method of successive approximation, in which small steps in the direction of the desired performance are rewarded — usually with food. The paradigms for these performances include: reference, sentence, Yes-No interrogatives, *Wh* interrogatives, negatives, class concepts of color, shape and size, compound or coordinated sentences, the copula, pluralization, quantifiers, the logical connective *if. . . then*; all of which problems she does correctly about 70% to 80% of the time. So far, however, these seem to be a set of independent language games that have not been shown to be integrated into a single system. The "words" in these games are plastic tokens varying in size, shape, color, and texture which adhere to a magnetized slate and which Sarah arranges into "sentences" on the slate vertically.

Unlike Washoe, Sarah has not taken up her token language as a medium of communication. She has almost never initiated communication with the tokens and when they are left in her cage she largely ignores them. Premack's paradigms often involve logical relations and other content not very relevant to Sarah's desires and Premack himself believes that Sarah's passive role is a direct consequence of training procedures which do not require initiating. But the absence of interest in initiating communication makes the performances seem very unhuman. Somewhere here, perhaps, lies the answer to the question of why, if chimpanzees have so much linguistic ability, they do not make more use of it in their normal environments.

There are two serious questions one must ask about the interpretation of Premack's demonstrations with Sarah. The first of these is whether the experimental paradigms which Premack has devised preserve the essential properties of the linguistic processes they are designed to represent. Has Sarah really shown comprehension of the sentence, of the copula and so on? One may recall that in the laboratory of B. F. Skinner (1962) pigeons were trained, by a shaping procedure, to play something that looked very much like a game of ping-pong. But, in certain ways that we think of as being essential to the game, the pigeons' performance was not ping-pong. They did not keep score, or stop when one had "won," or develop strategies for misleading one another. This problem of superficial resemblance must also be raised with Sarah's performances in linguistic games. The general technique in these games was always the same: to set up three-term contingencies in which reward depended upon the emission of the right response in the presence of the correct stimulus pattern, with the stimulus patterns getting progressively more complicated.

Consider the demonstration of comprehension for an imperative compound sentence. In prior training, the tokens symbolizing *apple, dish, pail,* etc., had been linked with their referents by a kind of exchange process. Then simple sentences like "Sarah insert banana dish" and "Sarah insert apple pail" were presented side by side in all possible pairs with reward being made contingent on the correct double response. Then all possible pairs were arranged one above the other in the equivalent of full coordination; e.g., "Sarah insert banana pail Sarah insert apple dish." Then the subject *Sarah* was deleted once in each coordination and next both subject and verb were deleted ("Sarah insert banana pail apple dish."). The deletions caused Sarah no trouble; she continued to perform correctly between 75% and 80% of the time. Finally, transfer tests were made involving substitutions for the verb or the object and locative nouns, and Sarah's performance was unimpaired. Evidently Sarah has made certain responses which were appropriate to all the problems she was presented, but is the range of problem and response near enough to the range available to humans to justify attributing linguistic capacities to her? It is easy to think of things that humans can do with (say) coordination that Sarah has not been shown to be able to do. But whether she has done *enough* is not really possible to say at this point.

The differences between Sarah's performance across all the paradigms and the human performance in the real case that seem most important are *(a)* possible dependence of terminal accomplishments on specific atomic preliminary programs; and *(b)* a great difference in systematic scope of performance. Processing a sentence which comes to you as simply one from among the almost infinite possibilities of a language seems to be a very different matter from processing that sentence when it arrives as the crowning problem in a pyramid of training which has made one familiar with most of the components involved and put them in a state of readiness. Sarah has almost never had sessions in which she received several sorts of sentences and apparently never had sessions in which any one of all the kinds of sentences she presumably understands might be presented. I am reminded by her training of the two weeks of "total immersion" in Japanese I had at Berlitz. I, like Sarah, had a very ingenious teacher who programmed her lessons in an almost Skinnerian way. On the day I finished my course I was met outside the Berlitz door by a Japanese friend who asked me in Japanese: "Where is your car?" I was completely floored and could make nothing of the sentence except that it called for a reply. I realized then that my peak accomplishments had been narrowly adapted to a particular drill procedure in which almost all of a sentence was so well practiced as not to need to be processed at all, leaving all my attention free to focus on some single new element that I could get right. Sarah may be as narrowly adapted to her language as I was to Japanese, but fluent speakers of a language — even young children learning it — are not thus narrowly adapted. The difference is an important one for how sentence processing is done.

Even more important is the difference in limitation in systematic grammatical scope. The English sentence "Sarah insert banana pail apple dish," has well-defined negative, interrogative, and imperative counterparts. None of these is limited to some small family of sentences and, furthermore, the relationship across these modalities is completely general and systematic for the whole languge. Any affirmative declarative whatever can be mapped onto another modality by means of the same abstract transformation. This is an order of systematic generality immeasurably beyond that demonstrated in Premack's compound sentence paradigm, and such differences in scope probably matter in terms of how the operations upon the language are performed.

The second serious question that must be raised about Sarah's accomplishments is whether her several trainers, all of whom in the major experiments knew the answers to the problems they posed her, may have unintentionally signaled the correct choices to Sarah. There are many ways this can happen; one that has been found with small children is that the trainer looks at the object to be selected and the child looks at the trainer's eyes. Premack has recognized this possibility and done some experiments (1971) to check on it. He introduced a new trainer who did not know which answer was correct in any given problem. In several dimensions Sarah's performance deteriorated under these circumstances; e.g., instead of placing tokens more or less under one another she tended to let them sprawl across the board as she had done early in her training. Her overall level of correctness in these problems fell to 70% or less, but Premack concluded it remained well above chance. However, since at least some (possibly all) of the problems were familiar to her, this study does not allow us to conclude that Sarah's accomplishments were not cued by her trainers. Might she not originally have learned the correct answers from nonlinguistic cues emitted by knowledgeable trainers and then, at length, committed to memory the tokens that would bring reward in the presence of this or that problem configuration? The controls reported by Premack do not rule out this possibility.

Despite the impressive accomplishments of these two chimps, the differences between their performances and those of human children should incline against concluding that it has been demonstrated that they have mastered language. While both Washoe and Sarah indicate fairly high levels of semanticity, the scope of their productivity and their degree of displacement seem still to be open issues. Perhaps it is not possible explicitly to train high levels of linguistic productivity and displacement in an organism that is not innately disposed to operate on materials having the universal properties of language with the sorts of information-analysis programs humans probably have. If automatic internal programs of structure extraction provide the generally correct sort of answer to how a first language is learned by humans, then inquiries into external communication pressures are simply misguided. They look for the answer in the wrong place. That, of course, does not mean that we are anywhere close to having the right answer. It only remains to specify the kinds of programs that would produce the results regularly obtained.

REFERENCES

Bever, T. G., Mehler, J. R., & Valian, V. V. Linguistic capacity of very young children. In T. G. Bever & W. Weksel (Eds.), *The acquisition of structure*. New York: Holt, Rinehart, Winston, in press.

Bloom, L. *Language development: Form and function in emerging grammars.* Cambridge, Mass.: MIT Press, 1970.

Bowerman, M. Early syntactic development: A cross-linguistic study with special reference to Finnish. Cambridge, England: Cambridge University Press, 1970.

Braine, M. D. S. The ontogeny of English phrase structure: The first phase. *Language,* 1963, **39** 1–14.

Brown, R. *A first language: The early stages.* Cambridge, Mass.: Harvard University Press, 1973.

Brown, R., Cazden, C., & Bellugi, U. The child's grammar from I to III. In J. P. Hill (Ed.), *Minnesota symposium on child psychology: Vol. 2.* Minneapolis: University of Minnesota Press, 1969.

Brown, R., & Fraser, C. The acquisition of syntax. In C. N. Cofer & B. S. Musgrave (Eds.), *Verbal behavior and learning: Problems and processes.* New York: McGraw-Hill, 1963.

Brown, R., & Hanlon, C. Derivational complexity and order of acquisition in child speech. In J. R. Hayes (Ed.), *Cognition and the development of language.* New York: Wiley, 1970.

Cazden, C. B. Environmental assistance to the child's acquisition of grammar. Unpublished doctoral dissertation, Harvard University, 1965.

Chomsky, C. *The acquisition of syntax in children from 5 to 10.* Cambridge, Mass.: MIT Press, 1969.

Chomsky, N. *Syntactic structures.* The Hague: Mouton, 1957.

Chomsky, N. Formal discussion of W. Miller and Susan Ervin, The development of grammar in child language. *Monographs of the Society for Research in Child Development,* 1964, **29**, 35–40.

Chomsky, N. *Language and mind.* New York: Harcourt, Brace, 1968.

de Villiers, J. G., & de Villiers, P. A. A cross-sectional study of the development of grammatical morphemes in child speech. *Journal of Psycholinguistic Research,* 1973, **2**, 267–278. (a)

de Villiers, J. G., & de Villiers, P. A. Development of the use of word order in comprehension. *Journal of Psycholinguistic Research,* 1973, **2**, 331–341. (b)

de Villiers, P. A., & de Villiers, J. G. Early judgments of semantic and syntactic acceptability of children. *Journal of Psycholinguistic Research,* 1972, **1**, 299–310.

Fillmore, C. J. The case for case. In E. Bach & R. T. Harms (Eds.), *Universals in linguistic theory.* New York: Holt, Rinehart & Winston, 1968.

Fraser, C., Bellugi, U., & Brown, R. Control of grammar in imitation, comprehension, and production. *Journal of Verbal Learning and Verbal Behavior,* 1963, **2**, 121–135.

Gardner, R. A., & Gardner, B. T. Teaching sign language to a chimpanzee. *Science,* 1969, **165**, 664–672.

Labov, W. The study of language in its social context. *Studium Generale,* 1970, **23**, 30–87.

Lees, R. Formal discussion of R. Brown and C. Fraser. The acquisition of syntax. And of R. Brown, C. Fraser, and U. Bellugi. Explorations in grammar evaluation. *Monographs of the Society for Research in Child Development,* 1964, **29**, 92–98.

Lenneberg, E. H. *Biological foundations of language.* New York: Wiley, 1967.

Lovell, K., & Dixon, E. M. The growth of grammar in imitation, comprehension, and production. *Journal of Child Psychology and Psychiatry,* 1965, **5**, 1–9.

Miller, W., & Ervin, S. The development of grammar in child language. *Monographs of the Society for Research in Child Development,* 1964, **29**, 9–34.

Premack, D. The education of Sarah. *Psychology Today,* September, 1970, **3**(9), 54–58. (a)

Premack, D. A Functional analysis of language. *Journal of the Experimental Analysis of Behavior,* 1970, **14**, 107–125. (b)

Premack, D. Language in chimpanzee? *Science,* 1971, **172**, 808–822.

Schlesinger, I. M. Production of utterances and language acquisition. In D. I. Slobin (Ed.), *The ontogenesis of grammar.* New York: Academic Press, 1971.

Skinner, B. F. *Science and human behavior.* New York: Macmillan, 1953.

Skinner, B. F. Two "synthetic social relations." *Journal of the Experimental Analysis of Behavior,* 1962, **5**, 531–533.

Slobin, D. I. *Cognitive prerequisites for the development of grammar.* Edmonton, Alberta, Canada: Linguistics Research, Inc., 1971.

8

SOME VALUES OF COMMUNICATION TECHNOLOGY FOR THE FUTURE OF WORLD ORDER[1]

Colin Cherry
Imperial College, London, England

Of all the revolutionary changes which have come upon us since the Second World War, few are likely to be of greater long-term significance to the world than those deriving from our vastly increased power of communicating. I say this, not thinking of specific gadgets like telephones, aircraft, television, computers, satellites and—whatever next? Nor from conjecture about what each is likely to do to us. I say it rather from consideration of the nature of human communication itself, of the basis of social existence and awareness, and of the real nature of technology. Indeed I would define "society" as "people in communication," the means of communication which are possessed being a major determinant of the form of the various social institutions in any society, whether it be a peasant society, a nomadic society, or one which we flatter ourselves in calling an "advanced society."

To take an example, money is a technical means of communication, the invention of which permitted totally new forms of social organization. Printing is another, whose social consequences I need hardly mention. Both are ancient technologies; yet, far from being outmoded, both are coming into increasing and more widespread use, nationally and internationally. The coming of the telephone in the last century was equally revolutionary, not just because it raised the speed of communication, in one step, from that of the horse to that of electricity, but because it enabled people to move about with greater security—it added as much to personal mobility as did the wheel, inasmuch as it made *conceivable* the movement of our bodies while our minds could remain at home. Again, the

[1]Some of the material presented here has appeared in the author's book *World Communication: Threat or Promise?* published by John Wiley (United Kingdom) Ltd., London, 1971.

primary importance of the invention of radio, at the turn of the century, was that it immediately changed the future of naval warfare because ships could disperse out of sight of one another.

The introduction of reliable intercontinental telephones after the Second World War, using both cables and satellites, whose message traffic has grown so explosively, together with international Telex, has removed certain constraints upon action, leading to the most globally dispersed industry of all time—the international airways. Figure 1 illustrates the principal cable and satellite routes of intercontinental telecommunication (as in 1970), while Figures 2, 3, 4, and 5 show a few of the rapid growths of traffic—telephone, Telex, and air traffic (Cherry, 1971).

These new systems of international communication have not merely removed the constraints of time and distance, as is so often said, but they have also altered the constraints upon political action. There are already obvious signs of effects of these newly acquired liberties upon governmental and diplomatic relations, upon international business and manufacturing industries, upon news services, and upon public attitudes and political aims. It is in this sense that technology, communication technology above all, is a political matter. Technology is a means, not an end; it offers new potential for choice of action and compels us to make decisions; it must be reckoned with, adapted to. Technology is thus power: power that is sometimes real and sometimes only in the imagination. And the only control over this power is wise law: law that is sufficiently flexible and humane to allow us to adapt socially to the creation of new technological power. Yet it continues to be taught within colleges and universities as though it were nothing more than abstract exercises in mathematics, physics, and chemistry, or as though it were an end in itself—fascinating, no doubt, and intellectually stimulating—like crossword puzzles. I would argue that this attitude is immoral.

Communication has today become a subject of great popular interest and often concern, for these very reasons. The various new "media," as they come in, offer a certain feeling of threat, because they all imply a possible disturbance of the familiar social order, a change of social relations, and hence a threat to one's own feeling of self. Many questions are anxiously raised: Will world communication help to unite or to divide us? Do radio, TV, and the Press control us or not? Is TV really increasing juvenile delinquency? In recent years, millions of transistor sets have poured into countries of Africa and the Middle East; what effects will they have upon these traditional societies, for better or worse? There is now a whole mythology of so-called "mass communication"; for mythology, in the sense of "popular wisdom," is the natural outcome of situations which are not understood by large fractions of a population. This mythology has arisen because of a pressing concern over what modern communication is doing to us and what new media are around the corner. Will increasing national and global communication services inevitably lead to greater centralization of power and so to loss of the individual? If this is feared by some, then why should centralized "world government" seem to many to be a desirable aim?

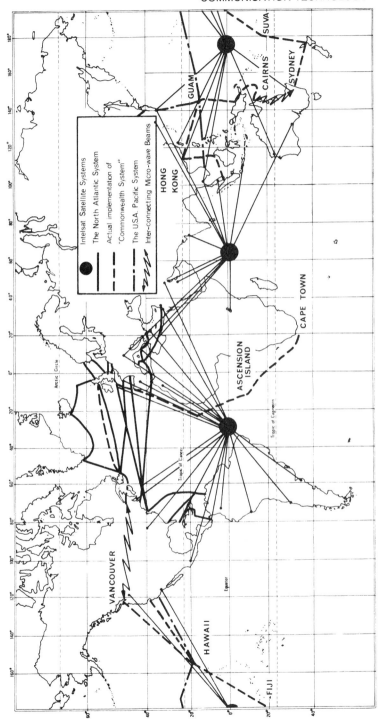

FIG. 1. The world's principal intercontinental trunk routes (cable & satellite) for telecommunication (telephony, Telex, etc.) as of April, 1970.

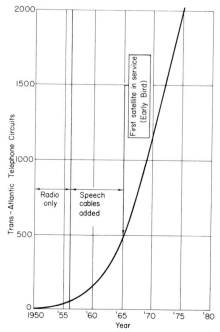

FIG. 2. Official prediction of telephone circuits on North Atlantic.

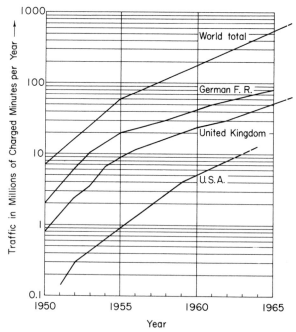

FIG. 3. The rapid post-war growth of international Telex traffic (incoming and outgoing). (With kind acknowledgement to the British Post Office.)

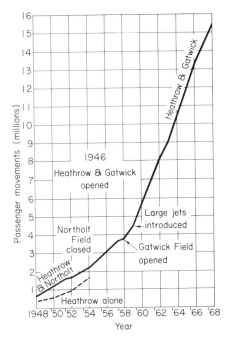

FIG. 4. Civilian air passenger movements in London. (Figures kindly supplied by the British Airports Authority.)

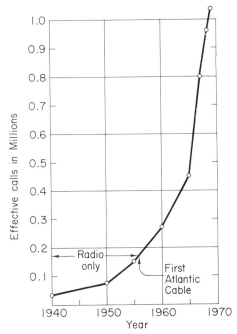

FIG. 5. Intercontinental telephone calls per annum from Britain, to countries beyond Europe.

Such questions cannot be fully answered, for we are still living in the early days of this technological revolution; money and printing we have had for centuries, but only for a flash of time have we seen the consequences of television, of computers, of global telephony and Telex, of data processing and data links, of satellites,—and of all the rest. In order to think about these endless social questions, it seems necessary to stand back a little and to consider them in a more general and philosophical way—in the form of two particular questions. The first is the question What is human communication? and the second is What is the true nature of technology?

First, then, what is communication? Strictly, the word means *sharing*. Communication is essentially social interaction. It is a sharing of a common language, cultural symbols, social habits, rituals, and many other forms of signs. It is a mistake to think of it as one person "sending messages" to another; the two persons may be sharing a language, but not necessarily sharing a common purpose. It is an even greater mistake to think of communication as necessarily being "goal-seeking," with the aim of bringing people together—for just as speech may sometimes bring people together, so it can equally well keep them apart. With language we can discuss amicably or we can quarrel. We can be both self-expressive and inquiring. We can unite or divide—and human division is vitally important.

When a child is born, it is part of its own mother who, by verbal and other play, begins to teach the child its own separate existence and identity. Within a few months that child is babbling mainly in the phonetics of its mother and has already set off on mental railway lines, separating it for life from children of other cultures, languages, and countries. The power of acquiring language not only distinguishes man from other animals by a gulf, which the American philosopher Suzanne Langer (1957) refers to as "one whole day of creation," but also inevitably ensures his adherence to his own kind, his group loyalties, and much of his thoughts, his basic beliefs, his attitudes, and his feelings, and so ensures, in turn, his segregation from other groups. To exist as a man, each man must *belong*—and belonging to any group implies exclusion from some other group. A man must *belong*, largely as he has been taught when young, to a country, a social class, an occupational group, a family, a religion—within which he plays his varied roles, thereby seeing others as being, somehow, different.

Among others, the great physicist Erwin Schrödinger (1964, p. 69) has pointed out that any person's private image of the world, what he sees and notices, or does not, what is important and what is unimportant, what are his relations to other people, to the sun, the moon, and the stars, are not the result of his own immediate and unaided observations. They are what he has been *taught* to see and understand, first by his mother teaching him to speak, with legends and fairy stories, and then by others, through the language and symbols of his culture. If he lives in a literate community, he will partly build his image of the world through books, giving him a continuity with the past, a sense of change, of the "historic arrow," and perhaps the sense of "progress." In acquiring his knowledge and thoughts about other countries of the world through literature, he cannot fail, at the same time, to acquire outmoded views of them; for it is a sad fact that our knowledge of foreign peoples must always be, to some extent, great or little, old-fashioned. It is sad, too, to think that tourism may do little to update our views of other countries and their institutions, for we are likely to visit them not to be *retaught* by them, but merely to observe, to "see for ourselves" what we have already been taught to see, and so to confirm our antique beliefs.

As a child is taught to speak with its mother, its family, and others, so it can talk to itself. All language is socially acquired and used for, as Charles Sanders Peirce (the onetime teacher of William James) pointed out 70 years ago, even talking to oneself is a form of communication (Gallie, 1972; Peirce, 1950). Thinking, that is to say, is also a social activity, so that one's knowledge of oneself is fundamentally no different from one's knowledge of other people. "Knowledge" means articulated or expressed ideas, shared socially through language, as distinct from uncorroborated introspection, feelings, or vague daydreams. "I," "me," and "myself" as objects of knowledge are all the creations of society. It was the great sociologist Emile Durkheim who first argued that an individual and his society are absolutely inseparable, that a person cannot have any concepts of his separate existence and nature other than those taught him by the society, through its language, symbols, and signs (Tiryakian, 1962). Whether these concepts number among them the concepts of *choice*, of *change*, or of *challenge*, however, will depend upon conditions of life within that society. It may be that, within some preindustrial communities wholly absorbed in backbreaking labour, scratching out the barest necessities of existence, the ideas of "choice" or "change" would arise in no one's mind, nor perhaps would they have much idea of individual existence. For only inasmuch as any choice exists, either conceptually, or physically, or morally, can that choice be acted upon.

Where such freedom of choice exists, challenge and change are possible. It is the man who says "No!" or "You're wrong" who is the source of progress, for he can be required to give his reasons, or to state new ideas: that is, to be challenged. Language serves both for assenting and for dissenting, both for agreement and for dispute. And dissenting, or disputing, are vital to change, though frequently they make us uncomfortable. If language served only the purposes of social integration, of unquestioning agreement, it would lead to a world of authoritarianism, a world ruled by clichés and slogans. And authoritarianism is not communication; it is its denial, it is a refusal to communicate—just as assuredly as war is not "an extension of diplomacy," but rather is a denial of diplomacy.

True communication is, then, always an act of *courage*, of daring, however slight or unnoticed, even in our daily conversation. What you say, you cannot *unsay*. You can, of course, apologize, withdraw, or want to sink through the floor—but it is irreversible; you are committed, however little.

This, then, seems to be man's inevitable fate. He is born and raised in groups; to be a "person," he must *belong*: to a language community, to a country, to a class, to an age group, to many different groups, within which he plays his roles, adopts his loyalties, and sees himself as "one of the others." Of course, he may be a refugee or a voluntary immigrant, in which case he may deliberately adopt new communities and roles, because he has both purpose and social experience. But a foreigner must work very hard to learn another language and a new cultural code, which may perhaps give him an interest in its people. He may travel and visit them and feel closely with them, but he cannot really *be* one of them. I may struggle half a lifetime to learn Chinese—but I can never be a Chinese.

Then what about the possibility of "world language"—a *lingua franca*? It certainly would have many practical values (as does English over a wide area of the world now, or Arabic, or written Chinese, say). But there is no one single *culture* existing to sustain a "world language" and to give it cause for change and development. However, these practical values are, in my opinion, of the very greatest value, and I shall refer to them again. A people develops the language it *needs*, just as it evolves the moral code it needs—to enable it to adapt to its particular environments. And these environments vary greatly in different parts of the world.

It is upon such a varied world, with its immense variety of languages, of physical, social, and political conditions which have evolved and changed over the centuries, that technological inventions have sprung. Inventions happen suddenly. Even though the social *milieu* of some societies is far more encouraging of individual inventiveness than that of others, inventions are often the creations of individuals, and they usually come in advance of social needs and readiness for them. The two worlds, the human and the technological, are different in their natures in this way: man is evolutionary; technology is revolutionary. All modern "technological societies" must therefore develop under constant shock and strain, at least until we have learned to develop institutions (of government, education, and law, especially) which will have vastly greater abilities to adapt than those we have inherited today. For the scientific traditions of the past 300 years have led us to an overwhelmingly greater understanding of material and impersonal things than they have of people and institutions. With our accelerating technology today, we are reaping the bitter fruits of this discrepancy—an ever-mounting number of moral problems and dilemmas, a constant state of crisis.

This brings me to my second question: What is the true nature of technology? I should like to answer first with a denial, and say that, in my opinion, it is essentially *not* the study of things, nor is it meaningful to define it as "applied science." It concerns invention, design, and the making of artifacts, but always *artifacts for persons*. Technology is a social study.

Furthermore, technology is irreversible. What has been invented cannot be uninvented. It may remove constraints upon the society, open up new modes of acting, living, and feeling, and the social adjustment to these new possibilities may be painful; for, as we have seen most clearly with the invention of the Pill, such adjustment can violently disturb existing traditions. For technology is not simply a matter of *things*: it concerns things in relation to people, and so, inevitably, it has major control over human relationships.

Again, technology is always purposeful: it always raises questions about values; it is economic; it involves responsibilities. The criterion of success of any manufactured artifact is not expressed by how it supports or denies a theory, but by people's opinions and often by whether it sells or not. It is always open to criticism. In other words, technology, unlike science, does not contain within itself its own success criteria—unless we regard technology always within a social context. Its criteria are essentially *social*. An artifact is designed *for* a person, or for a class of persons, and the design will depend upon who those people are, upon their conditions and needs. To take a simple example, the transistor set came upon us, when it did, not just because somebody knew about solid-state physics and decided to "apply" it; it was successful at a time when millions of young people could afford the luxury, and also because, being small and light, it suited a generation which, for the first time in Western society, could travel about extensively; it brought pop entertainment in a cheap and portable form.

However, taking this same example, cheap transistor sets are now pouring into areas of the world whose social conditions are very different from those of the Western industrial countries which first *created* these artifacts. They are being taken up within tribal societies and, increasingly, within the traditional societies of the Middle East. What will be their consequences there? Nasser once claimed that radio now counts far more than literacy, meaning that, for promotion of change and political awareness, at least, a backward country did not now have to wait for massive literacy.

So it is with all today's technologies of communication. It is quite wrong to think that a Western film has the same effect upon, say, an African village audience as it does upon us. We may see "the plot," or speak disparagingly of "horror" or "violence," or "sex," and wonder what effects these will have upon Africans, while they may be far more fascinated by the film star's clothes, or just by the sheer movement going on, or by details trivial to us. To some extent such realization is comforting, as it is when we remember that many East African schoolchildren have been taught to read and write through such apparently unsuitable literature as *Pride and Prejudice,* or *Great Expectations*, or the writings of Shakespeare or Thackeray. Happily, many African authors are now appearing, and they may soon have their own literature. If so, this will enrich us too — but perhaps not in ways that their authors intended.

What, then, is technology? It was the existentialist thinker, Heidegger, who saw its real nature, when he called it "mediator between Man and raw nature" (Tiryakian, 1962). Technology is a *mediator*. It determines our conceivable freedoms of action, or liberties of choice—though we may not always be able to actually *take* these actions, say, for economic, educational, or moral reasons. A new invention offers us, in principle, new conceivable modes of action, of thinking, and of feeling which may or may not be adopted; in practice the taking of these actions may inhibit us in other ways. Invention is not to be equated with "progress."

Nevertheless, it is worth noting that the introduction of a new communication medium has not usually resulted in abandonment of earlier ones. Thus the telephone has not ousted the postal service; television has not destroyed the cinema, nor the newspapers; the coming of radio in the 1920s even boosted the gramaphone industry. Contrary to popular belief, the coming of television has not destroyed reading—nor, in my opinion, will it (Luckham & Orr, 1967; McColvin, 1956). For example, the lendings of books from public libraries rapidly increased after the introduction of television (in Britain, the U.S.A., and elsewhere), for the standards of education of a major section of our population also rose rapidly (see Figure 6).

The expression "this shrinking world" is a commonplace today but, to my mind, a deceptive one. The world is shrinking only in the sense that travel is much faster and that events in, say, Vietnam, are reported in New York and London and everywhere else, and seen on TV News Bulletins within the hour. That is, the world has shrunk as a result of faster communication, only in *time scale*. On the contrary, in the sense of personal experience and existence, the world has vastly expanded—at least, in the minds of those people who have access to books,

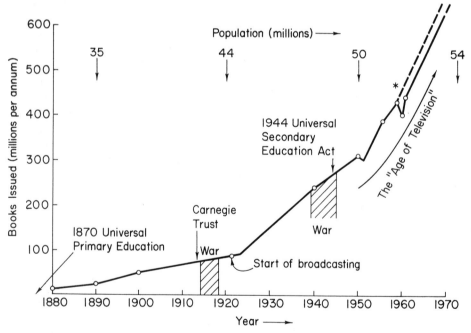

FIG. 6. Books issued by the Municipal Public Libraries in Britain. (*After 1958, school library issues excluded.)

newspapers, radio, or television, or who are able to travel more or fly overseas. To such people, in their increasingly greater numbers and with their rising educational standards, the world has vastly expanded. There is far *more* to read about or to see today. We who can read, or travel, are increasingly called upon to make more and more critical assessments, to take more and more personal views upon more and more issues, to try to understand the doings and affairs of more and more peoples in ever more regions of the earth. The world increasingly expands and faces us with more dilemmas; but our emotional capacities do not expand. We may read the news about millions of people, or see their faces on the TV screen—but we do not always feel *personal* relation with those images. We can put the paper down, or turn to the crossword puzzle, without a qualm, just as we can switch off the TV set, blot out the news, and get on with our dinners.

How many friends can a man have—in the sense of real personal involvement and with compassion? A dozen? A hundred, maybe? Something on a village scale of size. On no account can he have a million or a thousand million friends, known as persons by name, and with their individual hopes and tragedies. *The world can never be my village.* It is true that, on very special occasions, some special person is brought to the attention of millions simultaneously by a communicational medium—as with the assassination of a President. But these events are very rare, and these people are special "public figures." World communication offers no possibility of bringing together millions of people into a sense of personal involvement, each with every other. Nothing integrates a community like disaster. But news is mostly news of other people's disasters, in which we and our own community are not, in a direct and personal way, involved. The ever-mounting volume of news that presses upon us, brought by modern technology from most corners of the earth, requires us to adopt some personal attitudes towards millions of different people. We cannot see them as individual persons, but only as institutions, as abstractions. We speak of "*the* Indians", "*the* Chinese", "*the* Americans"—that is, not as *people* at all, but as *personifications*. I am certainly not suggesting, however, that it would be better for us if we stopped having the news, merely because it cannot be personal. If nothing else, news can be the antidote to what would otherwise be rumor.

Today's fast-expanding technology of communication and transport is something new which has sprung upon us, for it is not confined to single countries, language groups or cultures, as was much of our past technology. It is essentially global, and it is upon these global implications for the human race that I would like to offer opinions now.

But first let me summarize. I have here argued against prediction of the future through conjecture about what the various technological inventions that we have—television, radio, telephones, Telex, satellites, computers, aircraft, cars—even money—may be doing to us now, let alone by guessing what future gadgets may spring upon our future forms of society. I have argued that those people who are concerned about so-called "mass communication," or about what these various technologies may do to us (to education, to international relations, to employment, to the developing countries, and to other major affairs) should draw back before plunging into the bottomless morass of technical speculation and, instead, address themselves to two major questions, both of a philosophical nature and neither yet fully answered: First, what is communication? And second, What is technology?

Briefly, I have argued that "communication" does not mean "sending messages," nor, least of all, "bringing people together." Human language may sometimes bring us together in agreement, but it can equally well keep us apart. You may breathe words of love into a telephone, or you may shout abuse. When communicating, you can agree or disagree, assent or dispute. And I have argued that disagreement and dispute are prerequisites to change. I argued further that, through man's unique power of speech, we are each of us taught from birth our own individual identities, but essentially as members of various social groups. That is, to exist, we must *belong*.

With regard to the second question—What is technology?—I accepted the view of the existentialist thinker Heidegger that technology is "mediator between Man and raw Nature" (Tiryakian, 1962). It is a means of increasing our power of acting, of thinking, and of feeling, through which power, according to the level of technology we happen to possess, we are able to come to terms with the world and to form our own views of it and of each other. Technology is not an end but a means, and, unlike Science, it cannot pretend to be amoral. It involves us in decisions, in choices, and in increasing numbers of dilemmas. The criteria of success and failure of any technology are social, not scientific. So, too, in the public eye it is the social values of technology that are seen and so often criticized.

I should now like to bring together these opinions upon the questions, What is Communication? and What is Technology? and offer some views on the real human values of our communication media, now and in the future, especially with regard to the explosively growing systems of global communication. Every year shows additions to international and intercontinental *means* of communication— new oceanic cables, new satellites, new airways. Will these bring us closer together or drive us further apart? And for what reasons?

Even to discuss such questions lays one wide open to misunderstanding, because "communication" is a highly emotional subject, and one which personally affects us and our feelings of security. Mention the words "overseas broadcasting," and back comes the reply "propaganda"; mention "the Press," and you are challenged with the words "advertising" or "slanted news." How can one argue rationally within a field that is so filled with popular wisdom and emotion?

For a start, it is absolutely essential to recognize that all media of communication serve two distinct functions. These may be termed the private and the public, or the domestic and the institutional, or the personal and the social, or, more broadly, the emotional and the organizational. These functions correspond to one's inner personal life and to the structure of one's society, and it is the organizational values of the media—not the emotional values—that seem to me to dominate the future. Certainly, radio and television, books and newspapers, telephones and the post, can affect your emotions profoundly; but your particular feelings will depend upon who you are, your particular circumstances, your particular views of the world and of yourself, as your own social institutions have taught you. From such a point of view, emotions are seen not as primary causes, but rather as consequences of the particular freedoms of action or the particular frustrations that bear upon one within one's society. Thus, it is the enormous powers for *organization* offered by communication media, today and in the future, that seem to me of primary value. They offer us the potential, the means, for forming and operating many new types of organization, especially on a global scale, if we now so wish.

Let us look for a moment at what is actually happening. Certain forms of international industry have grown fast—since the Second World War, for example, the News Services and the Airways (both being dependent upon the international Telex and telephone). The Transatlantic telephone service has led to new kinds of industry and business, with legs on both sides of the ocean. One thing is certain about the future: some industries will become increasingly dispersed around the globe. Our International Airways are the most globally dispersed industry in history. We are already witnessing the frustration of international trade and industry caused by the inadequacy of one particular medium of international communication—that is, a workable international currency system.

Ownership of the greater part of the global communication systems of today lies in the hands of the affluent Western countries. Only they, at present, can afford the necessary capital. Furthermore, it is cheaper for these richer countries to use these systems, because their traffic demands are high. The higher the traffic on any route, the cheaper becomes each message (Cherry, 1971). A kind of "capitalism" of communication may then develop; for communication, if regarded as "organizing power," like money, can create itself, unless some means are found to control the explosion and to direct some of this power to the service of the poorer developing countries.

Fortunately, there is a long and fairly happy tradition of international cooperation in communication services. Over a century ago, the postal services and the telegraphs were organized on an international basis in ways which have not substantially changed since. Modern long-distance communication services, like the telephone and other public services, do present new problems, to a great extent financial problems, but the international organizations that are needed to own, operate, and use them are working fairly well. But there will always be room for improvement.

There is no denying the fact that, at present, it is only the "advanced" countries which have the technical potential and the capital needed to design and install the major global systems. It is only they who also have the traffic demands to justify the creation of such systems. We can speak lightly of "world communication," but we should remember that the bulk of the traffic is at present confined to one particular route—the North Atlantic—both message traffic and air transport (see Figures 1 and 2). Thus, 80% of all the world's intercontinental telephone traffic passes between North America and Europe. Nevertheless, the communication channels themselves are not confined to the North Atlantic, for within only the past few years, complete round-the-world installations have been introduced, connecting all the continents, and so are available for use by the less rich countries with their present low demands for international traffic.

I have used the expression "developing countries." What is a "developed" or an "advanced" country? It seems to me that the difference lies not only in the possession of things, but also in the different concepts of trust. In a "developing" country, people may each place their trust in specific individuals, whom they know personally; whereas, in a so-called "advanced" country, people place trust also upon abstract institutions and upon their representatives, who they may never have met. They trust "the Manager" or "the Secretary" or "the Inspector," unknown to them as persons. And when their institutions fail this trust, they are righteously indignant. They *oughtn't* to fail us; Heaven intends that they should operate well. Industrialization requires this essential change in the people's concept of trust. One of the great values of modern communication media could be to help with this change within developing countries; but, unfortunately, they are expensive not only to install, but also to operate day by day. The United Nations has stressed in numerous reports the importance of countrywide communication services for "developing" countries—especially the media of the Press, radio, film and television—and has laid down minimal targets (United Nations Organization, 1948, 1960, 1966; UNESCO, 1964). The U.N. has urged the importance of these media not only for the development of national institutions for economic growth, government, and education, but also for assisting change in people's attitudes and for instilling the sense of "nationhood"—and what is a sense of nationhood but a feeling of trust in one's own national institutions? In the so-called "advanced" or industrialized countries, we take this state of affairs for granted, and we can so easily forget that a large part of the world does not yet live with much of the feeling of security that we have. We may too easily scorn "nationhood" (for liberty to criticize it is one of its ingredients) and speak of it as undesirable by confusing it with "nationalism." "Nationhood" is simply a social fact; it is a sense of identity with a community, whereas "nationalism" is an ethnocentric valuation—a belief that my nationhood is better than yours.

In the "advanced" industrial countries, it may well be that we have carried the process too far by now, in the sense of becoming overcentralized. Roads and railways first enabled areas of economic action to expand and central government to operate over whole countries. The coming of telegraphs and telephones continued the process by extending and tightening central control. The Press, radio, and television carried it yet further. It is certainly true to say that our technologies of communication have so far led to a very great increase in centralization, which has advanced us economically. It has, so far, been the price we have had to pay in order to grow richer, a price which may have included much loss of local values, traditional institutions, and identities. But it would be a great mistake to take the gloomy view that communication technology inevitably must lead to increased centralization *alone*.

Furthermore, such "loss" of local variations is nothing new, and nostalgic lament cannot help us. The blame certainly does not fall wholly upon our modern means of communication; they merely contribute to our centralization. The whole Western world has certainly increased its forms of centralization, which has required diverse powers, including those of finance and capital, transport, urbanization, education, mass production, law, and a host of others—in brief, industrialization itself. Communication is a contributory factor and part of the inevitable price. As Emile Durkheim himself argued, many years ago, there is no real mystery in the apparent paradox: Why can our real liberties increase as the powers of the centralized State increase? Isolation, individualism, disorganization are not liberty, but anarchy.

So far, or at least until the middle of this century, we have indeed used our enhanced power of communication largely for centralization, and the organized State has increased in power. In Max Weber's terms, we have greatly added to our domination by rational action directed toward *goals*. But there are signs now that, perhaps as a consequence, we can afford to consider increasingly Weber's other form of domination—that of rational action directed towards *values*. Voices of criticism and dissent are nowadays more likely to be heard. Perhaps we can now *afford* to use our technology of communication for decentralizing.

Technology, per se, has no powers, for it is dead stuff; the powers lie in the hands of those who use it. It must always involve us in decisions, political decisions. It can give us the powers both to centralize *and* decentralize, according to our political wisdom. Centralization and decentralization need not be antagonistic. We can have both at the same time, and they can be mutually advantageous. Increase in strength of national government need not necessarily weaken local government, but may indeed strengthen it, and may eventually assist development of local variety. The two forms of government, central and local, are concerned with different institutions, with different social purposes, but they can and should be mutually supporting.

In my opinion, we are now at a watershed and are beginning to develop the decentralizing powers of our communication media, the values of which once seen by people, will be demanded increasingly. At least in industrial countries, we can now *afford* to. The point is that we do not have to be members of one community only, but can identify with two, or with ten—or with very many. We may be members of a large community for certain general purposes, while at the same time identifying with smaller communities for local or personal purposes. Thus, for us in Britain to join Europe, because of the economic advantages of belonging to an enlarged community, does not require us to shed *all* aspects of being British. Or, again, in Britain (which I know best) and no doubt elsewhere, we have drives for greater provincial autonomy today, for more local broadcasting based upon local interests, for greater participation in local affairs. And such varieties can, in principle, be achieved better within federation. Federation does not mean identity, nor some colossus of overcentralized power. It means searching for and separating out those elements of common interest, elements which change over the years. And federation cannot be built without communication services. The "communication explosion" may lead some people to fear this colossus of overcentralization as an inevitable creation of our expanding technology. If it happens, which I obviously doubt, the fault will lie in ourselves and not in our communication media.

The reason that so many have such fear may arise from the early history of the "communication explosion," which has witnessed great and rapid growth of centralization in many forms. We have seen rapid expansions of many areas of control or influence, at many different levels and with very varied organizations. I am thinking not only of government, but of areas created also by unified educational systems, or by national broadcasting, or by the Press, and by other forms of so-called "mass communication." But what is far more important, yet less dramatic for the lay public, is that the mid-twentieth century has seen other forms of centralization, such as in the remarkable growth of such international organizations as the WHO, the IMF, UNESCO, and some 25 others within the United Nations sphere, together with 3,000 or so outside their sphere—but each with a precise and prescribed function, and each federating different groups of countries according to these functional needs (see Figure 7).

At the same time, the mid-twentieth century has witnessed another phenomenon—that of decentralization—in the appearance of many new and very small nations, each seeking to run its own affairs such as are unique to its people and their feelings of identity. It is a sobering thought that half the countries of this world have less than 5 million inhabitants. Alexis de Tocqueville, after the French Revolution, predicted that there would soon be very few and large countries in the world. I feel that he would be astonished by the truth!

I would like to end by giving my own conclusions as to the values of world communication to the development of "world order," and how our fast-growing global systems will contribute towards rationalizing these two apparently opposing postwar drives—that for centralization and that for decentralization.

I have argued earlier on that, in order to exist as a person, a man must *belong*, not to one community but perhaps to many. He may pretend to be a citizen of the world, but he also belongs to a race, to a country (or to a community of stateless persons), to a village, to an occupational group, to an age group, to a social class, to a family and ancestors—endless groups, each involving him in different acts of trust, different forms of loyalty, and different purposes. It may be argued, with some truth, that because of today's widespread travel and communication, all cities will soon look alike, much as do airports and just as you can already buy

Coca-Cola everywhere. But this is trivial in our present context. These growing similarities need not make us love or understand one another more. Neither does their mere possession mean that they have the same *significance* everywhere. Furthermore, I do not believe that our world communication systems of the future will either, just because all countries possess the same ones—each has radio, television, newspapers, airlines, etc. These are shared *things* but are not shared *symbols*. They function differently in different cultural contexts.

One of the present-day threats arises from this very possibility—a high-powered satellite system which is able to pump the same television program directly into every home in the world, and into every native village. This would no more be a sharing than have been, say, Western films and books sent into Africa in the past. Many poorer countries are already forced into transmitting to their people our Western TV programs much of the time—not because they can create nothing more suitable themselves, but because they cannot afford anything else. But again we should not assume that they *mean* the same to peoples of different countries.

No; I do not believe that the real and positive contributions of global communication to world order in the future will arise mainly from their emotional powers, at least not directly. Closer world harmony will not be gained by trying to persuade other national groups to be like us, because any attack upon the institutions or the communities with which a person identifies (i.e., to which a person belongs) is an attack upon himself. It seems to me that the real and positive values of our rapidly increasing power of world communication are practical ones, stemming from their organizing powers. It is now possible, technically speaking, to organize many formal institutions on a global scale for specific purposes, and this we have been doing very fast, though only since the last War (Mangone, 1954). Certainly, when any new technique of communication has been introduced in the past, its first applications have usually been to warfare or moneymaking. But there is some evidence to suggest that in the past the development of more fruitful international institutions has been frustrated partly by lack of adequate technical media and channels which are practical prerequisites for their creation, communication, organization, and operation (see Figure 7).

The first international organization was a result of the Treaty of Vienna, following the Napoleonic Wars, when the crowned heads of the European States met. Among the questions dealt with was Who owned the rivers of Europe?—for the same waters flowed through several countries and were shared both as "stuff" and as "value." During the nineteenth century, the number of international organizations grew as different specific common interests became identified, but the First World War more or less saw collapse of the whole process. It was after the Second World War, only 25 years ago, that the growth began again in a world so needing it, and in a way truly "explosive," to use the word once again (Mangone, 1954). We now have some three thousand organizations, each dealing with specific and defined interests common to various overlapping groups of countries, whose representatives share a common expertise but may belong to countries of varied

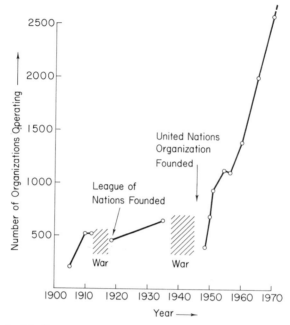

FIG. 7. Growth of the listed International Organizations, since 1900 (see "Yearbook of International Organizations," pub. by the Union, 1 rue aux Laines, Brussels).

political systems. They deal with the practical constraints of life—trades, law, scientific knowledge, finance, navigation, health, and many others, each having a separate and defined *function*. It is by virtue of such practical institutions that international law is increasingly operative—not because we are "better people." There seems as yet no check to their growing numbers.

As I see hope for the future, then, it is not through enforced shedding of national autonomies, political differences and cultural distinctions, nor by creation of some centralized "government" based upon analogy with our concept of a national government. For what an unthinkable extent of bureaucracy and concentration of power would such an overcentralized organization imply! And under what political system would it operate? The United Nations is an institution which is sometimes spoken of as a potential world government. But in fact it is not. It was not created as such, and it has never set out to be so. It does indeed provide a talking-house and an organized Secretariat. But to compare its debates with the operation of, say, the British House of Commons, or the House of Representatives could only lead us to endless disappointments—for it can be nothing of the kind. To express my personal view, the real and great practical value of the United Nations Organization lies in the existence of its specialized agencies. Rather than through a hypothetical centralized world "government," I see the possibility of better world order through varied and flexible federations of countries, according to a host of specific, defined, mutual interests; that is, through continued growth of the international organizations, leading to greater dispersal of power in many of its forms and with varied *functions*, as these become identified and defined.

And it is to this end that the technology of world communication allows us to go, if we choose, and it is along such a path that our emotional attitudes to one another in this world have some chance of converging.

REFERENCES

Cherry, E. C. *World communication: Threat or promise?* London: Wiley, 1971.

Gallie, W. B. *Peirce and pragmatism.* Harmondsworth, Eng.: Pelican, 1972

Langer, S. *Philosophy in a new key.* Cambridge, Mass.: Harvard University Press, 1957.

Luckham, B., & Orr, J. M. Broadcasting and public libraries. *Library Association Record,* 1967, **69** (January), 11.

Mangone, G. J. *A short history of international organizations.* New York: McGraw-Hill, 1954.

McColvin, L. R. *The chance to read: Public libraries in the world today.* New York: Oxford University Press (London: Dent), 1956.

Peirce, C. S. *Selected writings.* (Ed. by J. Buchler) London: Routledge and Kegan Paul, 1950.

Schrödinger, E. *My view of the world.* London: Cambridge University Press, 1964.

Tiryakian, E. A. *Sociologism and existentialism.* Englewood Cliffs, N. J.: Prentice-Hall, 1962. (An excellent account of Emile Durkheim's philosophy is included.)

UNESCO. *World communication: Press, radio, film, television.* Paris: UNESCO, 1964. (In French, 1966.)

United Nations Organization. Statistical yearbooks. New York: UNO, 1948, 1960, 1966.

9
THE HISTORY AND THE FUTURE
OF VERBAL MEDIA[1]

Walter J. Ong, S.J.
Saint Louis University

There is a great deal of talk today about the media of communication and a widespread interest in what effect these media are having on man. Nor is this interest misplaced. For the relationship of man to man, of man to society, of man to his entire life-world, can be seen in new and refreshing detail if we attend to the history of communications. Only we must be clear that by communications we understand here not simply new gimmicks, enabling man to "contact" his fellows but, more completely, the person's means of entering into the life and consciousness of others and thereby into his own life. Communications in this sense obviously relate to man's sense of his own presence to himself and to other men.

The development of communications is one of the central activities of man—indeed, in one sense, it is his central activity. Not only does society depend on it, human thought as we know it in the individual himself seemingly cannot come into existence outside a communications system. A child does not learn to think first and to talk afterward; he learns both together, and the two processes of communication and thinking remain correlatives throughout life.

Communication strikes deep into the consciousness. It is inadequate to think of communication, as we sometimes do, in terms of "contact." "Contact" suggests relationship in terms of surface. Communication is not the surface of life, but one aspect of life's substance. It is not expendable decoration, something added *ad libitum* to existence. Rather, when existence itself reaches a certain pitch with the advent of man, it entails communication. Man is a communicating being. Com-

[1]The present article incorporates material from the following publications by Walter J. Ong: *In the Human Grain* (1967, copyright the Macmillan Company), *The Presence of the Word* (1967, copyright Yale University Press), and 'Media Transformation: The Talked Book,' *College English,* 34 (1972), 405–410 (copyright National Council of Teachers of English), used with permission of the respective copyright owners.

munication brings the human person himself not only to knowledge of things and other persons, but also to his own self-awareness. Although I myself am unique, and in a way closed in on myself—for no other man knows what it feels like to be this "I" that I am—nevertheless I become aware of myself as myself only through communication with others.

Man communicates through all his senses, and in ways so complicated that even at this late date many, and perhaps most of them, have never been adequately described. But in some mysterious fashion, among all forms of communication—through touch, taste, smell, sight, or what have you—communication through sound is paramount. Words have a primacy over all other forms of communication. No matter how familiar we are with an object or a process, we do not feel that we have full mastery of it until we can verbalize it to others. And we do not enter into full communication with another person without speech. Verbalization, speech, is at root an oral and aural phenomenon, a matter of voice and ear, an event in the world of sound. Written words are substitutes for sound and are only marks on a surface until they are converted to sound again, either in the imagination or by actual vocalization. The work of an electronic computer, too, is merely a mechanical operation like any other until it is decoded into words, and if the words are typed or printed, they, too, are only marks on a surface without meaning until their reference to sound is established. Meaning thus focuses in a peculiar way in sound itself.

The curious primacy of sound in establishing meaning, the situation which makes the primary sensory correlative of our thoughts words, events in time, is obvious enough but very difficult for us today to grasp. The original, and permanently fundamental, spoken word has become all but inextricably entwined with writing and print and even with exactly reproduced pictorial statement—printed illustrations—to which print often refers. When we talk about words, we are seldom sure whether we mean spoken words or written words or printed words or all these simultaneously, and when we talk about verbal description, we have difficulty in separating the verbal description from the visually presented illustration which so often accompanies it. We have to make a supreme effort to establish a sense of vocalization as such. And yet, if we lack this sense, we cannot understand the development of communications systems in any real depth. For this reason, to get to the roots of our condition today, we must indulge in a little cultural history.

Over the past few decades, it has become evident that, in terms of communications media, cultures can be divided conveniently and informatively into three successive stages: (a) oral or oral-aural, (b) script, which reached critical breakthroughs with the invention first of the alphabet and then later of alphabetic movable type, and (c) electronic (cf. Ong, 1967a). If these stages do not have to do exclusively with verbal communication, since at certain points in the evolution of the media nonverbal visual devices such as diagrams and illustrations increase in use and effectiveness, and if much else can be said about verbal communication outside this framework, nevertheless these three stages are essentially stages of verbalization. Above all, they mark transformations of the word.

Awareness of the succession of the media stages and wonder about the meaning of this succession are themselves the product of the succession. We have come into this awareness only as we have entered the electronic stage. I do not mean by this simply that we have become aware of how different the electronic stage is only as we have entered into it. This would be only a truism. I mean much more: Only as we have entered the electronic stage has man become aware of the profundity of differences, some of which have been before his eyes for thousands of years, namely, the differences between the old oral culture and the culture initiated with writing and matured with alphabetic type. Apparently it was impossible for man to understand the psychological and cultural significance of writing and print and of oral expression itself, with which writing and print contrast, until he had moved beyond print into our present age of telephonic and wireless electronic communication. As late as the 1930s, the differences between speech and writing were still impossibly occluded for even the most astute scholars.

We know now that when changes in the media take place, the implications of what is communicated is in some way changed and often the substance of what is communicated is itself altered. What comes through in writing and print is something of a somewhat different order from that which "comes through" or, more properly, resonates in purely oral-aural communication. Changes in the media of communication restructure man's sense of the universe in which he lives and his very sense of what his thought itself is. They restructure, moreover, his own psyche (which has been defined for us quite conveniently as "what a psychiatrist deals with professionally").

For example, writing, and even more alphabetic print, helps change man from a "traditionalist," largely driven by forces which he shared with others in his society and which he accepted uncritically, to a more interiorly driven, reflective, and analytic individual. With writing, the word becomes something that can be privately assimilated: No person other than the reader need be there, only the book. The student, as we know him, is born, the learner who labors with words and concepts alone. This new state of affairs changes the role of guilt feelings in psychic drives, the structure of personal responsibility. The new media effect these changes not simply because they diffuse knowledge better but because they change man's feelings for what knowledge is and what actuality is. As the media of communication centered around the word—the ones with which we are here chiefly concerned—evolve, man's sense of his own interior and of its relationship to the exterior world evolves too.

Because our concept of what words are is so tied up with a feeling for words as written or printed, a basic difficulty in thinking about words today is our tendency to regard them largely or chiefly or ideally as records. Once we can get over our chirographic-typographic squint here, we can see that the word in its original habitat of sound, which is still its native habitat, is not a record at all. The word is something that happens, an event in the world of sound through which the mind is enabled to relate actuality to itself. To understand more fully what this implies, we must examine in some detail what an oral-aural culture in general is like.

The differences between oral-aural culture and our own technological culture are of course so vast and so profound as to defy total itemization. We can here hope to touch only on some points relevant to our present interest in the word itself as sound.

Perhaps one of the most striking and informative differences is that an oral-aural culture is necessarily a culture with a relationship to time different from ours. It has no records. It does have memory, but this is not by any means the same as records, for the written record is not a remembrance but an aid to recall. It does not belong to us as memory does. It is an external thing.

In an oral-aural culture one can ask about something, but no one can look up anything. As a result, in an oral-aural culture there is no history in our modern sense of the term. The past is indeed present, as to a degree the past always is, but it is present in the speech and social institutions of the people, not in the more abstract forms in which modern history deals. In verbal accounts of the past in an oral-aural culture, the items that we should isolate as facts become inextricably entangled with myth—to be disentangled partially and with great difficulty perhaps only thousands or tens of thousands and even hundreds of thousands of years later, after the advent of writing develops our curious latter-day probes into preliterate ages.

Oral-aural culture was of course to a degree in contact with its past. But the contact was infra-intellectual, embedded in institutions, in customs, and in language itself. Primitive man thought the way he did because of his cultural past, but he had no explicit access to his past. The only way he could find out anything he did not know from experience was to ask someone else. And the one who was asked had no records to consult. In this situation, all but the most immediate past was a wilderness in which fact was inextricably entwined with myth. And this situation set up a feedback: Even witnessed facts in the immediate past and the present were seen in a mythological context.

Words for oral-aural man were powerful things. For those who understand what verbalization is, they still are. A word is a sound, and sound always indicates an actually operating source of power, as the object of no sense other than hearing does. A buffalo need only be passively there—even dead—to be seen or felt or smelt or tasted. If he is bellowing, something is going on, he is *doing* something, one had better watch out.

Anthropologists like to make the point that for primitive man words are somehow of a piece with actuality. Primitive man commonly feels that one can use words to hurt people as one can use an arrow or spear: hence various magic formulas. But if one thinks of words as primarily and always and inevitably spoken words—as anthropologists and other scholars seldom do—the primitive's case is a little more plausible. And if his magic does not work, neither do some of the anthropological explanations of his belief in magic. Basically, he believes that words are powerful because he thinks of them always as events, as something going on, and he feels that, since they come from men, who are free agents and unpredictable, they have an unpredictable potential. He is aware, as post-Gutenberg technological man is likely not to be aware, that words, basically, are not "things" lying passively on a page, but are something someone *does*. This aspect of the word has been progressively obscured at least since Plato (as Eric A. Havelock's *Preface to Plato* 1963, has brilliantly indicated), although it is being made the object of explicit attention in our day. In the oral-aural past it was an object of keen awareness, but not of explicit, scientific discussion.

Oral-aural man, with his keen sense of the word as an indication of action and power, tended to think of the universe itself in terms of operations and sound. For technological man, actuality tends to be an "object"—something to be seen (and to some extent touched), something passive, something man operates on. For earlier oral-aural man, actuality, his life-world, the universe, tended more to be a "word," a manifestation and a power, something one interacted with, not a passive object of visual study and manipulation. Early cosmologies, which persist vestigially through the manuscript age and into the early typographical age, present the universe as a harmony with an insistency strange to us. The late Leo Spitzer (1963) has documented the fact massively in his now posthumously published *Classical and Christian Ideas of World Harmony*, and the concept is familiar enough to us all in the classical notion of the "harmony of the spheres" and in the Old Testament, where we read, for example, in Psalm 18:2-3, "The heavens declare the glory of God, and the firmament proclaims his handiwork. Day pours out the word to day, and night to night imparts knowledge."

To experience the universe as a unity conceived of by analogy with auditory harmony is to relate it not to quiescent Platonic forms (visualist conceptualizations, encouraged by the functional literacy of the Greeks, new in Plato's day, as Eric A. Havelock, 1963, has also shown) but rather to relate it to a present source of power. Such a concept of the universe remains a permanently serviceable insight, capable of supplementing our also serviceable, but ultimately limited, view of the world as a picturable and palpable "object." Milič Čapek's book *The Philosophical Impact of Contemporary Physics* (1961) calls for physicists to supplement their view of the world as basically a "picture," which is certainly not all it is, and to avail themselves of auditory phenomena, with their strikingly dynamic character, as models of physical phenomena, so as to open the way out of certain dead-ends in present physical sciences.

The breakthrough from oral communication to script occurred only around 3500 B.C., when there appeared in the Mesopotamian region the first scripts we know of anywhere. This breakthrough seemingly occurred under the stimulus provided by the need for keeping records as society became more concentrated and highly organized in the urban centers developing at this time on a limited scale. By script we mean a system of writing which in some way represents words, not merely things. Many scripts originate in picture writing and maintain some sort of immediate link with pictures, as Chinese script does. These mark advances, but not the great advance. For pictures do not refer to words as such, but to things. A picture of a bird can elicit any number of words, depending on the language the viewer speaks. The great breakthrough that has made modern technology possible came not with picture-writing but with the alphabet.

Something of the psychological revolution involved in alphabetic writing can be sensed from two facts. First, the alphabet came into being only around 1500 B.C., which means that it took man around 500,000 years to invent it. Secondly, the alphabet was invented only once: There is, strictly speaking, only one alphabet in the entire world. All alphabets in use or known ever to have been in use—the Hebrew, Greek, Roman, Cyrillic, Arabic, Sanscrit, Tamil, Korean and all the rest—trace in one way or another to the alphabet developed, perhaps in some way out of Egyptian hieroglyphic writing, in the ancient Syria-Palestine region.

Some hint of why the alphabet was so hard to come by can be gathered if we attend for a moment to the nature of the word as sound and to what alphabetization does to sound, or pretends to do to it. Sound is a time-bound phenomenon, which exists only as it is passing out of existence. There is no way to preserve sound as sound. If I stop a sound, I have only its opposite, silence, from which all sound starts and in which it ends. A word cannot be present all at once. If I say "present," by the time I get to the "-sent," the "pre-" is gone—and it has to be gone, or I cannot recognize the word. No one has ever measured sound as sound, for to measure it would be to apply to it a spatial existence which it does not have. We measure spatial equivalents of sound—oscillograph patterns or wavelengths—but these measurements can be carried on by deaf-mutes, who do not know what sound is, quite as well as by a Mozart or a Bartok. Our scientific dealings with sound are magnificent achievements and altogether necéssary, but they are always indirect.

Words exist in this mysterious realm which eludes direct scientific treatment. And, since words are the intimate sensory equivalents of our thoughts—not the "vehicles" or "clothes" of thought, but, more accurately, its matrix or even its alter ego—our thinking itself is intimately related to this realm of sound, a realm of existence on the edge of nonexistence, a realm of the living present instant, the only purchase on actuality we have, slender and fragile but alive and real.

Words, then, being sounds, exist only while they are going out of existence. The alphabet implies otherwise. It implies that the whole word is present at once, that one can cut it up into little segments, spatial segments (which it really does not have), and that one can reassemble these segments independently of the flow of time. I can write the letters "p-a-r-t" in that order, but pronounce them in the reverse order to get "t-r-a-p," "trap." This kind of performance is utterly unthinkable in a world of sound. The alphabet is, in other words, an elaborate pretense, in actuality untrue to the real state of affairs, as the modern science of linguistics is acutely aware.

In our culture, we are trained, generally during childhood, to believe in the alphabet. The work of Carothers (1959), and Opler (1956) has shown the effect of this training on the psyche. Massive repressions are set up, which differentiate literate from illiterate man, detribalize him, force him back upon himself, and encourage reflection, analysis, and a large store of guilt feelings different from those of illiterate man. Literate man often characteristically seeks relief from his tensions in schizophrenic delusional systematization, setting up a self-consistent dream world into which he can retire from anxiety. Illiterate man, a large number of studies show, is rarely capable of such withdrawal. Under comparable tensions, he seeks relief from them by a sudden outburst of overwhelming anxiety, fear, and hostility, externally directed and terminating in violence: This is the rioting Congolese soldier, or the old illiterate Scandinavian warrior gone berserk, or the Southeast Asian warrior run amok (it is significant that there are in oral-aural cultures terms for this characteristic pattern of behavior). In other ways, some of which Marshall McLuhan treats in his remarkable book, *The Gutenberg Galaxy* (1962), illiterate man discernibly faces outward, toward the tribe, and literate man inward, toward his own ego, shrouded in new defenses, defenses necessary if society is to move on in its evolutionary course, but entailing strain.

The invention of letterpress printing or alphabetic typography extends and intensifies the reduction of sound to space which was initiated by the alphabet. Significantly, it too was invented only once, in mid-fifteenth century central Europe. Elsewhere, even when breakthroughs to alphabetic type appeared inevitable, they failed to occur. The Koreans had both the alphabet and movable type, but they failed to go beyond word type. It did not occur to them to put separate letters on separate pieces of the type material. The same was the case with the Uigur Turks. On the threshold of a world-shaking invention, they were immobilized. We are obviously here in the presence of another breakthrough which entails a tremendous reorganization of the psyche, although, brought to maturity in a typographical culture, we are unaware of the reorganization to which we ourselves have been subjected, and we take the strains it entails as normal dimensions of life. The alphabet situates words in space, or attempts to do so. Printing literally attempts to lock them there, after interposing between the spoken word and the locked-up form eight or so operations in space and another five or more between the locked-up form and the printed word ready to be restored to the world of sound. The spoken word thus receded into the background so far as to make it unnecessary for those engaged in the typographical operation to know the language they are dealing with or even be able to speak at all.

The emergence of alphabetic typography is associated with a great intensification of spatial awareness in the European culture where alphabetic typography developed. The fifteenth and subsequent centuries mark the age of full linear perspective in painting, of maps and the concomitant sense of the earth's surface as a spatial expanse to be covered by exploration, of Copernican cosmology and Newtonian physics, which plotted the universe with charts more than ever before and reduced the old nature philosophy in the physical sciences to ineffectiveness. It was the age that made an issue of observation—that is, of the application of sight or of other senses conceived of not as they are but by analogy with sight. One cannot "observe" a sound with one's ears: One can only *hear* it.

The heightening of the importance of vision which accompanied typography changed man's sense of the universe about him. Vision depersonalizes. This truth can be grasped rather immediately if we reflect that to stare at another person, to treat him merely as an object of vision, is intolerable, for it reduces the other to a mere thing. One can, on the other hand, look at an individual as long as one wishes provided one talks to him at the same time. Speech personalizes. The movement from the old oral-aural world to the new visual world of alphabetic writing and typography can be understood largely in terms of this polarity between speech and vision. The old oral-aural culture was highly personal, nonanalytic, dramatic, oratorical, and full of hostilities, some natural and some cultivated—cultivated, for example, in the practice of dialectic and rhetoric, to which the academic system clung for almost all its teaching, despite writing and print, until the advent of the romantic age. The newer chirographic culture, matured by typography, and at long last relatively victorious, depersonalized the world.

For the ancients, the universe exhibited a sense of unity or "tunedness" working out from the world of sound to all actuality. Motion was not communicated in the Aristotelian universe mechanically through the different spheres. These spheres (of the moon, Mars, Mercury, Venus, etc.) were taken to be alive and were united as a community of persons, not as a machine or "system." The "harmony of the spheres" was like that of human voices, though it was beyond the human ear's hearing (today we might think of it as like the sound of a dog whistle, which dogs can hear but the human ear misses). But by the eighteenth century the new post-Newtonian world was being thought of in quite a different way, that is, as the silent universe. This new concept was no more accurate than the old, since extraterrestrial bodies can give off deafening sound waves (though these may dissipate in relatively empty space). But true or not, the imaginarily devocalized physical world had in a profound sense moved out of relationship with man's own personal, social, vocal world. Henceforth, man will be a kind of stranger, a spectator and manipulator in the universe rather than a participator. In the eighteenth century God himself had become silent. Many persons, following the devocalization recipe used for man and the physical universe, no longer considered God as a communicator, as someone who tells man something, but as the Great Architect, a kind of supernatural beaver. They tended to think of creation as something like piling bricks on each other. They forgot that in Genesis, one of the accounts reads "and God said, 'Let there be light,' and there was light," because he said it. God's word, conceived of as analogous to man's spoken word, signaled the application of power.

The past century has seen the word enter into a new stage beyond orality and script and print, a stage characterized by the use of electronics for verbal communication. There has been a sequence within this state, too: telegraph (electronic processing of the alphabetized word), telephone (electronic processing of the oral word), radio (first for telegraphy, then for voice; an extension first of telegraph and then of telephone), sound pictures (electronic sound added to electrically projected vision), television (electronic vision added to electronic sound), and computers (word silenced once more, and thought processes pretty completely reorganized by extreme quantification).

How can the status of the word in such a world be described? The changes in today's sensorium as a whole have been too complex for our present powers of description, but regarding the fortunes of the word as such one fact is especially noteworthy: The new age into which we have entered has stepped up the oral and aural. Voice, muted by script and print, has come newly alive. For communication at a distance, written letters are supplemented and largely supplanted by telephone, radio, and television. Rapid transportation makes personal confrontation, interviewing, and large-scale meetings or "conventions" possible to a degree unthinkable to early man. Sound has become curiously functional with the development of sonar, which is used even to catch fish for commercial purposes. Sound has become marketable, if indirectly so, through the use of (nonelectronic) disk recordings and, even more, through the use of electronic tapes. Recordings and tapes have given sound a new quality, recuperability.

Relying on the theorem that tribal life was basically oral-aural and thus rooted in constant interchange of communally possessed knowledge, and that writing and print isolate the individual or, if you prefer, liberate him from the tribe, Marshall McLuhan (1962) has described our present situation as that of a global village. And that it is. But a global village is not a tribal village.

There is a vast difference between tribal existence and our own, for tribal man either did not yet know or at least had not yet fully assimilated writing and print. Present electronic culture, even with its new activation of sound, relies necessarily on both. For the media in their succession do not cancel out one another but build on one another. When man began to write, he did not cease talking. Very likely, he talked more than ever; the most literate persons are often enough extraordinarily fluent oral verbalizers as well, although they speak somewhat differently from the way purely oral man does or did. When print was developed, man did not stop writing. Quite the contrary: only with print did it become imperative that everybody learn to write—universal literacy, knowledge of reading and writing, has not been an urgent concern of manuscript cultures but only of print cultures. Now that we have electronic communication, we shall not cease to write and print. Technological society in the electronic stage cannot exist without vast quantities of writing and print. Despite its activation of sound, it prints more than ever before.

One of the troubles with electronic computers themselves is that often the printout is so vast that it is useless: There are not enough attendants to read more than a fraction of it.

Nevertheless, it is true that what is said and written and printed may be determined more and more by the shape that electronics and sound give to social organization and to human life generally. What we are faced with today is a sensorium not merely extended by the various media but also so reflected and refracted inside and outside itself in so many directions as to be thus far utterly bewildering. Our situation is one of more and more complicated interactions. The radio telescope is an example. It has largely supplanted the earlier more direct-sight instruments. Yet it does not exactly return us to a world of sound. Rather, it provides data for a basically visual field of awareness, but does so by elaborate indirection. One looks at charts instead of at a galaxy. The code transmission of a picture of Mars is another example: The picture is constructed on Earth from electronic impulses transmitted from outer space and recorded as a series of numbers. Vision here is more and more disqualified as providing direct access to information. The electronic processes typical of today's communications world are themselves of their very nature infravisible—not even truly imaginable in terms of sight. To think one knows what an electron looks like is to deceive oneself. It is not something like the things we see, only smaller; rather, it is the sort of thing that cannot be registered directly at all in visual terms, or, indeed, directly in any sensory terms, although it is part of the substructure of the sensory world.

When we say that the present age validates voice again in a new way, as it certainly does, we must also add that the visual or the visual-tactile, which were so intensified with the emergence of alphabetic script and print, are being further intensified as never before. Quantification, reduction to parts outside parts in space, is the key to the computer's operations. And, although the computer is far from being the dominant factor in human life which the popular mythologies make it out to be, it is certainly a characteristic and critical factor. Computers are manipulators; they juggle items in space, quantified items only. What cannot be reduced to a spatial arrangement directly or indirectly cannot be digested in computer "language."

Furthermore, while the present age has in a new way validated the use of sound and thereby in a new way validated time, since sound is time-bound, existing only when it is passing out of existence in time, the present age has also established man in a radically new relationship to time. Developing further his theorem of the global village, McLuhan has pointed out in *The Gutenberg Galaxy* (1962) that a sense of simultaneity is a mark of both early oral culture and of electronic culture, while a sense of sequentiality (one-thing-after-another) with a related stress on causality is the mark of chirographic and typographic culture. Certainly, living in an oral-aural universe, the village consciousness has to live in simultaneity in the sense that it lives in the present to a degree unknown to man who can relate to the past circumstantially through writing and concomitantly to the future through highly controlled and sophisticated planning. Primitive life is simultaneous in that it has no records, so that its conscious contact with its past is governed by what people talk about. As Havelock (1963) has pointed out, if Homer and his associates had stopped singing, the knowledge their works impart would have largely disappeared in Homer's Greece.

But today's simultaneity is not due to absence of records, to the need to keep talking about our conscious possessions acquired in the past in order not to lose them. Rather, it is a simultaneity based on the most massive accumulation of records ever known. Today, with our knowledge of history and need for planning, the past and the future are forced into the present with an overpowering explicitness unknown to early man. Compared with that of earlier man, our sense of simultaneity is supercharged, and our reflectiveness supercharges it even more. Moreover, unlike earlier man, we achieve our sense of simultaneity in a sequential fashion. The computer is actually the most quantified and most highly sequential or linear of all instruments: It creates a sense of simultaneity only because its inhuman speedup of sequences makes it appear to annihilate them.

For all this to have happened, something must have happened to the word. To bring us where we are, the word must have been transplanted from its natural habitat, sound, to a new habitat, space. Writing and print and, later, electronic devices must have reshaped man's contact with actuality through the word. Only through the patterned sequences of shifts in the media and corresponding changes in the sensorium can man come into possession of his past. The word in its purest form, in its most human and nearest to divine form, in its holiest form, the word which passes orally between man and man to establish and deepen human relations, the word, in a world of sound, has its limitations. It can overcome some of these— impermanence, inaccuracy—only by taking on others—objectivity, concern with things as things, quantification, impersonality.

The introduction of electronic communication has certainly realigned the worlds of sound and sight and has brought the former into a new prominence. This new ascendancy of sound also favors a reinstatement of a sense of simultaneity. But there is no "return" here to an earlier world of sound, as we have seen. Time is one directional. There is no road back. The simultaneity of our present culture is qualitatively different from that of our oral-aural beginnings. Of the many questions raised by our heightened awareness of the new electronic orality of our society one of the most anxiety provoking is whether this orality will render irrelevant the highly differentiated literacy of the typographic age and whether or not it will destroy the old media. A particularly urgent form of the question is, will television wipe out books? Two different and indeed polarized answers are often given to this question. One answer is that electronics is wiping out books and print generally, whether you like it or not. The other is that books are books, and they are here to stay—or, with a slight variation, books are books and we'd better help them to stay, for we can no longer live without them.

Any more considered answer which takes cognizance of the facts of history and of technological activity will have to be more complex than either of these. Much of the writing about present-day orality assumes that, since primitive man was highly oral and we are likewise more oral than our immediate ancestors, we are back in the state of preliterate man once more. Certain points of resemblance between orality-related present-day phenomena and orality-related primitive phenomena are startling enough. Sound has certain built-in coefficients. It tends to socialize. Modern man has a strong group sense and a desire for participatory activities which suggests the traditionism of primary oral cultures. But when we compare our secondary oral culture (the oral culture historically emerging from and dependent upon writing and print, which make electronic orality feasible) with primary (prechirographic) oral cultures, at every point where we detect a startling likeness, we find equally assertive differences. Primary oral cultures have a strong group sense because they cannot help it: Individualism is a serious threat. Often enough, in our secondary oral culture we have a strong group sense because individually we feel an obligation to develop it, as our sociological and psychological as well as journalistic writings make clear.

Sound also relates to happenings, for it is itself an event, something ongoing. For primary oral cultures, the cosmos itself, as we have seen, tends to be thought of in more oral terms, not as merely a thing, "out there," in a visually conceived field, but as a kind of happening or event, something evoking response rather than inviting maximum control. We are receptive to happenings today, too, but again in an inner-directed, reflective way. With all the interiorized compulsiveness we can muster we plan unplanned events carefully so that we can be sure that they are spontaneous. And we videotape them so that we can have the spontaneity permanently on record. Our orality here shows itself clearly to be a secondary orality, founded upon, at the same time it departs from, the individualized introversion and sense of fixity fostered by writing and print.

Nor does our secondarily oral culture make use of formulary devices in the way that primary oral culture did. Preliterate societies needed standardized verbal expressions—proverbs, adages, apothegms, proverbial phrases, and the like—as knowledge storage and retrieval devices. In the absence of writing, primary oral culture could not "look up" anything, could not use its eyes to find utterances or even words as such. If words were to be retrieved, they had to be re*called*.

The poetry of primary oral cultures is made up almost entirely of formulary devices, but formulary devices are not the specialty of poets. Poets use, with unusual and exquisite skill if they are good poets, what at least those individuals in the sensitive places of the society all must use if the society is to survive. To get a complicated message from one village to another in pre-alphabetic Homeric Greece, the sender would have to think it out in highly mnemonic formulary fashion, or the messenger could not remember it for delivery nor the receiver retain it once it was told him. Moreover, in a culture without writing, the sender of course could not first think out his message in non-mnemonic patterns of words and *then* put it in mnemonic form. If it were worked out in non-mnemonic patterns, he could not recall it in order to give it a new mnemonic shape. Thought itself has to be mnemonically generated in oral cultures—which means that no thinking can take place without close dependence on formulas.

In the present age of sound, the formulary device no longer has this functional relationship to life. Very little of our knowledge is stored in formulas or retrieved by such means. It is largely structured for visual retrieval, not for being "*recalled*" but for being "looked" up. We go so far as to write elaborate memoranda to ourselves, as even medieval man, despite his high literacy, had apparently not learned to do. Our most sophisticated knowledge storing and retrieving tool, the computer, is essentially a visual device, with a printout.

Today's formulary sayings are cliché themes exploited to induce feelings or orientation to the past, to bring audiences into exaggerated confrontation with the cliché as an object of humor, or to produce slogans for action with short-term goals. Where formulary devices of a primary oral culture are conservative devices, ordered to the treasuring of hard-earned lore, today's advertising clichés are action-oriented; not reminiscent but programmatic, ordered to the future and thus even to something new. Our secondary oral culture is an irremediably literate oral culture. The more oral it gets, the more literate it becomes, at the same time that its orality invests its literacy with an orality all its own.

The new media of communication we use today are certainly not destroying books. There are more books on sale and being read today than ever before. Our survey of what has gone on in the past development of verbal communication and what is going on now has shown that a new medium of verbal communication not only does not wipe out the old, but actually reinforces the older medium or media. However, in doing so it transforms the old, so that the old is no longer what it used to be. Applied to books, this means that in the foreseeable future there will be more books than ever before but that books will no longer be what books used to be. If you think of books even today as working the way books did for Aristotle or St. Thomas Aquinas or Chaucer or Milton, you are out of touch with the way things are.

A revealing example of this transformation can be found already in books which are not written by anybody. They are talked books. Of course, we have had talked books before. Oral epics which in the past somehow got themselves transcribed are books not "written" by anybody—they are transcriptions of something someone said or sang. But our talked books work differently from these. They are superimpositions of electronic orality, writing, and print on or through one another. The new kind of book, once it is printed, may look like older books, may not have a recording or tape in a cover pocket, but it does not sound or work the same way.

I was recently interviewed for such a talked book. The supervisor of the book, as we might style him, or the production manager—he is not the author nor am I; there is no author in any earlier sense of this word—called me first in St. Louis by telephone from New York to arrange an interview with me in Bethlehem, Pennsylvania, where I was going to lecture at Lehigh University (rapid transportation is a communications device, implementing personal relations). He brought a tape recorder to the interview and taped my answers to questions which he put to me. Then he slept on the tape in a Bethlehem motel and came back the next morning with supplementary questions for a fill-in interview, which he also taped. He took all the tapes back to Brooklyn and had them transcribed. Of course the stenographer edited the tape a bit in transcribing it. The supervisor or production manager edited the transcription some more, after which he sent it to me for further editing. When I had reworked it and sent it back to him, he called me in St. Louis by long distance telephone from New York and once again, this time over the telephone, taped my answers to additional questions which had occurred to him after the two or three revisions. Then he had these additional questions transcribed, edited them, fed them back into the revised manuscript, and sent the whole to me for further revisions. When the book comes out, what do we have? The "book" is presented as an interview, with his questions and my responses. But in fact the total is something that neither of us said and that neither of us ever wrote. We have no term or readily available concept for this sort of thing. Perhaps we could call the end-result a "presentation" or "production." More and more books are "productions" of this sort. So are more and more magazine and newspaper "articles."

History books provide another good example. History in our sense of the word has been made possible by writing. But now historians of all periods after about A.D. 1900 will have to reckon with oral history. Interviewing to secure historical information (or something as near interviewing as possible) from those who can recall events in their own past has become a major academic enterprise since around 1948, when Allan Nevins began serious work with it at Columbia University. Oral history is of course no more accurate than written history. Neither is it like written history. It has a whole new set of problems with new kinds of inaccuracies as well as accuracies. It has been suggested that what the oral memoir gives the scholar is mostly not incontestable "facts" but simply an "incredible sense of immediacy." History written with an "incredible sense of immediacy" is certainly going to be a special kind of thing—perhaps it will be even incredibly true. One thing is certain, however, namely, that oral history is also going to interact vigorously with writing (typewriting) and print. The Oral History Association is not sure what this interaction ought to be or how to control it, as they clearly show in their notes on their Fourth National Colloquium held November 7–10, 1969, at Warrenton, Virginia. [2]

The interaction, then, is intense between the media. Not only is there talking, writing, and printing going on, but each of these is being carried on with a conscious reference to the other. When the "production manager" was asking questions of me as reported above and I was responding, both of us knew that what we said was going to be taped, edited, worked over in writing, and finally printed.

[2]See William B. Pickett, "The Fourth National Colloquium on Oral History," *Historical Methods Newsletter* (University of Pittsburgh), **3**, 1970, 24-27.

Electronic orality was aimed at the typewriter, blue pencil, and linotype. What we had in mind as we talked was not simply good talk but good printed matter. However, paradoxically, we wanted the final printing to sound as though the production were not printing at all but informal talk. We were talking to make edited printed matter sound as though it were not edited or printed, knowing that the only way to do this was to edit and print it.

To make the situation even more involuted, we commented on this state of affairs in the interview itself. The production manager remarked to me while we were being taped that we did not seem to be just talking informally to one another. "Why should we seem to be?" I returned. "We aren't." How was I supposed to believe that I was communicating with only one man when both he and I knew—or hoped—that I was communicating with tens of thousands? Moreover, I was communicating with tens of thousands by pretending I was communicating with only one. This was the effective way to do it. It all sounded like Catch 23. In fact, it was Catch 24, for this exchange was not left as it actually occurred but was retouched to appear in the final printed book.

One might argue that these paradoxes are no greater than those involved in all writing, for in writing you communicate with an audience who ordinarily *must* be absent while you are communicating with them (and thereby pretending that they are present). For writers, the audience is always a fiction and must be. Nevertheless, the new admixture of orality, writing, and print made possible by electronics has complicated all paradoxes here. No literary form or thought processes of the crisscross sort we had been using could have been possible before it was possible to record the spoken voice directly for sound reproduction.

The electronic media are here working not at all to destroy books but to produce more books faster. But by the same token they are producing different books, books which are not "books" in the old sense of the word. This sort of nonauthored, nonwritten book has a quite different ring from other books because, as we have just seen, the voices of those in the books are refracted through all kinds of new conventions.

Moreover, the existence of this new kind of book is sure to affect the book that, in accordance with earlier practice, is composed by one author with pen in hand or with typewriter before him. For once the old-style author has read this other kind of orally tooled production, the ring of it will be in his ear. And he will be sure on occasion to match, consciously or unconsciously, some of its special effects, especially if he is a television viewer.

Here we see the full complexity of the interaction of the media as successive media evolve. We have already seen that a new medium reinforces the earlier media by radically transforming them or, if you wish, radically transforms them by reinforcing them. Now we can see that part of the transformation is effected because the new medium feeds back into the old medium or media and makes them sound like the new. The conventionally produced book can now sound to some degree like the orally programmed book.

Patterns of reinforcement and transformation have existed from the very beginning in the verbal media as we have already seen. When writing began, it certainly did not wipe out talk. Writing is the product of urbanization. It was produced by those in compact settlements who certainly talked more than scattered folk in the countryside did. Once they had writing they were encouraged to talk more, if only because they had more to talk about.

But writing not only encouraged talk, it also remade talk. Once writing had established itself talk was no longer what it used to be. Once you had writing, you could compose a scientific treatise—something, for example, such as Aristotle's *Art of Rhetoric*, a scientific tract on the art of persuasion. Before writing, many persons were skilled in persuasion but there was no scientific treatment of the subject. How could you have had anything like Aristotle's *Art of Rhetoric* in a completely oral culture? Or, to focus the question on a subject matter other than discourse, how could you have had any systematic treatise such as, let us say, a treatise on hunting in a completely oral culture? No one could possibly put his mind through the series of thoughts that such books can marshal.

The only way these thoughts could have been generated in an oral culture would be by having someone with no knowledge of writing, or even of the possibility of such a thing as writing, recite the entire *Art of Rhetoric* or a treatise on hunting chapter after chapter from beginning to end, composing it as he went along. Such a feat is impossible. The closest an oral culture can come to a systematic treatise is through stringing together series of aphorisms: "The early bird gets the worm." "All that glitters is not gold." "He who hesitates is lost."

This means that although oratory was tens of thousands of years old, the kind of thinking *about* oratory you have in Aristotle's *Art of Rhetoric* had never been done before writing. The human mind had never gone through this series of maneuvers, never traced this kind of trajectory of thought. But once you had produced, with the help of writing, treatises such as Aristotle's *Art of Rhetoric* or Plato's *Republic*, this kind of thinking and expression would ring in your ears. Now when you spoke you could echo, to some limited degree, the way it sounded when you read aloud something that could be composed, as a whole, only in writing. Moreover, you now were obliged to sound a little bit like writing quite regularly or perhaps even always, or you would not sound educated. You were expected—as we are expected today—to let your speech be colored by the way writing was or could be done. Talk, after writing, had to sound literate—and "literate," we must remind ourselves, means "lettered," or post-oral.

After writing, in other words, oral speech was never the same. In one way it was better off. For in speaking, the mind could now go through motions of the kind men had learned from using writing. Moreover, you could—and did—use writing to make notes to help your speech. But in another way oral speech was worse off. It was now regularly competing with writing. It was no longer itself—no longer self-contained. Men were aware that there were many things that writing could do verbally which oral performance could not do at all. Oral performance no longer monopolized the verbal field.

A comparable situation arose with the invention of letterpress printing from movable alphabetic type. Print reinforced writing. It made universal literacy imperative—that is, print made it necessary for virtually everyone to be able to write, to work in the older medium. But print also transformed writing. With print, writers wrote about other things, and in different ways. Print, as we have shown, made possible tight positional control such as could not be achieved with writing. With print, for the first time, a teacher could stand before a class and say, "Everybody turn to page 84, fifth line from the top, third word from the left," and everyone could find the word. In a manuscript culture the students might all have had manuscripts, but you would have had to pronounce the word and wait for them to locate it because it would be in a different position on a different page in virtually every manuscript. The transformation of writing by print was further accentuated by the widespread use of the index as an effective retrieval device. A book began to be viewed as a container in which "things" are neatly ordered rather than as a voice which speaks to the reader, and "facts" tended to be regarded as physical objects available without any reference to verbalization—as "facts" in fact never are.

Subtly but irresistibly, with print what one wrote tended more and more to be thought of as lodging eventually in a fixed place. This fact appears to have affected what we call plot "structure." All the forces at work are not clear here, but it appears certain that until print there were no prose stories that were organized as tightly in plot as drama had been from the time of the ancient Greeks. Drama had long freed itself from being a story "told." First of all, drama was not narration but action. And secondly, it had been controlled by writing from ancient Greek times—the first verbal genre to be so controlled. As a consequence, it often, if not always, had what lengthy narrative prose or poetry virtually never had till the effects of print had matured: a tight linear structure, building up to a climax resolved in a denouement. Prose narration, until around the romantic age, even in so highly organized and late a production as *Tom Jones*, always remained largely episodic—by contrast, for example, with the short story as developed by Edgar Allan Poe or with a Thomas Hardy novel. This means that prose stories were still thought of as "told" even in a manuscript culture, rather than as being strictly composed in writing. The frequently recurring "dear reader" shows that even the nineteenth century was hyperconscious regarding adjustment away from an audience hearing a story to readers assimilating it through the mediation of sight. Somewhere deep in the subconscious the fixity suggested by print was at odds with the more loosely discursive, fluid narrator-audience situation in which "tales" had normally been "told." "Dear reader" eases the tension or was thought to do so.

The fixity of print underlies Joyce's composition of *Finnegans Wake*. It is virtually impossible to produce two fully accurate handwritten copies of *Finnegans Wake*. In a work with thousands of portmanteau words and other idiosyncratic creations, every single letter calls for individual supervision such as could hardly be achieved in multiple manuscript copies. This means, of course, that the final composition of the work—as of most works in print today—is done on the printer's proofs.

Once you know the kind of control over discourse that print makes possible, the feeling for such control influences your writing even in such things as your personal correspondence. You can tell that Alexander Pope's letters were written by a man who knew the printed book and that Cicero's were not. Cicero's sound far more oratorical for one thing: The reader is felt in a more oral-aural way. You can tell that my talk and yours are profoundly influenced not just by writing but also by print. The Venerable Bede or Geoffrey Chaucer could not possibly have given a talk that would sound like this one would. Neither, for that matter, could St. Thomas More or John Milton or Senator Dirksen—print had not had its full effect on these people yet.

And so in the present and future, as we live with the electronic media, we are finding and will find that these have not wiped out anything but simply complicated everything endlessly. We still talk face to face, as we still write and print. The electronic media have reinforced print. As we have earlier noted, the computer produces printouts. And if you associate print with localization and space, with "linearity" or "sequentiality," there is no more linear or sequential instrument in the world than the computer, digital or analogue. It seems to be near-instantaneous only because it moves through sequences with lightning speed and thereby moves through more sequences than were ever before possible. Moreover, just as when you moved beyond writing to print, it became urgent that nearly everyone learn to write, so now that we have moved beyond print to electronics, it becomes urgent that nearly everyone know how to print, that is, to use the typewriter, which is a form of printing (making letters out of preexisting types). Again, electronics are even giving new forms to what used to be, we thought, "ordinary" typography. Photosetting is replacing linotyping.

A new medium, finally, transforms not only the one that immediately precedes it but often all of those that preceded it all the way back to the beginning. Thus, we still orate as did the orators before writing and print but our oratory is completely transformed not only by writing and print but also by our new electronic orality. On television we use public address to reach millions of people, but to reach each one as though we were having a face-to-face conversation with him. Our public speaking is private speaking now. Senator Dirksen was one of the last of a dying race.

With regard to the media as to so much else, we live in an age when everything is going on at once. This means that all the old media are still around us. They are working harder than ever. But they are also producing kinds of things they never produced before. We need to reinterpret the old as well as the new. No one will ever understand what print is today if he thinks of it only in terms of Gutenberg or Addison and Steele or Matthew Arnold. And no one will ever understand what present-day orality is unless he has some first-hand knowledge of the abiding effects of print and, far beyond that, some first-hand knowledge of what a primary oral culture, so like and so different from our own, once was or perhaps in a few places in the world still is.

REFERENCES

Čapec, M. *The philosophical impact of contemporary physics*. New York: Van Nostrand, 1961.

Carothers, J. C. Culture, psychiatry and the written word. *Psychiatry*, 1959, **22**, 307-320.

Havelock, E. A. *Preface to Plato*. Cambridge, Mass.: Belknap Press, 1963.

Lord, A. B. *The singer of tales*. (Harvard Studies in Comparative Literature, 24). Cambridge, Mass.: Harvard University Press, 1960.

McLuhan, M. *The Gutenberg galaxy: The making of typographic man*. Toronto: University of Toronto Press, 1962.

Ong, W. J. *Ramus, method, and the decay of dialogue*. Cambridge, Mass.: Harvard University Press, 1958.

Ong, W. J. *In the human grain*. New York: Macmillan, 1967. (a)

Ong, W. J. *The presence of the word: Some prolegomena for cultural and religious history*. New Haven: Yale University Press, 1967. (b)

Ong, W. J. *Rhetoric, romance, and technology*. Ithaca: Cornell University Press, 1971.

Opler, M. K. *Culture, psychiatry and human values*. Springfield, Ill.: Charles C. Thomas, 1956.

Spitzer, L. *Classical and Christian ideas of world harmony: Prolegomena to an interpretation of the word "stimmung."* (Ed. by Hatcher, A. G.) Baltimore: Johns Hopkins Press, 1963.

10
COGNITIVE AND BEHAVIORAL APPROACHES TO PERSUASION

Elliott McGinnies
The American University

The dictionary is not a bad place to begin some inquiries. If we look up the word "persuade," we find it defined in two ways. In one sense, it means to prevail on a person to do something; in another, it means to convince or induce to believe. These two definitions, the first behavioral and the second cognitive, represent in essence the two major theoretical positions that psychologists have taken on this matter. In general, when we attempt to persuade someone, we see ourselves as endeavoring to alter his beliefs or attitudes; and we usually expect our efforts to be rewarded by some change in his behavior. If the recipient of our arguments merely gives lip service to our point of view, without any concomitant change in action, we are apt to feel that we have failed in our essential purpose.

COMMUNICATION AND PERSUASION

Persuasion, then, involves changes in behavior that are achieved through communication. Since communication is functionally present in nearly every type of interpersonal exchange, persuasion becomes a rather ubiquitous aspect of social behavior. Speaking and writing are obvious forms of communication; but so is punching someone in the nose. Communication is achieved to the extent that a *source* exerts some control over the behavior of a *recipient* and is influenced by the recipient's response. Each communicant thus achieves some measure of control over the other.

What do we mean by control? B. F. Skinner has frequently been misinterpreted with regard to the notion of control. What he refers to in his writings (most recently in *Beyond Freedom and Dignity,* 1971) is not an authoritarian or devious manipulation of one person's behavior by another, but rather the simple fact that everyone's behavior is controlled by social or environmental stimuli in one way or another. The essential question is whether or not we shall learn to analyze human interactions so as to make more obvious the ways in which we control one another and thus achieve greater freedom to respond differentially and selectively. Freedom is relative, and the man who is most free is the one who can identify the social and environmental pressures that shape his behavior. If he discovers that a certain nexus of social forces is compelling him to respond in ways that are to his ultimate disadvantage, then by altering these conditions he achieves relatively greater freedom. He is not completely free, however, in the sense that his behavior is never determined by factors beyond his control. But he is free to the extent that he understands the functional relationships between the stimuli that impinge upon him and his reactions to these stimuli.

Thus, a person may discover that his behavior has been altered as the result of a communication to which he has been exposed. The sheer fact that he can identify this relationship means that he is less susceptible to the sort of control that might work to his disadvantage. To illustrate this point consider the fact that few individuals could, if pressed, identify the process through which they have acquired many of their basic social attitudes, say toward sex and religion. Quite obviously, one is not born with a sense of piety or an aversion to polygamy. Such attitudes are transmitted to the individual by other persons with whom he interacts. Others acquire quite different sets of values and attitudes as a result of the unique social interactions they have experienced. Social communication thus provides the very foundation of most of our behaviors. Our characteristic ways of eating, dressing, gesturing, and speaking are all products of human communication. Yet we seldom analyze the process by which such learning occurs.

Consider for a moment an example of "control" in the sense in which the behaviorist uses this term. Imagine a conversation between Tom and Harry—the topic is unimportant for the moment. When Tom is speaking, he controls Harry's behavior to the extent that Harry is listening to him. When Harry ceases to listen (or pay attention), this fact is betrayed by certain changes in his behavior; his eyes focus elsewhere than upon Tom's face, his bodily posture changes, and his replies become irrelevant. When these behavioral changes occur, we conclude that Tom is no longer communicating to Harry. Communication, in short, is a two-way process; it requires that one person be able to prompt some sort of behavior from another person. An individual may be speaking or gesturing, yet not communicating. Such would be the case with a boring lecturer who has lost the attention of his class. The speaker in this instance is exclusively his own audience, and his verbal performance is maintained not by the reactions that it evokes from the audience but by virtue of a well-rehearsed verbal repertoire that runs its course through a period of 50 or 60 minutes.

Not all communication, of course, is verbal. A smile, the raising of an eyebrow, or the lifting of a hand may all serve as effective devices by which one person communicates to another. If the gesture prompts response, communication has taken place; if not, there has been no communication. The entire area of gestures and "body language," so insightfully described by Birdwhistell in Chapter 11, is a matter of current interest to social scientists, since it represents an area of communication that has until recently been largely neglected by researchers.

Communication also takes place when the source and the recipient are not in direct contact. This is achieved by the so-called *mass media* of print, radio, television, and motion pictures. The principal difference between communication *via* the mass media and communication *via* face-to-face interaction is that the source cannot immediately be influenced by feedback from the recipient. The flow of information is temporarily one-way. Ultimately, of course, the recipient must react in a manner that reinforces the source, otherwise the source would go "out-of-business." Readers must buy newspapers, viewers must tune in certain TV programs, and listeners must patronize radio advertisers if the activities of these various communicators are to be maintained. In these and other ways the subscribers to the mass media make known their preferences and aversions. The television viewer who changes from one channel to another is behaving analogously to Harry when he stops listening to Tom and reveals his inattention by averting his gaze or impatiently shuffling his feet.

The word *communication* can be used, then, not necessarily to imply an exchange of ideas, but to designate a particular pattern of behavioral interactions. Following B. F. Skinner (1957), we are inclined to stress the functional relations that govern the behaviors in question rather than to assume that the term "communicate" must lead us to an investigation of "thoughts" or "meanings." Furthermore, we are concerned here not with the formal properties of communication, but with those communicative behaviors that may be considered as persuasive. What distinguishes persuasion from other forms of communication is the emphasis placed on changes in the recipient's behavior *as these reflect and, in turn, modify the behavior of the communicator*. For example, a professor delivering a lecture is frequently not seeking to persuade his students of anything (although he may occasionally do so). If he is simply transmitting information, it may be of little concern to him whether his audience is awake or asleep. The speaker's behavior in this particular instance is less under the control of the audience than of his own verbal repertoire. A political speaker, on the other hand, is finely tuned to the reactions of his audience. His verbal performances are designed to prompt certain kinds of behaviors on the part of the audience. Hence, his own behavior accommodates to the responses of his listeners (or readers); he is reinforced or punished by the reactions of his audience. The effective advocate is as much controlled by his audience as the audience members are controlled by the force of his argument.

Methodological Problems in Studying Persuasion

For the most part, psychologists have been satisfied to test theories of persuasion by garnering evidence of changes in verbal behavior rather than by seeking modifications in their subjects' nonverbal performances. The usual instruments by which such verbal manifestations of persuasion have been measured are the attitude scale and the opinion questionnaire. Whether a change in the subject's behavior on these instruments is ever translated into action is seldom investigated, or confirmed. People's attitudes expressed verbally rather than through action have constituted the arena in which most of the controversy over persuasion has centered. As a general rule, it can be said that experimental attempts at persuasion are remarkably successful under laboratory conditions and strikingly unsuccessful in the natural environment. There are several possible reasons for this. For one thing, attitudes in the social psychological laboratory are generally measured immediately after some persuasive manipulation; the long-term effects of the manipulation are seldom determined. In addition, the measured changes are often statistically significant, but relatively small in any practical sense. For example, a mean change of 3 or 4 units along a scale of 24 units might well prove to be greater than chance, but the average individual in this group would not have emerged from the experiment with attitudes markedly different from those that characterized him initially. Perhaps an even more important consideration involves what has variously been called the "experimenter effect," "demand characteristics," and a_ "social desirability" effect. These several terms, although referring to somewhat different phenomena, have in common an allusion to changes in attitude that occur as a result of certain artificialities inherent in the experimental situation. Changes in attitude that occur because the experimenter has unintentionally communicated his expectations to the subjects, because the subject is behaving in a manner designed to please the experimenter, or because the subject is doing what he believes is socially desirable are essentially *artifacts* of the experimental situation. By artifactual change we mean an apparent modification in attitude (or behavior) that is restricted to the immediate research setting in which it has been induced. A "real" change in attitude, on the other hand, would generalize to situations other than the one in which it had been generated.

This is not to imply, of course, that all attitude-change experiments have produced artifactual results. Many studies have been done under carefully controlled conditions that have tended either to eliminate or greatly reduce the impact of such confounding factors as these. In such instances, it is generally assumed that the rather small absolute changes in attitude that have been observed are suggestive of much larger changes that could presumably be generated under the more powerful contingencies that operate in the natural environment. A small but statistically significant change in attitude attributable to the relatively greater credibility of one communicator over another should show up more dramatically under naturalistic circumstances where more powerful persuasive forces are operative. For example, a candidate for political office will, if elected, have at his disposal substantial resources for rewarding his constituents. The psychologist working in a laboratory, however, has a relatively meager store of reinforcers to offer his subjects; he may pay them a small fee or credit them with fulfilling a course requirement. Any attitude change produced by the manipulations of the psychologist, therefore, would probably be greater under more naturalistic conditions where the agencies of persuasion control more effective contingencies of reinforcement, such as money, jobs, power, or peer-group approval. The results of laboratory investigations provide us with predictors of the type and extent of attitude change that might be expected under conditions where natural rather than artificial contingencies are present.

COGNITIVE APPROACHES

Why should attitudes change at all under persuasion? This question leads us to the heart of the theoretical issues surrounding the entire area of attitude change research. Like the definitions of "persuade" that we mentioned at the beginning of this chapter, attitude change theories can be divided broadly into those that stress cognitions and those that stress behavior. As we shall see, however, these two conceptual orientations are not as far apart as they might seem at first blush. They have in common the assumption that individuals who exhibit a change in attitude do so either because of positive or negative incentives. Suppose we look briefly at some of the theoretical assumptions underlying the cognitive position.

Dissonance and balance theories. One theory, first propounded by Festinger (1957), states that a condition of "cognitive dissonance" is aroused whenever an individual is forced to entertain two or more incompatible ideas, or cognitions. This state of cognitive dissonance has some of the motivating characteristics of any arousal state, such as hunger, thirst, or fear, and there is activity on the part of the individual to relieve, or reduce it. In the examples used here, we stress conflicts between an attitude toward an issue and a "feeling" toward a person or group, rather than contradictory attitudes towards issues. While the latter class of dissonance is handled in the same way by the theory, it raises the difficult question (for cognitive theorists) of whether we are trained from childhood with rewards and punishments to "be consistent." For example, if Individual A denies Cognition X, and thereby finds himself in disagreement with Individual B (whom Individual A greatly respects, but who affirms Cognition X), then Individual A would presumably experience cognitive dissonance. (Imagine a person who opposed our military involvement in Vietnam, but whose brother served there and feels the effort was worthwhile.) This uncomfortable condition would be relieved if Individual A could view Individual B as lacking credibility on this particular issue, or if Individual A could somehow modify his own attitudes and beliefs so as to be more in agreement with Individual B. Fig. 1 shows this situation, with "likes" and "dislikes" expressed as + or −.

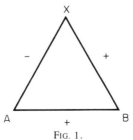

FIG. 1.

Sometimes referred to as the A, B, X system, this particular theory of cognitive balance and imbalance has been expressed by such psychologists as Heider (1946) and Newcomb (1953). A balanced system is one where the product of the signs is positive, and an unbalanced system is one where the product is negative. An unbalanced system is in a state of stress and tends to readjust itself in such a way as to restore balance. The situation that we diagrammed in Fig. 1, for example, would come back into balance if Individual A were to adopt a more positive attitude toward X (the Vietnam war), and thus, achieve agreement with Individual B on this issue. All signs would then be "plus." Alternatively, the system would be restored to balance if Individual B should come to agree with Individual A by developing a negative attitude toward X. Still a third possibility is for a state of "dislike" to develop between Individuals A and B; the two negative signs and single positive sign would yield a positive product, signifying balance.

Field theory. The language of balance theory has the merit of identifying the major components in a social situation involving conflict of attitudes. By borrowing some terminology from Lewin (1951), we can describe attitudinal conflict in terms of field theory. Lewin employed an elliptically shaped space, or "egg," within which the various elements that influence the individual could be represented. Forces impelling the individual either to approach or to withdraw from objects and persons in his psychological environment, or life-space, are shown as vectors, or arrows. Consider the following situation, pictured in Lewinian terms.

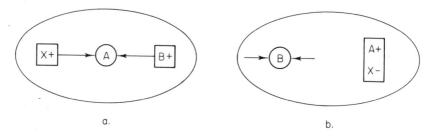

a.   b.

Fig. 2.

Individual A is shown here in conflict, represented by vectors that push him simultaneously toward X and B. (For example, he likes his wife (B) but he also likes to smoke cigars (X), which his wife abhors.) The situation is pictured for Individual B (the wife) in the second diagram of Fig. 2. She is also in conflict, being attracted to A (her husband) but repelled by X (the cigars he smokes). Individual A cannot simultaneously approach both B and X; that is, he cannot smoke a cigar while in the presence of his wife. The conflict will be resolved when one of the field forces acting on him becomes stronger than the others. He will then either maintain his attraction to X (continue to smoke cigars) and move away from Individual B (disregard his wife's objections), or he will move toward Individual B and abandon X (forego smoking in his wife's presence). Of course, if Individual B should move close to Issue X (the wife accepts her husband's cigar smoking) the conflict for A would disappear.

Balance theory and field theory, as we have briefly outlined them in this example, are not very far apart conceptually. A common feature is the congruity or incongruity that exists in an individual's relationship with other persons and the social issues that engage them both. A rather sophisticated model for quantifying these relationships and for predicting the outcome has been developed by Osgood and Tannenbaum (1955). In the present instance, we can see better how this particular model works if we look at it from A's viewpoint. Think of Individual A as having rated both the Supreme Court and legalized abortion along an attitudinal continuum that ranges from very positive to very negative. (See Fig. 3.)

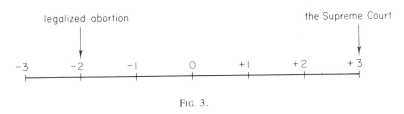

Fig. 3.

In this figure, Individual A's dispositions toward both legalized abortion and the Supreme Court are shown as points along the assumed attitudinal continuum; minus 2 in one case, and plus 3 in the other. Incongruity for A exists to the extent that the following assertion can be made: "The Supreme Court approves of early abortion." The incongruity arises from the fact that although A is quite favorably disposed toward the Supreme Court, the Court has acted to legalize early abortion, which is anathema to A. The discrepancy between these two attitudinal objects, or referents, along A's subjective attitudinal continuum generates stress, or imbalance. The system, according to Osgood and Tannenbaum, generates pressure toward congruence. Such congruence can be achieved by a shift in Individual A's attitudes toward either abortion, the Supreme Court, or both. The direction and extent of such a shift is computed from a formula in which the major variables are the extremeness of scale values of the two attitudinal referents and the amount of pressure toward congruity for each. Without going through the computation, we will merely state that the point of equilibrium will be reached at + 1 on the scale. In effect, what will happen is that the less polarized (i.e., distant from zero) of the two concepts, in this case legalized abortion, absorbs more of the pressure toward congruity. In the final analysis, the Supreme Court should lose somewhat in A's estimation and legalized abortion should improve its position. Individual A will accept legalized abortion more than he did previously and will like the Supreme Court somewhat less, but the latter change should be a smaller one.

A BEHAVIORAL ANALYSIS

We have expounded, briefly, several features of cognitive theory in attitude change to illustrate what is probably the more popular of current viewpoints in this area. Because attitudes have traditionally been thought of as "cognitions," it is not surprising that cognitive psychologists have dominated both theory and research on attitudes and attitude change. There is, however, another approach that is conceptually quite distinct from that of the cognitive theorist. This is the approach of the behavioral psychologist, who prefers to deal with performances rather than with "dispositions" to perform. The term attitude, in its strictly behavioral sense, covers not just a single performance but a wide range of behaviors under the control of stimuli of a particular class. A "religious attitude," for example, might be manifested in a certain pattern of church attendance, in the statements one makes about certain moral and ethical issues, and in the behaviors relevant to religion that one rewards or punishes in one's children. If we know what a person's attitudes (or typical behaviors) are on a variety of matters, we feel that we can better understand that person and predict his future behavior in similar situations. Because attitudes and evidence for attitude change are most typically measured from verbal performances, we need to consider briefly the role of language in behavior theory.

The role of language. Behaviorally, language is dealt with as a form of behavior that is acquired and maintained largely by its effects on other persons. This approach, pioneered by B. F. Skinner (1957), is not concerned with the problem of "meaning" in language. Rather, a verbal utterance is viewed both as a response and as a discriminative stimulus that, in turn, prompts a response from the listener. A verbal episode designates a chain of verbal performances that are both prompted and maintained by the participants. When the responses of one fail to reinforce or become aversive to the other, or when other factors intervene (such as a phone call or the time for another appointment) the episode is terminated. The process of persuasion is seen as involving a verbal episode in which the most reinforcing consequence to the speaker is some predetermined change in the verbal or nonverbal performance of the listener. The nature of this change is specified in the remarks of the speaker; in less technical language we refer to an attempt to modify someone's attitude.

The ontogeny of attitudes can thus be seen as, in large part, the ontogeny of language. As Skinner puts it: "A child acquires verbal behavior when relatively unpatterned vocalizations, selectively reinforced, gradually assume forms which produce appropriate consequences in a given verbal community [1957, p. 31]." By substituting the word "attitude" for the term "verbal behavior" in this quotation, we may summarize in behavioral language the process by which attitudes are acquired.

The problem of meaning can be approached in the same general fashion; that is, words have meaning in the sense that they bear a functional relationship to other performances. If a listener is to respond appropriately in terms of "meaning," he must be influenced not only by the verbal performance of the speaker but also by the situational variables that have controlled the speaker's behavior. The word "boy," for example, might be emitted as a request for service in a hotel, as a derogatory way of referring to a Negro, or as an exclamation of delight. The "meaning" that the word conveys obviously is a function of all the stimuli that prompted its use, and its effects upon the listener will be partially a function of these same variables. That is, the use of "boy" may reveal to the listener a desire for something, a prejudicial attitude toward Negroes, or a pleased reaction.

It is obvious even from superficial observation that a parent may control his child's behavior by the appropriate use of verbal approval as a positive reinforcer. Or the parent may place his child under aversive control by criticizing his faults instead of praising his accomplishments; he reinforces the child for what he does not do rather than what he does. The child, in this case, accedes to the parent's demands in order to avoid or escape from punishment. We may assume that social attitudes are acquired, in general, in one of these two ways: through positive control or aversive control.

What reinforces the persuader? Behaviorally, persuasion can be seen as arising from a situation where the actions of one person are either *(a)* aversive to the other or *(b)* nonreinforcing to the other. Thus, a parent may find certain behaviors (verbal and otherwise) of a son or daughter in the areas of sex, drugs, or politics aversive. Or, he may simply discover that his own verbalizations on social issues are not echoed by his offspring; they do not reinforce him when he expresses his attitudes on a number of matters. He may then try to change their behavior through verbal exhortation involving the use of incentives, threats, or both. Attitudinal discrepancy, in short, reduces behaviorally to the fact that two individuals are doing or saying different things. For example, if the parent says, "I think there should be stiffer penalties for the use of marijuana," and if his son or daughter is more inclined to say, "I think there should be no penalties for the use of marijuana," there is an obvious discrepancy in their verbal behaviors. (We could also speak of imbalance or cognitive incongruity.) If one of these participants now engages in argumentation designed to bring the other person's behavior more into conformity with his own, we say he is engaging in persuasion. Note that in this description of the persuasive process, there is no need to analyze the intentions or motivations of the persuader. It is sufficient to say that the situation has prompted him to engage in a type of verbal performance that has, in the past, been successful in reducing the type of behavioral discrepancy (an aversive situation) that he now encounters. One way of avoiding further aversiveness is to effect some change in the other individual's verbal repertoire, so that it becomes more like his own. Thus, if the father succeeds in prompting his son or daughter to say "Well, now I agree with you; perhaps there should be some penalties for using marijuana," then he has effectively reduced the aversiveness of his offspring's attitude on the issue. In addition, he is positively reinforced by hearing at least a partial echo of his own viewpoint. We assume here that confirmation of one's attitudes and opinions is reinforcing, and, indeed, there is experimental evidence that such is the case.[1]

The oft-noted "generation-gap" refers to the discrepancies in attitudinal behaviors that seem inevitably to occur between parents and their children. Some of these differences may be minor, as in the conflict over whether the son's hair should be worn short or long. But such seemingly petty disputes are also symptomatic of underlying discrepancies in the attitudes of parent and offspring toward the conventional values of society. These discrepancies and conflicts loom larger in the case of attitudes toward such issues as drugs, sex, and politics. One may ask how it is that a parent loses control over certain features of his children's behaviors that are important to him. The answer, oversimplified, is that primary groups other than the family and subcultures other than the ones to which the parents belong have acquired preemptive control over some of their children's behaviors. Teenagers, in short, are strongly reinforced by their peers for dressing in a particular way, for using drugs or for engaging in premarital sex, and their parents cannot summon up sufficient positive or aversive control to offset these other social influences.

Why some individuals are persuaded to adopt "deviant" patterns of behaviors is a question that psychologists are not yet prepared to answer in full. However, it seems highly probable that the mode of control exercised by the parent is a crucial factor in determining whether or not an offspring becomes compliant or rebellious. One tenable hypothesis is that adherence to the parents' value system is more likely when the parents have used positive rather than aversive means of inculcating these values in their children. Aversive control, or the use of threats and punishment, is more likely to engender resentment and escape behavior. These reactions, in turn, increase the likelihood that the young person will come into more frequent contact with those who will offer him immediate, positive reinforcement (i.e., praise, acceptance) for engaging in the very behaviors of which the parents disapprove. These various interactions between young people, parents, and peer groups illustrate in a very real sense some of the more dramatic aspects of persuasion.

Does information persuade? The persuasion process, of course, is not as simple as this discussion might indicate. Assume that an extreme discrepancy exists between the attitudes of two individuals. They may engage in a prolonged and heated discussion and, in the end, be exactly where they started so far as their initial attitudes are concerned. All that this proves, of course, is that persuading another individual is no simple matter; that the contingencies that reinforce one's attitudes are generally more powerful than those which can be brought to bear by an antagonist. The frequent futility of persuasive argumentation can be very puzzling, especially when each protagonist has supplied the other with logic and factual information that seems ineluctable. However, a good deal of research has shown that the correlation between retention of new information and attitude change is

[1]A good example of such evidence may be found in Newcomb, T. M., *The Acquaintance Process,* (1961). Newcomb shows many instances in which the probability of affiliative behaviors is strengthened by having one's opinions agreed with.

negligible. In short, simply understanding and remembering factual material brought to one's attention has relatively little impact on one's related attitudes. Abelson (1972) cites an example of the failure of new information to modify attitudes. He observes that during the 1963 New York City newspaper strike, many commuting bankers and businessmen accustomed to reading the conservative New York World Telegram and Sun had to make do with the New York Post, a notoriously liberal publication. When the attitudes of a sample of these readers were surveyed at the conclusion of the strike, they were discovered to be no more liberally inclined following this period of exposure to a liberal newspaper than they had been initially. Apparently these individuals simply had a reading habit to be served, and they were quite impervious to any social or political bias in the content of a newspaper they had read for lack of one they would have preferred. There is also evidence to show that information from a "distrusted" source tends to produce little alteration in a person's attitude because such information evokes counterarguments in the recipient. Such counterarguments cannot be rebutted by a message in print or on the airways and, hence, the recipient's own views are self-reinforced by the belief that he has successfully countered an opponent's arguments. At the same time, there appears to be a strong habit of not "decoding" (i.e., responding differentially to) some of the more important information coming from a distrusted source.

Does emotion persuade? If information, per se, does not lie at the root of attitude change, then what does? Perhaps the affective, or emotional, impact of a persuasive argument is what influences the audience. Evidence on this point is somewhat scanty and inconsistent. However, it is established that words having reference to attitudes and beliefs will provoke an autonomic, or emotional, reaction in the listener. Recently, Dickson and McGinnies (1966) have shown that religious subjects respond more emotionally (as measured by the galvanic skin response) to antichurch statements than to prochurch statements, and much less emotionally to neutral statements. In a related study, McGinnies and Aiba (1965) found that Japanese students who supported American foreign policy during the Vietnam conflict gave higher galvanic skin responses when listening to passages from a speech by Nikita Krushchev than when listening to passages from a speech by Adlai Stevenson. The interpretation of both sets of findings is that exposure to counterattitudinal material is more apt to prompt an emotional reaction than exposure to supportive messages. Both positive and negative communications, however, seem to evoke more of an emotional reaction than neutral material.

Is persuasion more readily accomplished when one uses positive appeals or when one attempts to influence the target audience through the use of threats for noncompliance? We have, as yet, no definitive answer to this question. However there is some evidence that fear-arousing appeals may be effective only so long as the message provides the recipient with some strategy for reducing or relieving any discomfort that he has experienced. The general ineffectiveness of fear appeals to smokers—suggesting the danger of cancer, high blood pressure, and other physical disorders — is well known. On the other hand, it is widely believed by political figures that emotional arguments are more effective than rational arguments so far as the average voter is concerned. In fact, in this area, it is quite probable that characteristics of the speaker outweigh to a considerable extent the content of what he says.

Communicator credibility. This brings us to one of the more interesting variables in persuasion, namely, the credibility of the communicator. Credibility can be viewed as having two basic components: expertise and trustworthiness. The expert communicator is one whom the listener or viewer perceives as possessing accurate and authoritative knowledge of his subject matter. A trustworthy communicator is one who is seen as having no ulterior or self-serving purposes. The greater effectiveness of a more credible as opposed to a less credible communicator is reasonably well-established. Cognitive and balance theories would interpret this finding as indicative of greater pressure on the individual to modify his opinion because of discomfort engendered from hearing an incongruent point of view expressed by a highly credible communicator. The tension, or dissonance, can be reduced in one of several ways: by disparaging the communicator (so that his arguments are rendered unacceptable), or by bringing one's own attitude more into conformity with the viewpoint to which one has just been exposed. Derrogation of the communicator, however, is difficult to accomplish when he is perceived as both expert and trustworthy. The main remaining avenue for dissonance reduction, therefore, is a change in the recipient's attitude so that it becomes more consistent with that of the communicator. This analysis, of course, involves assumptions of inner processes, such as cognitive dissonance, that are unobservable and, hence, troublesome to a behaviorist.

An alternative view of why persuasion is more often accomplished by a highly credible and trustworthy source could be stated in terms of incentives. It is sometimes difficult to say what reinforces an individual who is moved to accept a viewpoint with which he disagrees. Initially, the experience of hearing such argumentation is probably aversive to him. In order to account for the fact that his attitudes sometimes do change so as to become more consistent with those advocated by someone else, we must assume that the communicator offers him some incentive, either explicit or implicit, for modifying his stand. One incentive might arise from the fact that agreement with highly credible sources has, in the past, been positively reinforcing, (e.g., through social approval). Alternatively, one might, by agreeing with an influential communicator, avoid certain aversive consequences of not agreeing, (e.g., being fired from one's job, losing a friend, suffering scorn or ridicule). Behavior acquired or maintained through the avoidance of aversive consequences is said to be negatively reinforced. One merit to this particular interpretation is that incentives and reinforcers are commodities that can be identified in the environment. They need not be tangible, as in the case of social approval, but they can be measured and manipulated.

It should be pointed out, however, that a large incentive offered someone as an inducement for him to engage in counterattitudinal behavior may actually produce a smaller change in his attitude than a small incentive. As elaborated by Festinger (1957) and his students, this effect is due presumably to the fact that receiving a large reward for saying something that one does not really believe provides the person a rationalization for having behaved in an incongruous manner. A small reward, on the other hand, would provide insufficient justification for engaging in counterattitudinal behavior and the person, therefore, would be more likely to believe what he has said or agree with what he has done. This line of reasoning assumes a state of *cognitive dissonance* which is induced whenever one's behaviors are inconsistent with one's attitudes and is reduced under certain conditions by a change in attitude. Because different predictions about the direction and amount of attitude change generated in such circumstances can be made from cognitive theory and from reinforcement theory, these two theoretical approaches have come to grips in a number of recent experiments. Space does not permit us to go into this particular controversy in greater detail, except to note that a careful specification of the nature and timing of incentives (offered before) and reinforcers (presented after) the counterattitudinal performance seems crucial to the nature of any attitude change that occurs.[2]

In the same way that balance and field theories have their visual models, we can construct a diagram that shows, in a crude sense, the behavioral events that occur in the course of persuasion. The general format of this model is adapted from B. F. Skinner's (1957) analysis of verbal behavior. The symbol (S^D) stands for "discriminative stimulus," or a feature of the environment that prompts a response, or performance. The symbol (R^{op}) means "operant response," or a performance emitted by an individual in the presence of an S^D. An aversive stimulus is shown as (S^{av}) and a reinforcer, or reinforcing stimulus, as (S^{rein}). A performance that effects the removal of an aversive stimulus, as we have noted, is said to be negatively reinforced ($S^{neg\ rein}$).

The following diagram (borrowed from McGinnies, 1970), attempts to combine these various behavioral symbols into a simplified description of the events that occur when a credible communicator interacts with a recipient who initially disagrees with him.

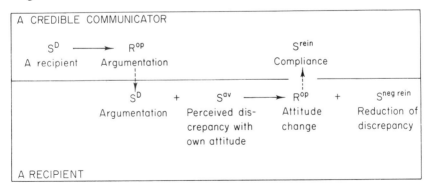

Fig. 4.

<hr />

[2]A particularly insightful review of this literature is given by Elms (1967), who delineates previously unnoticed sources of positive and negative incentives produced by the relationship of the experimenter and the subjects in these studies. Another valuable and comprehensive review can be found in McGuire (1966).

Reinforcement of attitude change. It is a basic postulate of behavior theory that a response must be emitted before it can be reinforced. In order to be emitted, the behavior must be in the individual's repertoire. A child can read only when he can recognize individual words; he can understand words only when he recognizes the letters of the alphabet; he can learn the alphabet only when he can utter the component sounds. In short an individual must have the elements of a complex performance in his behavioral repertoire before he can emit that performance. This generalization is equally true of attitudes and attitude change. Persuasion is simply a process of rearranging certain verbal behaviors that the person has already acquired.

One technique of the effective communicator is to nurture those small elements of agreement that he may touch upon in his listener. He then provides the listener with sufficient incentive to enlarge these areas of agreement. For example, two-sided arguments have been found to be more effective than one-sided arguments when the recipient initially disagrees with the communicator. By incorporating elements of the opposing viewpoint in his presentation, the communicator manages to reinforce some of the attitudes that are already part of the audience's repertoire. He endeavors, however, to suggest alternative verbal performances (attitudes) that can be emitted by his audience members, since the component parts are already present. Most importantly, the communicator provides incentives for the audience members to emit these new performances. Thus in an experiment where we tried to convince Japanese university students that it might be to their advantage to have American nuclear powered submarines visit Japanese ports, several of the advantages of such visits were pointed out to them. This argument was effective, however, only after we acknowledged their quite reasonable fears and doubts about such a proposal. This essentially two-sided approach was more successful in modifying opinions than a strictly one-sided argument, which simply stressed the advantages to Japan of being protected by the American nuclear umbrella (McGinnies, 1966).

There are several possible explanations of this effect. One is that a two-sided communication increases the "attention" that is paid to it because of the positively reinforcing elements that it contains. Another is that the presentation of some statements with which a recipient agrees reduces his tendency to rehearse counter-arguments to those statements with which he disagrees. The problem of what a person is "saying to himself" while listening to a persuasive communication is, of course, difficult to investigate.

BEHAVIORAL AND COGNITIVE APPROACHES COMPARED

Perhaps the foremost advantage of a behavioral approach to persuasion is that it avoids the speculative question: "What is an individual's real attitude?" The literature on attitudes is replete with instances in which "verbal attitudes" are found to differ from "action attitudes." That is, individuals are prone to express attitudes on a questionnaire that are not always reliable predictors of what they will do in a naturalistic situation. For example, Linn (1965) measured the willingness of white subjects to pose for a photograph with a Negro in a social situation. He then obtained a comparable behavioral score based on the signed level of agreement to pose with a Negro. The prejudiced subjects were more consistent; that is, 72% of them not only expressed unwillingness to pose with a Negro but refused to sign an agreement to do so. On the other hand, only 30% of the ostensibly less prejudiced individuals behaved consistently with their expressed attitudes; 70% of them refused to sign the photographic agreement.

Cowdry, Keniston, and Cabin (1970) report similar inconsistencies between the attitudes of students who opposed the Vietnam war and their actual behavior with respect to this issue. Many strongly antiwar students refused to sign a Military Service Resolution, which would have put them on record as both opposing the draft and as willing to serve only under protest. These investigators conclude that the disposition to act publicly in support of one's private attitudes is a separate variable which may be independent of both the content and the intensity of the attitude. Behaviorally, we would say that answering a questionnaire and signing a commitment are entirely different situations which present different contingencies of reinforcement. There is little chance that any aversive consequences will follow from simply indicating what one's attitude is on an issue. However, a signed agreement to engage in behavior related to the attitude may result in consequences that are aversive to the signer. There is no "true" attitude in this case. Rather a person has different behavioral dispositions (i.e., to reply to a question or to sign an agreement) that are controlled by the reinforcement contingencies that operate in different situations. Situational factors are paramount in controlling attitudinal behavior, and a testing situation may not prompt the same kind of performance that occurs in direct confrontation with another person. Apparent inconsistencies in attitudinal behavior are thus explained in terms of specific agents of stimulus control.

I should not want to leave the reader with the impression that the behavioral approach to persuasion for which I have argued is characteristic of most social psychologists; it probably is not. This fact has been expressed succinctly by Abelson (1972): "The more mainstream social psychological view of attitudes is one which recognizes closely interrelated affective, cognitive, and conative components, and which interests itself deeply with the details of cognitive structure and persuasive communication — that is, with attitude as a mediating construct with a complicated life of its own. The componential, mediational view is central not only for most social psychologists, but also for the colloquial view of attitudes: you knowingly feel a certain way about something, and this determines how you act about that something when you get the opportunity [p. 20]."

The behaviorist, of course, would translate such expressions as "knowingly feel a certain way about something" into a person "talking to himself." An individual, in other words, interacts with his own verbal repertoire; he is both speaker and listener within the same skin (McGinnies & Ferster, 1971). Whether his self-administered verbal prompts result in a particular course of action depends on the situation in which he finds himself. The person who harbors latent prejudices toward blacks may act with exaggerated politeness in the presence of a black. Even his score on an attitude scale may not reflect his "true attitude," since he might be performing in a way designed to evoke positive reinforcement from whoever is administering the scale. His "true attitude" might appear, however, in conversation with his close friends, who are inclined to voice similar sentiments and, thus, reinforce his prejudices. It is fruitless therefore to argue about the "real" nature of his attitude. He has a number of attitudes, or better, *performances* with respect to blacks. He behaves in one way on an attitude scale, in another way in the presence of blacks, and in still a third way in the presence of individuals who share his convictions about blacks.

By conceptualizing attitudes as performances prompted by relevant social situations and maintained by social reinforcement, we avoid contention about the nature of a person's "real" attitudes and about the causal relationship between attitudes and behavior. We need not speculate on whether behavior causes attitudes or attitudes cause behavior; rather, we can simply speak of the probability that a certain kind of behavior will occur in a particular kind of situation. These are variables with which we can deal objectively. The behavioral approach, in general, promises an understanding of the nature of attitudinal behavior that circumvents speculation about cognitive processes which, by their nature, can reveal themselves only indirectly to our scientific scrutiny.

REFERENCES

Abelson, R. P. Are attitudes necessary? In B. T. King & E. McGinnies (Eds.), *Attitudes, conflict, and social change.* New York: Academic Press, 1972.

Cowdry, R. W., Keniston, K., & Cabin, S. The war and military obligation: Private attitudes and public actions. *Journal of Personality,* 1970, **38**, 525–549.

Dickson, H. W., & McGinnies, E. Affectivity in the arousal of attitudes as measured by galvanic skin response. *American Journal of Psychology,* 1966, **79**, 584–589.

Elms, A. C. Role playing, incentive and dissonance. *Psychological Bulletin,* 1967, **68**, 132–148.

Festinger, L. *A theory of cognitive dissonance.* Evanston, Ill.: Row, Peterson, 1957.

Heider, F. Attitudes and cognitive organization. *Journal of Psychology,* 1946, **21**, 107–112.

Lewin, K. *A dynamic theory of personality.* (Trans. by D. K. Adams and K. E. Zener) New York: McGraw-Hill, 1935.

Linn, L. S. Verbal attitudes and overt behavior: A study of racial discrimination. *Social Forces,* 1965, **43**, 353–364.

McGinnies, E. Studies in persuasion: III. Reactions of Japanese students to one-sided and two-sided communications. *Journal of Social Psychology,* 1966, **70**, 87–93.

McGinnies, E. *Social behavior: A functional analysis.* Boston: Houghton Mifflin, 1970.

McGinnies, E., & Aiba, F. H. Persuasion and emotional response: A cross cultural study. *Psychological Reports,* 1965, **16**, 503–510.

McGinnies, E., & Ferster, C. B. (Eds.) *The reinforcement of social behavior.* Boston: Houghton Mifflin, 1971.

McGuire, W. J. Attitudes and opinions. In, *Annual review of psychology*. Palo Alto, Calif.: Annual Reviews, 1966.

Newcomb, T. An approach to the study of communicative acts. *Psychological Review*, 1953, **60**, 393–404.

Newcomb, T. *The acquaintance process*. New York: Holt, 1961.

Osgood, C. E., & Tannenbaum, P. H. The principle of congruity in the prediction of attitude change. *Psychological Review*, 1955, **62**, 42 – 55.

Skinner, B. F. *Verbal behavior*. New York: Appleton-Century-Crofts, 1957.

Skinner, B. F. *Beyond freedom and dignity*. New York: Knopf, 1971.

11

THE LANGUAGE OF THE BODY: THE NATURAL ENVIRONMENT OF WORDS[1]

Ray L. Birdwhistell
The Annenberg School of Communication
University of Pennsylvania

Human communication is much broader than the exchange of words in discrete messages with silences between them. My premise is that communication is a continuous multisensory process. In this view, words occur in and are important in a natural and interdependent environment. The entire body provides them with that environment through personal appearance, gestures, posture, and paralanguage ("tone" and pattern of voice) as well as other activities of the total sensorium. Present research indicates that fascinating and complex relationships are operative in the patterned activities of the various sensory modalities utilized in the communicational process. These relationships are active in the structures which control the meanings necessary to social interaction. However, in order to discuss these relationships sensibly, some traditional myths about communication must be put into perspective as these myths stand in the way of our being able to conceptualize communication, much less describe or analyze it in a refutable manner.

From one point of view the two world wars can be used as historical markers to gain *a* perspective on the development of present stances in *social* communicational theory. I say, "from one point of view" because a very different perspective could be provided by the examination of developments in mathematical or psychological theorizing. And, obviously, these are not discrete perspectives. However, a crude diagram could be drawn illustrating the invasion of theorists and essayists with a social science leaning into a province of thought previously dominated by the humanist, philosophical, or literary. My own generation of

---

[1]Some of the material dealing with kinesic analyses is drawn from more detailed accounts in R. L. Birdwhistell, *Kinesics and Context*, Philadelphia: University of Pennsylvania Press, 1970.

young sociology and social or cultural anthropology students were cognizant of and influenced by an array of such men. H. L. Mencken (1936), Ogden and Richards (1938), Korzybski (1941), Hayakawa (1951), Stuart Chase (1938), Thurmond Arnold (1937), and, in particular, G. H. Mead (1934) and Edward Sapir (1951) were listened to, read, and argued about. With the exceptions of G. H. Mead and Edward Sapir, who (like Margaret Mead, 1964, and Gregory Bateson, 1936) were to be forerunners of the post World War II developments in social communication theory, these theorists were primarily concerned with word and sentence-sized universes. They were aware and critical of the clumsiness, if not the inherent deceptiveness, of the written and spoken word as exclusive carriers of meaning. In their writings, pleas for improved logics, more flexible and contemporary epistemologies, more dynamic and consistent grammars, clearer and more reliable lexicography, and, above all, more precision and specificity in language usage alternated with admonitions for a healthy skepticism about language as a reliable depository for meaning and its transmission. For me, as a student, this was heady and reassuring. Their writings were reassuring perhaps because their conclusions were consistent with my great uncle James Madison Bell Birdwhistell who, when I left for college, warned "and remember one thing, Ray, paper will lie still and let you put anything on it."

While the attention of the pre World War II theory was to a large extent focused upon the word, the thought of this period set a direction of research away from the word as a container and transmitter of all meaning and away from simple manipulation of philosophical considerations of meaning, and thus communication. And, comparable to the brilliant theoreticians who were in the post World War II period to develop cybernetic and information theory, the work of the twenties and thirties demonstrated clearly where the answers were not.

For me as a student, and as an embryonic investigator, this was the intellectual climate which in post World War II led me toward an alternative model of theory and research, toward an alternative which would seem more relevant to the understanding of the passage of thought and action-ways between generations, between social classes and between and within whole social systems. However, if I am honest in my attempt here to give perspective, I must not pretend that my theorizing has purely scholarly antecedents.

When I originally moved North, I talked in a marked Southern drawl, and when I took my first teaching job at the University of Toronto, I talked about anthropology in that drawl. I soon discovered that my students weren't paying a bit of attention to the content of my lectures. The truth of the matter seems to be that you cannot talk science to a Northern audience with a Southern accent. A lecturer knows that you had better talk in "Standard Professor" if the content of your words is going to be attended to. Otherwise he is at best attended to with a spectator's delight in the anomalous. And probably you should stand in "scholarly formal." It helps in speech style to approach the reliability of modulated monotone. If you happen to be relatively loose jointed and you talk other than standard American English, Eastern Seaboard variety, you are highly likely to go unheeded. This was of vital interest to me and I knew that to become an academic I had to get rid of my accent, but I couldn't get rid of it all (or the feeling of the essential rightness of it). I say /minny/ and /pinny/ for "many" and "penny" and I say /y'all/ for my plural. I think in a Southern accent when I am angry or sexually excited, and I have the unshakeable belief that if you were to take a man from Oxford in England and wake him in the middle of the night that his first words would be in English, good standard middle Western English. The question of what this was all about, the effect of dialect, and the effect of the way one carries one's body in making certain points puzzled me, and that puzzlement shaped the direction of my scientific curiosity.

Later, I headed back South and taught the first course in evolution entitled "Evolution" south of the Mason-Dixon Line. Well, my aunts cared for me and for seven years I was interceded for at the local Baptist prayer meetings. With consistent missionary fervor, I lectured to those students at the University of Louisville, and I told them how the firmament had cooled and about the coming of the first little beastees, about the carbon-coagulates, and the complex hydrocarbons and the viruses that had gathered in that cooling firmament, and how we got some dry land and then came the beastees of the land and sea, and how the beastees finally stayed on the land and walked around on the land. The bold ones stood on their hind legs, and became mammals, and then you got humans, and finally humans overcame their animal past and invented society. And none of my students became perturbed by my revelations. No one got very upset, so I knew it was wrong. Somehow, the way I talked and the things I talked about and the central patterning of these things were so totally consistent with the basic assumptions of the kind of society that I and my cousins had come out of (totally immersed running water Baptists with a good sprinkling of Episcopalians) that the picture I gave of evolution in some way had to be a myth. When stated in standard scientese, evolution as a theory had been deemed very dangerous, yet when I discussed it in a familiar rhetoric it was a consistent myth and so familiar as to be unexciting.

Another question of interest to any anthropologist or folklorist is that of how our society, and only our society, came to possess the origin myth which in effect says, "In the beginning there was one adult male and one adult female, with no kinfolk or kithfolk, and no culture. We started from scratch, had offspring and were in the beginning cursed with self-awareness." What kind of a society would choose an adult dyad for an origin myth? This question was to haunt me even more when I became aware of the power of our society's second great dyad, the mother and the son, Mary and Jesus. This dyad came to special secular power under the aegis of modern psychiatry when the parent-child dyad assumed an importance rivaled only by the sexual one. When I began to try to understand and to study and to teach social communication, these two traditional attitudes exemplified by the traditional statement of evolution and by the particular emphasis within our society upon the dyad were underpinnings for thought ways that resisted any development of social communication theory. The dyadic model was a wonderfully useful myth for the development of information theory or for psychological models of interpersonal relationships. Unfortunately, however, the dyadic model so useful in the formation of elegant information theory has been inappropriately borrowed by those attempting to describe human communication. From my point of view there is a considerable divergence between information theory which is about messages and their transmission and communication theory which is about interconnectedness and its maintenance.

To understand the way in which information theory has been misused, we should look at the theories of communication following World War II to which it contributed. We held a simple image about communication which shaped our belief that communication can be understood through the analysis of the behavior of two people. Communication was seen as a dyadic process. Experiences with the radio and the receiver or with two people on the telephone or with letters being written and answered and, later, the TV camera and screen verified this position. With a sender and a receiver and essentially an action and reaction sequence you could rely upon good, clean, and uncomplicated nineteenth century Western European logic. Both the underlying epistemology and the presence of telecommunication technology diverted us from communication as a truly *social* process. We were interested in understanding fences but we focused our attention upon pickets and posts.

Perhaps more confusing to us at that time was the fact that our dyadic model was not really a social statement of two as a unit but was further complicated by our overriding assumption that since individual men invented society (the evolutionary myth discussed earlier), society was composed of the relationships between individual men. Thus, the dyad was made up of two ones, i.e., two individual men. And, whether one wished to study or to trivialize this, something relevant had to have happened *inside* each of the individuals. When I was starting as a student, that inside was called a telephone exchange; later it became a computer. Some people call it a brain; Gregory Bateson once said to me, "Let's call it macaroni because that is how much we know about it." But any American or Western European knows that something happens inside the individual human and "it" emits symbols somewhere through an orifice, each set called words, each word carrying meaning. The model is a very simple one to build. A little balloon filled with words comes out of the sender's nearest orifice, goes through the macaroni of a recipient, re-emerges, and another little balloon of words filled with meaning is returned to the original sender. Communication, then, is measured by the extent to which the second balloon can duplicate the first. If the analyst regards the process as more complicated than this, he can talk about the process of back and forth and recalibrated transmission as "feedback." "Feed-back" and "input" are words which I find very useful when dealing with information transmission. But this is not what I mean by communication.

From the point of view of an investigator concerned with *social* communication processes and theory there are several things wrong with these theoretical preconceptions. The first problem is that the model is exclusively a new-information model. Communication is viewed as that process whereby A, having information not possessed by B, passes that information on to B. B, being a *"tabula rasa,"* receives the new imprint or some aspect of it. Communication becomes an action-reaction sequence in which the task is to get the content of the balloon out of A and into B. This model is very fine for mechanical sequences but, except in very special circumstances, you cannot find humans who are either all knowledgeable or completely empty. To make it even more difficult as a communication theory, it won't work when we are talking about neonates gaining membership in a society. A friend of mine, using a computer, calculated the length of time required for these action–reaction sequences to take place, including the time for the physiological processes inside A, the duration of the message through time to B, the time for the physiological processes inside B, and the time for the connective processes. He decided that, if this is the way children learn, it would take three and a half generations to get to be a 2½-year-old human. Obviously, there are no serious supporters for such a simplified theory of enculturation or socialization. And yet there is comfort in such theory for those who poetically conceive of people (child or adult) as black boxes or machines. This order of thought can preclude the profanity that man did not invent society, but, rather, that society invented man.

A second difficulty is inherent in the use of a simplified information theory model to describe human communication. For such a model the final goal of the process results in *precision* of transmission. This is surely a good way to construct a door bell in which the information you stick into the button will come out at the bell. It is also fine for describing telegraphy. But it relegates to "noise" the imprecision and creativity which constitute a major proportion of all social communication. Precision is about signal transmission and not about the adaptive sharing of messages and messages about messages.

To reiterate, the premise that underlies and vitiates this order of model is the assumption that two is "social." If one is a determined protestant monadist, two looks complicated and, perhaps, "social." From this point of view the Adam and Eve myth is a literal statement and society is really made up of and based upon individuals and dyads. Obviously, if the ultimate building blocks of society are first of all individual humans and then dyads, then it is proper to look for information with regard to the communication processes in the behavior of a questioner and an answerer, or a sender and a receiver. Research leads us to believe, however, that, far from being basic, the dyad is an *extra*ordinary event anywhere in human or animal existence. In actual practice, the isolated couple seems to be, regardless of how important to the participants, a very short-lived relationship. Moreover, a fantastic amount of social work is required to isolate and maintain the isolation of two people. Our own society implicitly believes and acts as though any society performs in dyadic relationships and that social processes (and communication) are to be finally understood through the examination and comprehension of the behavior of the teacher and the student, the husband and the wife, the adult and the child, etc. The view that society is composed of the transactions of a whole series of primary dyads appears sensible because of our particular epistemology. A society that believes that there is something natural about tall and short, black and white, good and bad, also will believe that there is something specially natural about dyads. The ideational distance between dichotomy and dyad is not great. Dyadic situations, while easy to create experimentally (by taking over the social work), are very hard to find in nature. Certainly dyads are tremendously important for making love or fighting, but even these engagements last a matter of seconds, minutes at the longest. To stress this relationship as a model of communication is to limit the natural universe. The image of our modern Western bourgeois marriage or a love affair cannot be used as a model of the natural unit for our society, much less that of all societies. Such images are not measures of reality, but of our special social reality. To repeat, this is not to say that the dyad is unimportant, only that it is not basic, that it is not the fundamental unit of social process or organization. And, it is not the ideal situation to investigate if one wants to study social communication, for the simple reason that most of the relevant data about interaction will not pass exclusively between the two individuals involved. Such data are but part of the context of conditions under which the communicators are brought together, their interaction is maintained, and their separation is accomplished.

Even more serious than the strictures upon research posed by this insistence on the dyad is what we have done to the conception of the body as related to communication. One of the reasons that my Kentucky students were not upset during my lectures on evolution was that I unwittingly lied to them. I had told them that once we got mammals, we got anthropoids, and then man and, finally, man invented society. In the days prior to ethology, prior to the study of animals *in situ* (not crazy animals like laboratory rats or pets or caged animals, but real animals relating to one another in a natural condition), we failed to see that animals are and must be socially organized in order to survive. I know of no cross-speciational ethologist or anthropologist today who does not think that society (although, perhaps not culture) is at least as old as the fishes and may even go as far back as the fungi. Thus our conception of man is distorted if we conceive of man as inventing society because we are unable to see that social conditions made man possible. Society preceded Homo sapiens by thousands of socially dependent species. Social interrelationships are a natural condition of interdependency and, for me, of social communication. Communication as a dynamic aspect of interdependency precedes man by many thousands of species. Man calls himself Homo sapiens and this arrogance is supported by a myth wherein he sees the contractual relationships which men can make with one another as constituting society.

Related to all of this is another serious basic assumption that dominated, controlled, and, I think, until very recently foreclosed most studies of communication. This is included in myths about the nature of man's special emergence as a species. This myth claimed that man was to first animal capable of the first noninstinctual activity. Thus, all social animals were social, not on the basis of learning or on the basis of things that happened to them, not on the bases of accumulated or shared experience, but primarily in response to the drive of ''nature,'' where ''nature'' is described in terms of instinctive or genetic patterns. Perhaps these patterns were modified by ''habit'' or ''imitation,'' but essentially they were determined by the biological underpinning.

A basic conviction in our earlier myths was that man became man either through the act of an all-knowing deity or through some accident of the gene pool whereby, at some point in time, a particular anthropoid was suddenly touched in the central nervous system and those aspects of what was to become man began to evolve. The remainder of man remained animalistic, instinctual, and uncontrolled.

As late as the nineteenth century, the concept of man was essentially as a neutral body with an angel on one shoulder and a devil on the other. Then, philosophy became a little more sophisticated, theology reexamined a number of the exigencies of nineteenth century existence, anthropological data began to come in, and psychology began to look at man instead of at thoughts about man. This oversimple view was suddenly repealed, but we did not get rid of the angel and the devil. We located the angel from about the midbody up and the devil from the midbody down. The part above the midbody contains nice, clean, decent neuroprocesses which, if unadulterated by any bodily leakage from below, will not only be logical, denotative and objective but trustworthy, loyal, helpful, and probably quantitative, and commanding. Dirty words obviously come up from below, as does evil passion. All one needs is the ultimate conviction that there has been this order of asymmetrical evolution, with only the cerebroneural processes developing, for these neural processes to become the final location of good, of decency, of government, of knowledge, of information and, obviously, of communication.

Once this bifurcation is established, you then deal with a dualistic body out of which the head produces cognition or mentation and the rest produces affect or emotion. To be even more extreme we can imagine the good part of the body as separated from the bad part by a permeable membrane. The nether regions leak upward and distort the performance of the higher centers. However, at least in my background, the head and the will had some control over the membrane, and by self-control the membrane could be kept from leaking. And if you can just squeeze the midline orifices tight enough, then you can cogitate like crazy. The instinctual, basic, unsocialized, unteachable, untrainable, and unpatternable areas of the nether regions were assumed to continue in instinctual fashion. It is perfectly obvious that if you are a white, upper-class adult mathematician, you can really have it under control. And if you go backward from that down to a lower-class black child, who obviously is not as far advanced, there is a situation of continuous leakage.

It is very easy to go from this sort of theory about human nature to speak of *communication* as originating in the head, while from the remainder of the body comes something called *expression*. If you can accept this opposition as absolutely natural, you can believe that the upper part of the body communicates to people what it is you want to say and the remainder of the body expresses how you feel about it. By thinking of "meaning" as encapsulated in words, you can describe the central message as modified in an adjective-noun way by the remainder of the sensory apparatus.

Most of the people who studied communications in the past were professional lexicators, and were legitimatized as teachers or writers by proving that they could manipulate words. Their devotion to and involvement with words supported the separation of that which is in words from that which is "nonverbal," the separation of "communication" from "expression." Such a position inevitably leads to the conviction that all information, all knowledge, in the universe is stored in words, and that these are stored inside people's heads. However, because our midline diaphragm leaks, there is a variability in the way we talk about how we feel. "Feeling" is another word we use for "expression." Feeling obviously does not come out of the head. Feeling comes out of the glands and other non-evolved body parts. It has been in fashion again recently for many people to think that the lower part of the body tells the truth because it is more natural, that people can lie with words because they can control them. For the sentimentally "naturalistic" it becomes somehow more naturally honest, instinctually honest, animalistically honest, to have the message come out of the nonverbal part of our bodies. This is the same old puritan dichotomy, just turned on its head. But it is no less faithful than its opposite.

Now if one takes a look at the data rather than at the myth, he sees that there is no conclusive evidence for this dichotomy, for such an asymmetrical evolution. There are no data that I can discover to show that animals lived in a state of passion prior to man. Animals are systematically organized in their ways of life and, so far as we know, they learn to become members of their group as they become members of their communication system. We are aware even from our very limited studies that animals engage in highly elaborate ways of dealing with coded messages for recognizing familiars and aliens, for organizing concerted activity, for dealing with aggression, for coding and managing territory, and particularly, for organizing courtship, pairing and nonpairing. It is interesting that western man took the things that he despised most in himself and projected them upon animals. Or, in a perfect reversal, the romantic pastoralist position views the native, the instinctual, the animalistic as more attractive and only hampered by society through its agency in the central nervous system.

Data has dealt harshly too with the notion that the senses represent isolated pathways into storage places in the central nervous system. Most of us have, regardless of our training, regardless of our sensitivity to neurophysiology, a deep belief that the senses go into the center of the head and that in the brain are cupboards storing in separate compartments sights, sounds, odors, and so on. Long ago, William James (1890) was making fun of this position, saying that we do not see, or hear or taste or smell or feel separately except in poetry and psychological experiments; we see-hear-taste-smell. These are not separable variables. We have an organized whole neurological system. We do not learn to see, or hear, or taste, or smell; we learn these in bunches. (I use the word "bunches" because I do not know how they fit together.) They are, apparently, interdependent and they seem mutually reinforcing. It is clear, that by separating the senses into entities, it has been possible to support a concept of monosensory communication. From my point of view, the concept of a monosensory intermittent communication system is nonsensical. While it is useful as a model for information theory, it is counterproductive as a model for social communication theory. For most of us, introspectively and intuitively, it seems natural to think of ourselves as intermittently communicating when we are talking, and stopping when we are not talking. A model like this essentially sees communication as appropriately studied by experiments in which someone picks up a telephone after it has rung and says "Hello, this is Jack." "Hi ya', Jack." And the relevant behavior is concluded when the participation ends by saying "good-bye" and hanging up. In contrast, the model designed for the analysis of social communication is based upon the proposition that the moment you install the phone, the communicational context is established and, thus, communication processes are activated. The phone not ringing is a positive message. Anyone in a dormitory who has ever waited on a Friday night knows how noisy a phone can be that is not ringing. Anyone who has ever had someone dear ill in a distant city knows what the phone not ringing means. To offer you one other image to hold in your head, there is Gregory Bateson's story of flying into Philadelphia in a very thick fog and, because of a false circuit in the sound system, instead of receiving Mozart in his ears, all he was receiving was the radar beeps telling him he was on course, "beep-beep-beep-beep." And then the beeps stopped. Any violation of that pattern, any failure of the regular appearance of the next beep is just as meaningful, just as real, as the occurrence of the expected sound. Within such a view, to see social communication as intermittent is to ignore all pattern in communication. Communicational events are events in an ongoing process.

When I began to study communication, my hope was to find what it was that we did nonverbally that fleshed out words. But I do not think that is my question any longer. My question now is, "When is it appropriate to lexicate and in what classes of situation is the use of words, by custom, inappropriate?" I suppose that a research experience that I had about 20 years ago destroyed my earlier confidence that words were central to communication. After the completion of an intensive investigation of the family patterning in a small community and of its relationship to social mobility in that community, I was the recipient of a small grant designed to implement a study of "happy marriages" in that community. After a series of false starts occasioned by methodological naivete, a sample of 100 "happy" couples were selected for special examination. In short, the sample was drawn from couples (who had been married for at least 15 years) nominated by their neighbors, who in a joint interview testified as to the "happiness" of the marriage and who agreed to participate in the study. For one year data were collected about their conversations with one another. We were interested in the extent and duration of these conversations and not in the content, except in order to ascertain that the talk one person was doing had some adjustive relationship (a difficult methodological judgment) to the talk of the other. We eliminated all tandem monologues and all conversations including third persons. Again, in short, for I doubt the reliability of these methods but have invented no better ones, the methods used were biweekly interviews, diaries kept by either or both members of the couple, voice-operated microphones (when welcome), and cross-checks from other members of the family. The data were punched into Holorith cards and at the end of the year fed into machines which then gave us the answer. The *median* amount of conversation between these couples came out to the astonishing figure of 27½ minutes per week. I say "astonishing" because a statistically normal sentence in spoken American English is about 2½ to 2¾ seconds long, so that 27½ minutes contains a very large number of sentences. Still, this is far less conversation than any of the standard descriptions of behavior available would have suggested. The reader is warned that we did not count silences then. I now am much more aware of the unavoidable importance of not talking.

These data were so interesting (if only suggestive) that I followed them up in an attempt to find out when couples do most of their lexication. Analysis of some 50 interviews indicated that conversation seemed to be highest on the third date, before couples learned more appropriate means of communication, and in the last year before the divorce. But this does not mean that there is generally, if ever, a low *amount* of communication between married people. The way they occupy the room, the way they are aware of one another's breathing, even the sense that any married man has of how his wife feels by listening to her do the dishes, the click of the dishes, the quietness of them, is communicative.

This material was important for us as it directed attention to the difference between new-informational communication and what I hesitantly call integrational communication. The amount of truly new information that passes between human beings in a day is probably less than the impurities in Ivory soap. But there is a tremendous amount of relational information in the "I'm all right," "you're all right," "we're all right," "my belly hurts," "modify my last sentence because I feel this way," "I really don't want to do this," "I want to do that" behavior which may not require lexical transmission. These are the kinds of things that make it possible for human beings to orient and organize their relationships to one another. The overwhelming importance of integrational communication in the maintenance of social relationships led to other questions. I had the opportunity of studying such behavior in distinct ethnic groups. I ran preliminary studies in two divergent groups, one in Pennsylvania Dutch country, and another among families in northeast Philadelphia which were largely second and third generation middle-class Jewish. In the homes that were used in the Pennsylvania Dutch country, the *median* amount of *talk* per day within the family was about 2½ minutes. In northeast Philadelphia we ran out of recording tape every day. The talk ran somewhere between 6 and 12 hours of vocalization. For the anthropologist the significant point is that with 2½ minutes per day of lexication the Pennsylvania Dutch raised a good Pennsylvania Dutchman and, in many hours a day of lexication, the northeast Philadelphian Jewish family raised good northeast Philadelphia Jewish children. And insofar as we could ascertain, equal amounts of new information were customarily transmitted in the two types of families. However, when the *conditions* of communication were examined, it became evident that the lexical mode was used for different purposes in the two groups. In northeast Philadelphia a great amount of the conversation that you would hear went under the heading of "Kvetch," a ritual sing-song of complaint. When the mother is talking like this the signal says, "Look how I've suffered, I worked very hard, I went down to the store and the guy was bad to me and I didn't get the stuff you wanted and the traffic was bad and I'm having trouble getting this on the table," with that "nyahh" sound over all of it. Suddenly another child comes in and the mother changes her voice and says, "Oh, by the way, tell your father that the mail came." The signal was that the information passing under that sound was not to be attended to in the same way as the information going in under the other sound. At the present state of our knowledge we have no way of knowing whether the Pennsylvania Dutch or the northeast Philadelphia Jews are better communicators. (And I doubt that the question is important.) If the task of family communication is to rear people and to socialize them in terms of the values of their society and to leave them ready for meeting the outer society as representatives of their own society, obviously there is some equivalence there.

If communication is not exclusively carried on by people in words produced intermittently, words that are conceived in the head, produced by the mouth, heard by the ears with the meaning extracted from the words by the receiver's head, then we must know about the communicational behavior that is produced by the whole body and that is understood in terms of a variety of coordinated activity patterns of the entire body. The first class of data that emerges upon the examination of communication that goes beyond the actual (lexemes) words spoken by people is paralinguistic. This includes the patterning in *circum* lexical activity that permits people to modify the messages they send vocally by systematic variations of pitch, stress, spacing, rhythm, loudness, resonance, and so on. The lexical and nonlexical aspects of talking can be made congruent or incongruent, dramatic or funny, exciting or dull, hopeless or calm by these cues. However, even the most reliable tape recorder is insufficient to record conversation. A great deal goes into the body's social communication besides paralanguage. In fact, the study of paralinguistic storage and performance showed that it is possible to say so many different particular things with a very limited number of messages, and strongly suggested that we have the same kind of communicational powers for the communicational performance of the body in general.

Since the average American actually speaks words for only 10 to 11 minutes daily, we estimate (in pseudostatistics) that more than 65% of the social meaning conveyed in two-person interaction is carried by totally nonvocal cues. And it seems clear now that communication must be regarded in the broadest sense as a highly structured system of significant symbols from *all* the sensory based modalities. This is a *continuous* process that can make use of information received acoustically, visually, by touch, by smell, and so on. So we cannot investigate communication by isolating and measuring only one process, the acoustic (that is, sound-sending and sound-receiving). We can no more understand communication by the exhaustive investigation of language and paralanguage than we can understand physiology by, say, the exhaustive investigation of the circulatory system. However, it is methodologically proper to make entrance to the physiological system through the circulatory system, if we use physiological and not anatomic theory.

A number of important classes of nonverbal communications have been identified by students of communication: (*a*) bodily motion—gestures, limb movement, eye and mouth behavior, posture, and touching behavior; (*b*) proxemics—the use of personal and social distance from others; (*c*) physical characteristics—physique, personal odors, hair and skin color, hair style, etc; (*d*) artifacts—objects used in interaction with others, beauty aids, clothing, status emblems, etc. (*e*) environmental setting—locale, furniture, architectural style, lighting, music, noises, and traces of prior action. Kinesics is the discipline concerned with the study of all the bodily motions which are communicative and which may or may not substitute for and/or illustrate, modify, regulate and adapt speech. Kinesics is concerned with abstracting from the continuous muscular shifts which are characteristic of living physiological systems those groupings of movements which are of significance to the communicational process and thus to the interactional systems of social groups in general.

But linguistic and kinesic systems are only infra-communicational systems, and it is only in their inter-relationships with each other and with comparable systems from other sensory modalities that the emergent communication system is achieved.

A DEMONSTRATION OF THE BODY'S COMMUNICATION[2]

When you think of the motions of the body, remember that all of the body's parts can be seen as having varied functions. First, you must recall that even the so-called vocal organs are also the organs of breathing and the organs of swallowing. These let air pass out, causing a variety of sounds, a small number of which can be arbitrarily "chosen" by any society and used to carry the audible messages of that society. The vocal organs, like all of the body, are a set of moving parts and their movements make them

[2]The material in this section is taken directly from a lecture of Professor Birdwhistell's. While it lacks the visual presence of his body, for example, the informal style of the lecture was retained to convey some of the quality of the demonstration.

adaptable to varied communicative activity. Let us consider a number of other bodily parts that move, starting with the hair. The scalp, contrary to popular opinion, does not grow out of the skull, it is a moving part, which every baby begins to mold at birth as part of the determination of his appearance as he gets older. One primary task that every baby has is to convince the world to accept him and not to kill him or let him die. He has to behave sufficiently well during a checkout period, which may go on for quite awhile, either not to be killed or, in times of sufficient surplus, not to be institutionalized. That is, he must show himself to be worthy of membership by a minimal demonstration of ability to handle his society's system. One of the ways he does this is by how he looks.

Parenthetically, I know very little about when in this or any other society certain aspects of appearance are subject to social variation. I haven't the faintest idea *when* in the process of development the appearance tasks emerge, are completed, or are variable. We do not have these data and the particular sequence of body parts discussed below is a presentational convenience. In a society that says "Head to toe" this sequence is easier for lecture purposes than it would be for one that would begin with the heels or the elbows. The baby I am told has about three-quarters of an inch of variation possibility for the placement of his scalp. Nobody will directly teach him this, and he will not be aware that he is learning it, but he will learn it, sooner or later, even though he will probably never be aware of having learned it. He may keep the scalp mobile or may just rest it somewhere within the arc of potentiality. Wherever the scalp rests its position is of consequence to the appearance of the forehead. The forehead is a vast, beautiful, reflective surface that you can see for a great distance; it has a high broadcast capacity and it catches light and reflects it most communicatively. And it is framed by other mobile pieces of the face, and the nature of that framing communicates also. The way we appear to others is related to our eyebrows, for they too frame the forehead as well as the eyes. Again, they do not grow out of our skulls but are moveable. If one comes from, say, certain parts of England, the brows are carried way above the supercanthic ridge and produce a look which makes Americans think that the British are in a state of perpetual surprise. Two social classes and a few blocks away from that group you have people whose brows are carried below the ridges, yielding the familiar Welsh look. The way eyebrows are shaped, the way they grow, the way they are set is within a range consistent with those of a person's familiars. It looks as though people use their brows as do the people in their surroundings use them. If their appearance is too different from others around us, we may change them or at least we may be forced to be aware of them. While no one has to teach us these things, we do learn them as members of our community.

There is another area important for communication appearance that runs from the temple down to the cheekbone. If you take your fingers and put them against your temples and then squeeze your jaw, you will feel that area swelling. If you did that often enough, perhaps as a response to anger, you would have a fat forehead like the stereotyped Georgia sheriff because you would develop these muscles just as you do a bicep. If you come from my part of the country, where you never quite close the mouth, you would have a concave look in that area because you would have underdeveloped muscles there. Now take your eyelids. I grew up believing that what you did was that you slept behind them and they closed to keep stuff out and sometimes you winked with one. But it really took a lot of work on my mother's part to get my eyelids organized as those of a good clean decent American male. Don't suppose for a minute that when I was four years old she took hold of me and said, "Ray, honey, you gotta watch your eyelids, honey, 'cause if you're going to grow up and do male kind of things, you gotta do male things with your eyelids. When boy tikes close their lids and open them, they do it fast and all the way, they just don't go and leave them half closed. And, honey, watch your eyeballs, too, else they'll get you into trouble, because boy tikes don't move them while their eyelids are shut. Little girls do that." She did nothing of the sort, but I learned it anyhow. One of the early tasks anyone must learn is to send signals that are appropriate to his sex role. But do not jump too quickly. It's too easy to assume that a female eyelid signal from a man would mean he was sending a signal of homosexuality whereby men try to attract men. Such behavior can also be a useful device to keep females away; or it may very well keep at a distance all females of certain types that one cannot deal with. There are many such communicational devices. One of the things we are studying now is the developmental tasks of learning to be ugly or learning to be beautiful. That is, how do you keep from being selected for the wrong sorts of roles in the culture? How do you send the proper signals as to your appropriateness to be regarded as a success, or as a leader, or as sexually attractive? And one of the ways to keep a man from being regarded as a sexually attractive male, for any of a great variety of temporary or permanent reasons, is to make his face behave like a woman's.

If we continue down the face to the mouth, we find that it, too, contains a range of communicative potential. Did you ever notice that mouths are highly adaptive? They are much more interesting to me than are the eyes. Eyes may very well be less important than mouths in terms of signaling to one another a readiness or an unreadiness for activity. Mouths also display marked regionality. The kind of mouth that comes out of a part of the country that is around Tidewater, Virginia across through central Kentucky and some areas in western Maryland is to me (who has one) kind of luscious. It's full in the integumental aspects in the upper and lower lips but not quite as full as in certain types you see that come out of New York City that give a kind of unweaned look. If you go up around Rochester or Syracuse, New York, you get the lower lip carried over the upper teeth. If you come down to the South, and head up into the hills, the integumental aspect of the upper lip disappears and you just have a lower lip. Or you can go to New England and they both disappear. And, of course, you can come to Philadelphia in the Main Line and the area of the cold teeth appears, because the upper teeth in these mouths seem totally exposed.

Some interesting differences appear when we look at how the head is carried. When we were quadrupeds our spinal column fit right in the back of the cranium and we carried the head below the intersection with the spine. And when we stood up, that hole for the spine began to migrate anteriorly, but it still has not quite reached balance, so it's always work to hold the head up. If you come from certain parts of our society you learn certain styles of carrying your head as part of who you are. You learn to carry the back of your head posterior to the line of your shoulders. This is not, however, the same as the rigid extreme of the "Sunday School superintendent look" where everything falls along a line right straight through to the floor. When you come from other parts of the community, you may carry your shoulders high, concealing your neck. Humans do not have a wide range of longer or shorter necks; all of us have the same number of vertebrae. It's the way we carry our heads that makes much of the difference in appearance. If you grow up in the wrong community and carry your head as though you were an aristocrat, you'll get it knocked off. So you learn to carry it safely tucked away. And if you want to convince the family that they ought to make an intellectual out of you, you do not develop your pectorals and you walk around slightly concaved, which proves you can write poetry. These are all moving parts that we use to inform one another who we are, what we mean, and how we respond to those with whom we are interacting. And we do not limit such communication to the moving parts of the face. All of our moveable and visible organs are available for communicational purposes.

As anthropological linguists or kinesicists or, emergently, as students of communication behavior, our primary task is that of isolating and ordering vocal and other body behavior in a way which will make it possible for us to understand their structural properties. The linguists have understood this and have developed sophisticated systems of analyzing the structural units of vocal behavior. If we are to understand the meanings, attitudes, and feelings communicated through body movements in anything more than an impressionistic sense, we must analyze the structural units of movement and understand the component parts of the kinesic system itself. That is, we must grasp the nature of the building blocks of man's body communicational structure. We also need to know how the kinesic and linguistic systems are related to each other and what the emergent communicational units are. We do not, as yet, know enough about words or gestures or their association to know the shapes or sizes of the communicational units in which they both participate and which make up the meaningful units of social interaction. At present, we have only vaguely conceptualized them.

But we have made a beginning in the study of the structure of body motion and found that it is comparable in ways to spoken language. We have isolated basic kinesic units which seem comparable to the phoneme in linguistics. In describing the basic structural units of speech, we find that many variations in the acoustic sound of a letter, say /l/, can be used interchangeably without altering the communicational results, as when we say "let" or "long." If you feel the position of your tongue in your mouth as you say the /l/ in those two words you can tell that they are giving different sounds, but nobody notices these variations. But when the range of acoustic variation of the initial sound of a word is great enough to include the initial sound of both "let" and "debt," the change in meaning that results shows that we have moved from /l/ to a new phoneme, /d/. Similarly, a group of slightly different body motions which can be used interchangeably in a specific structural context without altering the communicational result is called a unitary kineme. We found in our study of American movers that we could identify 23 different positions of the eyelid but that only four of them altered messages in any way. The remainder were unnoticed, hence trivial, changes, though they could have been noticed (at the perceptual level of observation).

Careful analyses of motion pictures have shown us that middle-class American body motion language contains about 50 to 60 kinemes, 33 of which are located in the head and face. They can be described as follows:

3 head nod kinemes (single, double, and triple nod)
2 lateral head sweep kinemes (single and double sweep)
1 head cock kineme
1 head tilt kineme
3 connective, whole head motion kinemes (head raise and hold, head lower and hold, and current head position hold)
4 eyebrow motion kinemes (lift, lower, knit, and move eyebrows)
4 nose movement kinemes (wrinkle, nostril compression, unilateral nostril flare, and bilateral nostril flare)
7 mouth movement kinemes (compress lips, protrude lips, retract lips, apically withdraw lips, snarl, lax mouth opening, and large mouth opening)
2 chin thrust kinemes (anterior and lateral chin thrust)
1 puffed cheeks kineme
1 sucked cheeks kineme

Other categories of kineme are those of the trunk and shoulders, hand and fingers, hip and leg (including ankle), foot, and neck behaviors.

We have also delineated various tyes of kinemorphs which are formed by the combination of kinemes and which are further analyzable into kinemorph classes that behave like linguistic morphemes and morpheme classes. These, analyzed, abstracted, and combined in the full-body behavioral stream prove to form complex kinemorphs which are analogous to words. Finally, these are combined by syntactic arrangements, still only partially understood, into extended linked behavioral organizations, which have many of the properties of the spoken syntactic sentence. Interestingly enough, body movement systems have dialects, and regional and social-class variations, just as spoken language does. Some of this variation, with regard to typical facial settings, has already been discussed and, again, it applies to the entire body and its patterned action sequences.

To complete the story of the study of human communication, we must say a little about "social kinesics," the study of units and patterns of movement in relation to varying social contexts in order to determine their function in communication. There is one central point to be made here. I do not believe that we are going to be able to weigh the effect of either body motion complexes or words in interaction until we know enough about the matrices or settings of their occurrence to study them meaningfully. As our studies approach the point where we must deal with *social* meaning, we need clear statements regarding the structure of the social contexts of communicational occurrences. It is not enough to know the structure of spoken language and the structure of body language. It is difficult, if not impossible, to answer the question: What does this symbol or that gesture mean? Meaning is not imminent in particular symbols, acts, words, or sentences, but in the behavior elicited by the *presence or absence* of such symbols, acts, words, or sentences in particular sequences and in particular social contexts.

Each society seems to have evolved a coded system of gestures and of words related to each other and related to the other displays that are parts of the communication matrix of its environment. Just as the sound of a letter depends on the phonemic context and the meaning of any word depends on the sentence it is used in, and the context in which it occurs, so no body position or movement, in and of itself, has a precise social meaning. To assume that a woman crossing her legs indicates that she is sexually closing out those around her is just as dangerous as to assume that the word "table" always means a flat surface used for eating. How much is this danger amplified in the assumption that such a gesture has universal cultural meaning. Insofar as I know there are no universally identical communicational contexts. And for this reason there are no universal gestures. As far as we can tell, there is no single facial expression, stance, or body position that invariably conveys the same meaning in all societies. The derivation and comprehension of the social meaning of a body movement rests equally upon comprehension of the code and of the context which selects from the possibilities provided by the code.

REFERENCES

Arnold, T. W. *The Folklore of Capitalism*. New Haven: Yale University Press, 1937.
Bateson, G. (Ed.) *Naven*. London: Cambridge University Press, 1936.

Birdwhistell, R. L. *Kinesics and context: Essays on body motion communication*. Philadelphia: University of Pennsylvania Press, 1970.

Chase, S. *The tyranny of words*. New York: Harcourt, Brace, 1938.

Hayakawa, S. I. *Language in action*. New York: Harcourt, 1951.

James, W. *The principles of psychology*. New York: Holt, 1890.

Korzybski, A. *Science and sanity: An introduction to non-Aristotelian systems and general semantics*. New York: Science Press, 1941.

Mead, G. H. *Mind, self, and society*. London: University of Chicago Press, 1934.

Mead, M. *Continuities in cultural evolution*. (The Terry Lectures) Vol. 34. London: Yale University Press, 1964.

Mencken, H. L. *The American language: An inquiry into the development of English in the United States*. New York: Knopf, 1936.

Ogden, C. K., & Richards, I. A. *The meaning of meaning*. (5th ed.) New York: Harcourt, Brace, 1938.

Sapir, E. A. Speech as a personality trait. In D. G. Mandelbaum (Ed.), *Selected writings of Edward Sapir in language, culture and personality*. Berkeley: University of California Press, 1951.

12
LINGUISTIC CHANGE AS A FORM
OF COMMUNICATION

William Labov
University of Pennsylvania

Among the bewildering array of social facts that are hard to understand, the existence of language differences stands out as one of the hardest. It seems to be an irreducibly brute fact that our instrument of communication is defective: It works well only with the little groups around us, fairly well for the larger social world in which we operate, and not at all when we cross national boundaries and encounter "other" peoples. The long and painful years that we spend in language classes show that this is a disease that cannot easily be cured. Why should this be so? We can imagine many independent origins for human language, which are only slowly now converging to a single means of communication. But historical linguistics has demonstrated that just the reverse seems to be occurring, and that there is no limit to the differentiation of languages from a common core.[1] The Indo-European family shows vast differentiation among its members, from its eastern rim of Bengali dialects to the western edge of Gaelic spoken in the Aran Islands. Thus, we have to face the fact that languages have *become* different, and that in the course of time, they seem to have become less and less efficient means of communication between members of the human race. Here is a form of evolution which seems to be entirely without adaptive value; for language evolves but does

[1]This is the normal consequence of the family-tree model. Historical linguists have long been alert to the virtues of the opposing model in which change spreads in a wavelike fashion from one language to another, after they have become separate branches on the family tree. Such wavelike effects can reduce the amount of divergence, and sometimes lead to remarkable convergence of some languages, as on the Indian subcontinent. But on the whole, the basic operation of historical linguistics is to construct an original pattern out of which very different daughter languages have emerged.

not progress in any important sense.[2] It must originally have evolved from some more primitive forms, but we have not been able to trace its development back that far; what we witness in the historical record, and reconstruct from current day differences, is a continual differentiation without any clear advantage to the users.

We must immediately recognize the existence of multilingual societies where many people acquire many languages apparently with little effort. Switzerland, the Nigerian plateau, and the Vaupes basin of Venezuela can be cited as examples that cover the whole range of social types (Greenberg 1971; Sorenson 1967; Weinreich 1959). Recent studies in these areas have pointed out the extraordinary range of multilingualism and the astonishing facility that uneducated speakers show in learning and using their many languages. But the limiting case in any such society would be one in which children learn two languages just as easily as one and communicate in two as easily as in one.[3] On the other hand, we can locate vast areas of the world where children are now taught second languages in school with great effort and only fair success.

Causes and Effects of Dialect Differences

When we move from language differences to dialect differences, we see the same pattern on a smaller scale. Teachers in America, England, France, and Russia work hard to eliminate or compensate for dialect differences, as a way of helping children to communicate better in the larger social world.

One basic explanation for this unfortunate situation is that communication networks are discontinuous. As people move apart, as rivers or mountains intervene, or as roads or laws break down, languages diverge in the same way that species differentiate when they are isolated. Recent studies of Spielman and his associates (in press) with the Yanomama Indians in Venezuela have demonstrated close quantitative parallels between genetic and linguistic differentiation. Clearly genetic differentiation is the result of barriers to the free intermarriage of various groups; and the parallel linguistic differentiation would seem to be the result of barriers to communication. This is a clear demonstration of a basic pattern long recognized, that discontinuities in the pattern of communication bring about linguistic differentiation (Bloomfield, 1933: 403).

A necessary basis for such differentiation has to be the inherent variability of linguistic systems, just as the basis of genetic differentiation is the variable recombination and mutation of genes. We now know some of the fundamental

[2]For a clear statement of the accepted linguistic position that linguistic evolution means development but not progress, see Greenberg (1959). Hymes (1961) presents an opposing case, showing the extent to which modern world languages have developed a wider range of technical vocabulary, greater complexity of stylistic levels, and a metalanguage for linguistic analysis.

[3]There is a sense in which one can communicate better in two languages than in one, if the one has been overspecialized or limited in the domains in which it can be spoken. It is reported that young Javanese people in Indonesia find it easier to switch to the new language Bahasa Indonesia than to apply the elaborate etiquette of Javanese to new social situations.

mechanisms for genetic variation. There is less agreement on the mechanism of linguistic variation. Why are languages differentiated internally, and what is the source of dialect differences?

The traditional view ascribes dialect differences to two main sources: laziness and ignorance. The more neutral terminology for laziness is "The principle of least effort."[4] It is assumed that human beings articulate language with as little effort as possible, and only the need for clear communication prevents them from eventually slurring all sounds into a neutral vowel [ə]. It is believed that if this tendency is not corrected, uneducated speakers will gradually slur their words more and more until they cannot be understood by anyone but their close associates. Thus dialect differences are seen as products of the same corrupting influence that prevents children from learning their lessons properly, one of the basic forms of human corruption that teachers must be continually on the alert to correct.

The chief stereotypes of uneducated English illustrate this point: *th* and *dh* are not carefully articulated by holding the tongue in an interdental (or more typically predental) position, but are merged with the /t/ and /d/; the final /g/ is carelessly dropped in -*ing* endings; the /y/ glide is sloppily dropped after the consonant in *tune* and *new*, giving "*toon*" and "*noo*."[5] And quantitative sociolinguistic studies have confirmed that the higher in the socioeconomic scale a group of speakers stands, the less they are apt to do these things; and for all groups, the more attention paid to speech, the less they are apt to do them (Labov, 1966, 1972a; Shuy, Wolfram, & Riley, 1966).

But as soon as we look at a few more examples, the principles of ignorance and laziness fail dismally to explain linguistic change. Most of the linguistic changes taking place in the sound systems of British and American English require more effort, not less. Typically, the short, lax *a* in *bad, ask, dance,* or *bat* is lengthened, fronted, diphthongized and raised to $[\epsilon^{<}\!:\!ə, e^{<}\!:\!ə, \iota\!:\!ə]$. This is happening in at least some environments in every American dialect.[6]

The same kind of complication was observed in Swiss French dialects by Gauchat in 1899, who observed that "least effort" could not possibly account for these changes, and parallel changes can be seen in the history of dozens of Romance, Germanic, Balto-Slavic and Finno-Ugric languages (Labov, Yaeger, & Steiner, 1972, pp. 99-104). We sometimes see that vernacular changes produce

[4]For a review of the arguments on this principle, see Jespersen, *Language* (1922, pp. 261ff). Jespersen cites many of the objections to the principle, but concludes that "the instinctive feeling of all linguists is still in favour of the view that a movement towards the easier sound is the rule, and not the exception."

[5]This is of course the stereotypical view. In actual fact there are many dialects which preserve a small phonetic difference between *dew* and *do* without using a y-glide in *dew*, which in fact requires greater precision of articulation.

[6]A detailed account of the raising of short *a* in New York City is given in Labov (1966), and an instrumental study of the process in New York, Buffalo, Detroit, Chicago, and many other cities is provided in Labov et al. (1972).

grammatical simplification, as in the loss of English inflections; but we also see grammatical complication, as in the development of the periphrastic future *he is going to*; the dependent subject of *my brothers they don't know better*; and the development of a new specific indefinite article *this* which differentiates *I met this man downtown* from *He was a doctor*.[7] Nor is dialect differentiation confined to uneducated, lower-class people. It is well-known that some linguistic changes originate in the upper social groups. Many of these represent the importation of forms from high-prestige foreign languages or classical standards.[8] But some new developments seem to be pushed farther and faster among educated speakers, at least until the change becomes noticed and subject to strong social correction. Thus the raising of the open *o* in *long, lost, off, awful* in New York City and Philadelphia seems to be strongest among middle-class speakers (Labov, 1966).

Finally, we may consider another of the underlying assumptions on linguistic change as the product of ignorance and laziness: that it is really characteristic of illiterate societies, and that it is rapidly coming to a halt in modern society under the combined effects of mass communications and education. It is true enough that the traditional site of dialect studies shows such a process. Many of the rural dialects are receding, and younger speakers in farm areas shift more towards the standard language than their parents. But just the opposite situation seems to prevail for the great bulk of the population in our cities; as we will see, language change seems to be going on at a great rate in all the major cities we have studied.

The upshot of our present findings is that the clear and simple accounting of linguistic change as the product of laziness, ignorance, and isolation has broken down. And once we abandon the traditional view, linguistic change appears as increasingly mysterious and unproductive, the result of forces we do not understand. This paper will attack one facet of the problem, by challenging the notion that linguistic change and dialect differences are always barriers to communication. In many cases, linguistic change may promote communication rather than impede it.

Two Ways of Thinking about Linguistic Communities

There is no clear agreement about the boundaries of speech communities or just what a speech community is. The traditional approach is to take an individual as representative of a homogeneous group of speakers who produce and interpret the

[7]This *this* is a colloquial development in modern English which resolves the ambiguity of the indefinite article *a*. When we say *He went out with a girl*, the article *a* is indefinite: The listener usually does not know who we are talking about. But it may either be a specific girl that we know or some unknown girl that we do not know. *He went out with this girl* resolves the ambiguity and clearly refers to the specific case.

[8]In a study of linguistic change on the Indian subcontinent, Bright and Ramanujan (1964) point out that the upper-class Brahmin group innovates in the more conscious types of change but the lower castes do not. In Tulu, for example, they find that the Brahmins show semantic shifts, lexical borrowing, and phonological borrowing. The non-Brahmin dialects tend to innovate only in the "less conscious processes of phonological and morphological change involving native materials."

language in the same way. This abstraction has been defended explicitly in recent years, but it has long been assumed that any language differences in the population can only be the result of a mixture of several such ideal communities. For those who want to limit their study of language to the evidence given by one or two individuals, it is quite important to postulate such a homogeneous object; for otherwise, there would be no way to say what any particular bit of extracted evidence represents.

A different view has been forced on those who have entered into direct contact with the speech community, and studied the speech of many individuals interacting with one another. No sign of a homogeneous community has appeared; whenever this object is pursued, it vanishes. In 1899, Louis Gauchat (1905) began the study of Charmey, a small isolated village in the mountains of French-speaking Switzerland, as likely an example of an unmixed speech community as one could hope to find. But Gauchat concluded, ''The unity of Charmey is null.'' An intricate pattern of fluctuating variants appeared in which men and women of different ages spoke in very different ways. Since that time, every other accountable study of real speech communities has found systematic differentiation by style, social context, and social identity of the user, that is, his sex, age, socioeconomic class, and ethnicity.

What then would make a speech community one, rather than two, five or a hundred communities? The question is similar to one that linguists have faced in regard to sounds, morphemes, etc.; that is, when are two physically different sounds responded to as ''the same'' sound? The normal procedure is to show that the differences between them are linguistically insignificant, perhaps not even perceived by the speakers. But variation in the community structure is often quite significant, and it is impossible to disregard it in any reasonable approach. The conclusion of many sociolinguistic studies is that variation within the community is normal; and that it is used by speakers in many systematic and subtle ways to accomplish their social and linguistic needs (Weinreich, Labov, & Herzog, 1968). The present study begins with this finding: that orderly, heterogeneous behavior is normal within the speech community. From this standpoint, we will address the question posed on the evaluation of linguistic change: Can we conceive of any way in which linguistic change fits into the communicative economy of the speech community, or is it basically a disruptive and degenerative process? The title of this paper makes it clear that a positive direction will be pursued. We will consider a wide variety of linguistic changes to document the case.

SOUND CHANGE

The traditional view of linguistic change is that it is disruptive, and that the primary disruptive force is the mysterious and little-understood process of sound change. Conditioned sound changes are said to destroy the regularity of grammatical paradigms, and even wipe out the grammatical mechanism itself, while analogical re-formation builds up that mechanism again. Conditioned sound change also disrupts the system by creating great differences between the stem form of words and the derived forms, yielding such well-known alternations as *wise* /wayz/ vs. *wisdom* /wizdəm/ or *grave* /greyv/ vs. *gravity* /gravitiy/. Such alternations are responsible for the considerable complexity of English spelling, which is based on the morphemic principle that roots which mean the same should be spelled the same, but which produces a sound-to-spelling relation that is quite indirect or irregular and unpredictable in many cases. [9] This situation is largely the result of the Great Vowel Shift, which rotated English vowels in the sixteenth and seventeenth centuries. The mechanism of this process is still largely debated: how it proceeded, whether it was a gradual shift or a sudden one, and what were the causes that brought it about (Labov et al., 1972, p. 198).

Let us consider only the front half of the shift as it affected the vowels of Middle English ā in *sane* and āy in *say*, ē in *meet* and *see*, and ī in *bite* and *sigh*. The weight of the historical evidence leads us to reconstruct a phonetic progression such as:

	15th century	17th century	19th century
sigh	si:	sey	say
see	se:	si:	siy
say	s æ y	sey	sey
sane	s æ :n	se:n	seyn

Some think that the change was a discrete one, the result of a sudden reversal in the positions of *see* and *sigh*, for example. A father might then say "Can you see why I sigh" while a son might answer "Can you sigh why I see?" The situation would be even more confusing when we add *say* to the picture. When *sigh* became diphthongized to /siy/ and descended to /sey/, with a midfront nucleus, it must have coincided with *say*. If the father ever got the *sigh* and *see* situation straightened out, he would still find it impossible to tell whether his son was saying "I didn't sigh" or "I didn't say." The notion of a sudden reversal produces a chaotic picture, but the situation would not be much better with gradual movement. We still cannot say how a merger of *sigh* and *say* would be avoided in the seventeenth century, though as a matter of cold fact, the two word classes showed no evidence of affecting each other and went their separate ways. One remaining possibility was suggested by Chomsky and Halle (1968, p. 256): that vowels really do not count for very much after all, and perhaps people paid very little attention to their vowels in the seventeenth century.

A more rational view can be obtained by studying the current sound changes in our major cities which replicate quite closely the processes that operated several

---

[9]Developments among the high back vowels are particularly difficult to regularize in the aftermath of the vowel shift. Thus most Middle English ū descended to /aw/, except before labials and velars, and we have *Houston Street* in New York City as [haostın] but *Houston, Texas* as [hjustın]; the name *Cowper* is rightly said [kupər] but more often pronounced [kaopər], and so on.

hundred years ago. It appears that the Great Vowel Shift is a part of a long-standing trend which has rotated English vowels for several millennia; this process is in turn governed by two general principles of chain shifting (Labov et al., 1972, p. 106):

1. In chain shifts, long vowels rise.
2. In chain shifts, the lax nuclei of upgliding diphthongs fall.

We find remarkable parallels to the Great Vowel Shift occurring in a wide variety of dialects. Southern England, London, Norwich, Birmingham, and Southampton show us /iy/ falling to /ey/, /ey/ falling to /ay/. It also appears in the English of Australia and New Zealand (Burgess, 1969). In the United States, the same process can be seen operating in the Outer Banks of North Carolina, Atlanta, and central Texas. At the same time that these diphthongs fall, other tense vowels rise by Principle I. In some cases, the old short /i/ and /e/ become long or tense ingliding vowels. In almost every case, the short /a/ becomes tense and ingliding, at least in some environments. Furthermore, the nucleus of /aw/ becomes a tense [æ:] and begins to rise. We therefore have two sets of vowels, one rising by Principle I, the other falling by Principle II, quite parallel to the situation in the Great Vowel Shift.

Our spectrographic studies of these vowel shifts reveal a much more rational and regular view of linguistic change than the confusing and incoherent picture that results from that abstract manipulation of the Great Vowel Shift. Figures 1, 2, and 3 show the new vowel shift in progress in the sound system of three young males: Bob Frost, 31, of Southall to the west of London; Tony Tassie, 16, of Norwich in East Anglis; and Monnie O'Neill, 31, of Wanchese on the Outer Banks of North Carolina[10]. These figures show that there are two distinct tracks for the front (and back) vowels. The /iy/ and /ey/ phonemes are plainly descending along an inner, less peripheral track, while the tensed / æ / vowels and other (originally) short vowels are taking up more peripheral positions. In the chain shifts displayed here, tense vowels rise along the peripheral track and fall along the less peripheral track, descending in some cases to become the lowest vowels in the system.

If the Great Vowel Shift of the seventeenth century followed the same pattern, and we have every reason to believe it did, then the problems raised in this discussion are resolved. When *sigh* fell to /sey/, for example, it was differentiated

---

[10]The displays of the vowel system shown here are from spectrographic measurements of the first and second formants. These are bundles of harmonics which are selectively reinforced as the tongue forms various vowels, altering the shape of the mouth cavity. The first formant is the vertical axis: higher first formant corresponds roughly to phonetically lower vowels with more open tongue and jaw positions. The second formant is shown on the horizontal axis: higher second formants correspond to phonetically fronter vowels, with the high point of the tongue closer to the palate. Though phoneticians often write as if they perceived tongue position, their transcriptions probably correspond more closely to the perception of formant position. The acoustic record is about as accurate as the ear in the perception of height, the first formant, but much more so for the second.

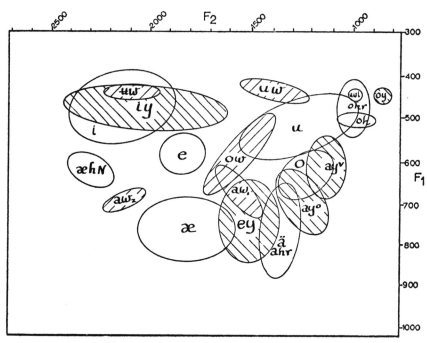

FIG. 12.1.   Bob Frost, 31, Southall, London.

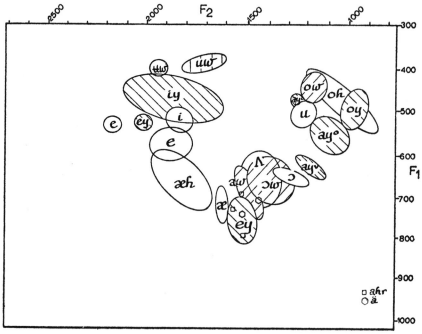

FIG. 12.2.   Tony Tassie, 16, Norwich.

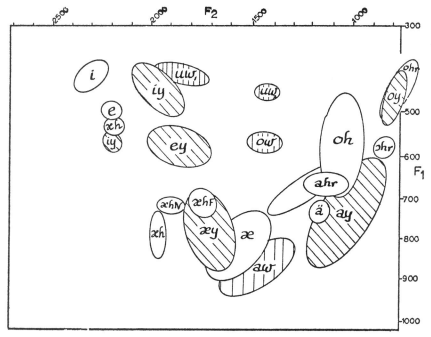

FIG. 12.3.   Monnie O'Neill, 31, Wanchese, North Carolina.

from *see* in more ways than one; as an upgliding diphthong versus a monophthong; and as a less peripheral vowel vs. a peripheral one. In the same way, the middiphthong /sēy/ which represented *sigh*, need never have been confused with the /sĕy/ that represented *say*. The first had a nonperipheral (lax) nucleus while the second had a peripheral (tense) nucleus.

Do we understand other dialects? The question naturally arises as to whether these dramatic differences in vowel systems are barriers to communication. Given the fact that London, Norwich, and Texas /ey/ is roughly in the position of New York, Detroit, and Chicago /ay/, how is it possible that one man's *pay* is not another man's *pie*? Strangely enough, speakers from one dialect area seem to understand speakers from the other tolerably well. It seems that the support of other meaningful elements in the context is normally great enough that no rotation of vowels or consonants, no matter how extreme, can lead to unintelligibility by itself. When we examine closely the reactions of Americans to tape recordings of rapid London speech, or Northerners to Texas speech, it seems that inability to understand almost always revolves around unfamiliar idioms, proper names, and unknown words from another lexicon. Thus, in a tape from Battersea Park, London, a boy talks about the game of "chaining": Americans almost always hear it as "China." A woman from Millwall speaks of the axe murderers known as the "Creigh twins"; Americans hear "cry twins." In Chicago, a 17-year-old boy named Tony introduced me to his friend [ǰ æ n]; it took me a few minutes to realize that this was not his girl friend, but a boy named *John*, since Chicago short *o* has rotated to the point of short *a* in other dialects.

The fact that context can give enough support to prevent confusion should not prevent us from seeing that the normal function of the phonemes involved is seriously impaired or even obliterated. A phoneme of English is defined by its capacity to distinguish words when it is the *only* difference between them, as in *John* vs. *Jan*. And it is not only proper names that can be confused. Ordinary nouns and verbs can also be confounded if the context does not make them entirely predictable. Here is Tony from Chicago, 17 years old, trying to tell me what happened to his friend Marty:

Tony: Well Marty, he went in the $\left[\text{l} \, \text{æ} \, \text{ks} \right]$
. . . and he got stuck in there, and they had to tow him out. $\left[\text{General laughter} \right]$
W. L. What do you mean . . . in the where?
Tony: In the $\left[\text{l} \, \text{æ}^{>} \text{ks} \right]$, you know, the $\left[\text{l} \, \text{æ}^{>} \text{ks} \right]$.
W. L. Whassat?
Floyd: For a boat, you know.

Even though I knew in general that Chicago short _o_ had shifted to something close to $\left[\text{æ} \right]$, it was a different matter to realize in the middle of a conversation that $\left[\text{l} \, \text{æ} \, \text{ks} \right]$ was not "lax" but "locks."

It is hard to say how much of a functional load a given vowel must carry in ordinary speech and how easily that load can be suspended. But we must conclude that the sound changes involved are not supported by any communicative function; and in so far as speakers of other dialects have to communicate with each other, these radical rotations of the vowel system run counter to the communicative function of language.

The relation of dialect differences to lines of communication. We have already referred to the well-accepted notion that linguistic differences are the results of discontinuities in the lines of communication, and pointed to some new evidence in the connection between genetic and linguistic divergence. It may seem quite natural then that dialect differences should interfere with communication, if they result from the lack of it. Tools grow rusty if they are not used. To see how much force there is in this reasoning, it is necessary to ask what empirical evidence can be obtained on actual patterns of communication. To what extent do people from one dialect area hear speakers from another? There is some contact on the mass media and some long-distance telephoning, but the most effective kind of communication is face-to-face communication, and this necessarily depends on speakers traveling across dialect lines.[11] If we could measure the number of persons who travel across dialect boundaries every day, we would have a fair estimate of the amount of contact between speakers of the two different dialects; and conversely,

---

[11]The emphasis here is on face-to-face communication rather than the mass media, since there is considerable indirect evidence to show that speakers are influenced much more by the former than the latter, at least as far as effects on their speech are concerned.

TABLE 1

Volume of Intercity Passenger Traffic in the United States, 1953

	Passenger-Miles	Percentage
Railways	34.7	7.2
Highways:		
carriers	21.1	4.4
private	410.3	85.5
Inland waterways	1.4	.3
Airways	12.6	2.6

some idea as to whether the boundary is actually determined by discontinuities in the pattern of communication.

One measure of the amount of travel across such boundaries is the number of primary highways that cross it.[12] The relative importance of highways in the United States appears quite clearly in Table 1: Highways account for 90% of intercity passenger traffic. The primary highways are distinguished from secondary roads on all road maps, and a more sensitive measure of relation to traffic flow is obtained by counting the number of primary highways that cross the line rather than the total number of roads.[13] This measure was applied to all of the major dialect isoglosses (i.e., boundary lines between dialect regions) of the eastern United States displayed in Fig. 4. It appears that most, but not all such boundaries, fall in troughs in the highway network. They are crossed by fewer highways than any parallel boundaries that might be drawn across the territory. Figure 5 shows the results of such a calculation applied to the important dialect boundary that crosses Pennsylvania, separating the northern tier counties from the rest of the state. The *Word Geography of the Eastern United States* (Kurath, 1949) shows that this is one of the most concentrated bundles of lexical isoglosses that we can find, separating the Northern from the Midland dialect area. Kurath and McDavid (1961) showed that it also included a number of phonological boundaries. North of this line, speakers distinguished *hoarse* and *horse* as /ohr/ and /ɔhr/; south of it they did not. North of this line, speakers distinguished *which* and *witch*; south of it they did not.

Figure 5 shows the Highway Index for this boundary; it is 360 miles long and is crossed by eight primary highways, or 2.2 crossings per hundred miles. If we make east-west transits across the state at 30-mile intervals, making only local deviations of ± 10 miles to avoid crossing highways unnecessarily, we get indices of 2.6, 2.1, 2.6, 2.5, 3.1, 3.3, and 2.3 going from north to south.

[12]The following material is based on an unpublished study of the relation of dialect boundaries to lines of communication in the eastern United States (Labov, 1962).

[13]A primary highway is one marked in red or green on most maps and distinguished from "secondary" roads. The distinction is based on traffic flow maps; see below for the utilization of this original data.

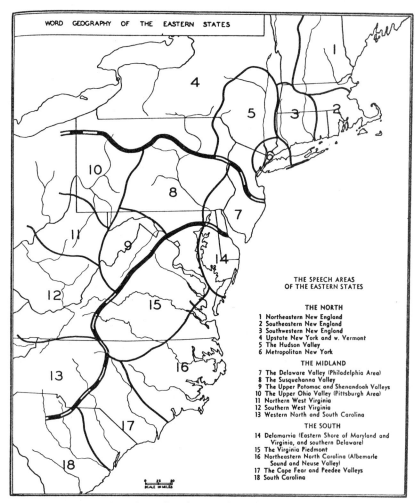

FIG. 12.4.   Speech areas of the eastern states.

On Fig. 4 we also see the traffic index for the actual isogloss which separates the North from the Midland: It falls at a low point in the profile. Because the isogloss is not exactly a horizontal line from west to east, it ranges over about 45 miles of our horizontal axis and appears as a line rather than a point on Fig. 4.

The division between primary and secondary highways is based upon traffic flow maps compiled by the state highway departments.[14] A more accurate index of the relation of these boundaries to lines of communication can be derived from the traffic flow maps themselves, which allow us to compute the average daily traffic

[14]For this information, I am indebted to P. Eckerson of General Drafting Corp., of Newark, New Jersey, who makes maps for *Esso*.

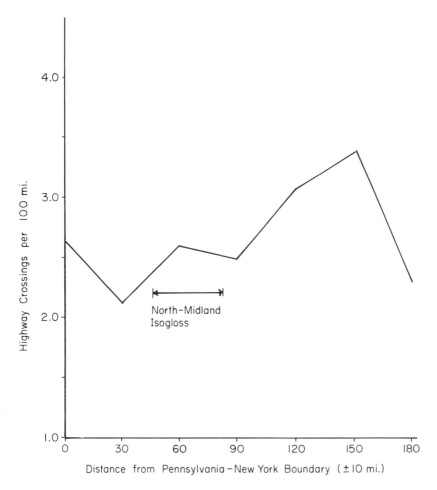

FIG. 12.5   Highway indices for seven east-west transits of Pennsylvania compared to the North-Midland boundary.

flow [ADT] across each dialect boundary. While the figures we have are based on traffic flow one or two decades after the dialect survey was made, they apparently preserve the pattern quite well. Figure 6 shows the Index of Traffic Density for seven east-west transits across Pennsylvania, and again we see that the actual dialect boundary falls in a trough, along with the lowest of the horizontal transits we would make without regard to traffic flow. This situation is repeated for most of the major isoglosses shown in Fig. 4. Figure 7 shows the placement of two dialect boundaries that divide Pennsylvania from north to south: a bundle of lexical isoglosses, and the phonological boundary that separates the merger of *hock* and *hawk*, as / ɒ / in the west from the two-phoneme area of the east. Both of these fall

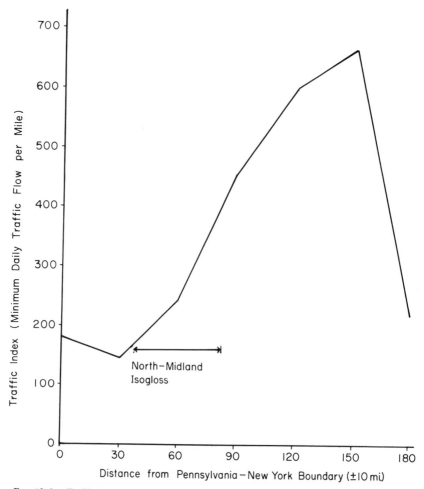

Fɪɢ. 12.6.   Traffic indices for seven east-west transits of Pennsylvania compared to the North-Midland boundary.

in the central trough of Traffic Indices; the phonological index seems to be spreading eastward, as we would predict from general principles.[15]

So far, we have given strong support to the notion that dialect differences are the result of isolation and the lack of communication. But as we continue our investigation of traffic indices, it appears that some of the most important dialect boundaries are radically different from those we have examined above. In central North Carolina, the boundaries that surround the upper and lower South pass through regions of high traffic density. And even more striking is the boundary

[15]When a region which has merged two phonemes is in contact with one which makes the distinction, the merger tends to spread at the expense of the distinction (Herzog, 1965, 211ff).

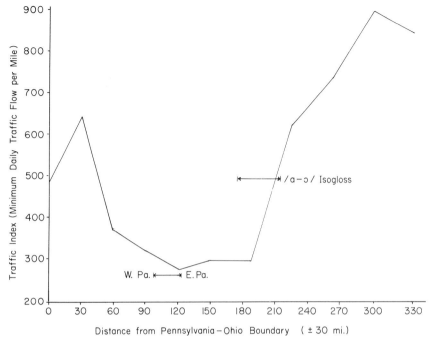

FIG. 12.7.   Traffic indices for north-south transits of Pennsylvania.

that surrounds the New York City dialect area. On Fig. 4, this appears as a small semicircle around the city, of a radius less than 50 miles. It passes through regions of very high traffic density, and by both measures, lies in an area of maximum communication. Table 2 compares a wide variety of dialect boundaries for their Highway and Traffic Indices. New York City stands out from the rest with an index of 9,000, seven times as great as the boundaries that pass by New Haven and surround Washington, and over 50 times as great as the Pennsylvania isoglosses we have been considering. In 1959, 718,000 people crossed the New York City boundary on highways every day, without considering train and bus traffic.[16]

The New York City isogloss is therefore a radically different type from the broader regional boundaries. It surrounds a compact speech community, almost the prototype of a concentrated metropolis. The boundary that constricts the New York City speech community has remained reasonably stable for a century and a half; while Boston, Charleston, and Richmond have expanded, New York speech remains confined to the suburbs of the city. During that long history, the New York City vernacular has enjoyed very low prestige, and many characteristic features of the dialect are heavily stigmatized. As a result, one would expect that the dialect is receding among younger speakers, and given the heavy contact with

[16]In this case, the relative proportion of highway transportation is probably much less than that shown in Table 1, and the exceptional character of New York City is understated.

TABLE 2

Relation of Dialect Boundaries in Eastern United States
to Primary Highways and Traffic Flow Patterns

Region	Linguistic feature	Length [miles]	Highway index[a]	Traffic index[b]
Vermont	Lexical, /r/, /Er/	180	2.0	77
Conn.	Lex	51	9.2	715
NYC	/r/	80	41.8	9000
Hudson Valley	Lex,/Or/,Er/ /WH/	273	5.3	300
Genessee Valley	/Er/	273	0.4	214
PA, E–W	Lex,/Or/,/WH/	361	2.2	164
PA, N–S	Lex,/WH/	119	4.2	285
	/ɔ/	130	4.6	448
PA-MD	/Ur/	268	3.3	326
VA	Lex,/r/,Er/, /AYr/	215	2.3	182

[a]Number of primary highways crossing per hundred miles.

[b]Average daily traffic crossing per mile.

the surrounding community, it would naturally follow that continued linguistic differentiation would come to an end.

To fully evaluate the force of such social pressures, we can turn to the study of the subjective evaluation of language and examine New Yorkers' reactions to their own dialect.

THE SUBJECTIVE EVALUATION OF LANGUAGE

The normal practice of linguists is to elicit a speaker's "competence" under formal conditions where language itself is the object under study. When we do so, we are dealing indirectly with the speaker's evaluation norms: what he considers "good," "proper," and "correct." The linguist will himself reject any overt expression of such ideas as nothing but "secondary reactions to language." But when he uses linguistic data produced under such formal conditions, the data are screened through such attitudes. Most native speakers do not know, or will not admit, how strong their attitudes towards language are. In our recent work in Philadelphia, we found people who consistently deny that they use the historical present, or the *got* form of the passive, when they have just proved otherwise in their own speech; and they still deny that they would ever bother to try to change their speech. Direct discussions of language elicit a small number of stereotypes, which are often weakly related to linguistic reality, or else firm denials that the person cares one way or the other about how people speak.

Because attitudes towards language tend to change rapidly when we ask people to think directly about them, it is necessary to transform them into judgments about personalities or social traits of individuals. This is done effectively in the "matched guise" technique developed by Wallace Lambert and his associates at McGill (Lambert, 1971, Ch. 8, p. 13). A subject hears a series of extracts from different speakers, usually reading the same passage; in this series, a bilingual or bidialectal speaker may be represented twice, using two different forms of language. The subject is asked to rate the speaker on a scale of personality traits, or on social characteristics such as the highest job he could hold. The subject is never aware that he is rating the same person, and his judgments of the same speaker are effectively independent; the differences in his judgments for two different linguistic guises of the same speaker show how the use of a given language or dialect influences his view of people.

Lambert's results show that attitudes towards language are extraordinarily uniform. Speakers of a stigmatized language or dialect typically agree with the community as a whole that those who speak in this way are likely to be less intelligent, less dependable, less honest, shorter, but possibly more religious or humorous. This pattern appears in studies of Continental French vs. Canadian French, of standard vs. nonstandard Canadian French, and many other bilingual and bidialectal situations. In New York City, our subjective reaction tests were aimed at isolating the evaluation of particular linguistic features, such as the pronunciation of final (r) or the raising of short *a* (Labov, 1966, Ch. XI). Subjects rated the speakers on a scale of job suitability and showed an extraordinary sensitivity to the sociolinguistic variables of New York City. New Yorkers of all classes agreed by rating speakers higher when they pronounced final $[r]$, and the fricative forms of *th-* and *dh-*, and corrected (æh) in *bad, ask, dance* to $[æ:]$ and (oh) in *law, chocolate, off* to $[ɔ:]$, and by penalizing speakers when they used the advanced higher forms of (æh) and (oh) in these words.

Most importantly, we find that the speakers who do use advanced forms such as $[i:ə]$ in *bad* and *man* are quicker to stigmatize speakers than those who use moderate forms. The pattern repeats for many variables. Table 3 shows the responses of speakers of various social classes to the (oh) variable in *lost, off,*

TABLE 3

Percentages of (oh)-Negative Response by Class

Socioeconomic class								
0	1	2	3	4	5	6	7–8	9
37	20	13	59	56	80	100	73	58

Note. From Labov, 1966.

awful, etc. [17] The lower middle class uses the highest values for this variable, and also shows the greatest tendency to downgrade speakers for their use of it.

New Yorkers also show extraordinary agreement in their general attitude towards New York City speech, at least as expressed in the interview situation. An overwhelming majority would not take it as a compliment if someone said they sound like a New Yorker, and many of the feelings about the city's speech are violent in the extreme. One head of a small advertising agency swore that he would never hire someone who said $[\text{lʊ}^\text{ə}\text{st}]$ for *lost*, though that was very close to the vowel he used himself.

The uniformity of subjective norms provides us with one answer for the question raised in Section 1: What is a speech community? Granted that New Yorkers talk in many different ways, they are also very similar. They share a common set of norms in regard to language, so that they all show the same direction of style shifting away from the vernacular in formal speech; and they show a common set of reactions towards the vernacular used by others.

In one respect, New Yorkers do not agree about subjective norms. There has been a change in the prestige pattern. The older prestige pattern was a borrowed one, based on English or New England pronunciation, where all final and preconsonantal /r/ is vocalized. After World War II, the prestige norm shifted rapidly to "general American," *r*-pronouncing netword English. We find that New Yorkers over 40 have no clear reaction to (r) in the subjective evaluation tests, but all those under 40 agree in rating a speaker higher when all occurrences of this (r) variable are consonantal $[\text{r}]$.

The only point on which New Yorkers seriously differ, then, is on which borrowed pattern should replace the New York City vernacular. The negative prestige of the New York City dialect is attested to in many ways. This low prestige is a social fact that cannot be altered by an individual declaring that he prefers the vernacular. Both New Yorkers and those outside the city agree in rejecting the dialect unless they give an ideological response. The stereotype of working-class New York City speech, under the name of "Brooklynese," is known and ridiculed by Americans everywhere. One element of that stereotype is the palatal upglide $[\text{əɪ}]$ heard in *bird* and *thirty-third*. It has been stigmatized as *boid* and *toidy-toid*, and effectively wiped out of the dialect: We rarely hear it in younger speakers, except in joking. Given the intimate contact of New Yorkers with the surrounding dialects, and the heavy pressure against the New York City vernacular, we might confidently expect that the other features of the dialect would begin to wither away as well. But nothing could be farther from the case. The New York City dialect is moving further along its evolutionary path with undiminished vigor; and this is true for any number of metropolitan dialects which are the subject of equally rigorous social criticism.

---

[17]The socioeconomic scale used here is an equally weighted index of occupation, education, and income, in which 0 is the lowest and 9 is the highest rating. Details are given in Labov (1966). Groups 0-2 correspond roughly to "lower class," 3-5 to "working class," 6-8 to "lower-middle class," and 9 to "upper-middle class."

THE VITALITY OF THE VERNACULAR

The general impression of most scholars is that local dialects are decaying and that regional and standard dialects are spreading at their expense: that we are entering a period of linguistic convergence after many millennia of divergence. This impression is based largely on the state of rural dialects, which are the only kinds that are generally studied by traditional dialectologists.[18] But when we enter the centers of our large cities, where most of the population lives in America and England, we find that linguistic change is going forward at a great rate: The local vernacular is thriving. In London, Birmingham, Glasgow, Edinburgh, Newcastle, Leeds, Southampton, Boston, Philadelphia, Detroit, and Chicago, the local vernacular has no shortage of young speakers, and it is showing the vigorous kind of internal evolution that carries it further and further away from dialects spoken by the highly educated, upper-class groups in the same city.

We then have many examples of continued linguistic divergence with no discontinuities in communication. Upper-class groups in these cities are quite familiar with the local dialects, and the mass media give all the contact with the standard dialect that one could ask for.

Let us consider the New York City dialect again. It is true that one of its features has been effectively stigmatized. The raising of the short *a* has also become a social stereotype: Most working-class New Yorkers are very conscious of it; in word lists, they frequently and irregularly correct it to a low front $[æ:]$. But the progressive raising of the vernacular vowel goes on, in spite of this social stigma. Figures 8, 9, and 10 show three stages in this evolution. In the oldest speaker, Chris Andersen, we can see that there is only one /æ/ phoneme, with some variants a little higher than others. The second stage can be seen in the speech of a woman of about the same age, since in general women are almost a whole generation ahead of men in this sound change. Here there is a clear split between some of the members of the /æ/ phoneme which are left behind in low position (*bat, pack, bang*) while others have been raised halfway up the vowel pattern. These form the (æh) variable: conditioned allophones with short *a* before nasals (*ham, man*), before voiced stops (*bad, bag*), before voiceless fricatives (*half, pass*). Most of these have reached the level of the mid vowels /ey/ and /ehr/. Figure 10 shows the most recent stage, in the speech of a 31-year-old working-class woman of Italian background. Here the (æh) variable has risen to high position, along with the phoneme /ehr/, so that *bad, beard,* and *bared* are all homonyms.

A glance at the right-hand side of Figs. 8, 9, and 10 will show a parallel development in the (oh) variable: the height of the vowel in *coffee, office, lost, awful,* etc. It begins as a low vowel, parallel to /æ/, rises to midposition, and in Fig. 10 shares with /uw/ the high back position. No more extreme raising of two

---

[18]Even the rural dialects may show much more life than the usual stereotype allows. It is common enough to read that "This is the last generation in which we can observe this dialect . . . ." but it is said so often that we are entitled to a certain scepticism.

vowels could be arranged. In addition, the New York City system shifts /oy/ to the same high back position, rotates /aw/ to the front, /ay/ and /ah/ to the back. It is only the oldest and most developed of these shifts which rises to social awareness; and even if speakers try to correct these, they continue to follow the more recent aspects of the change. Thus some middle-class New Yorkers try to correct the high vowel of (oh) in *office*, but no one tries to correct the same high vowel which has followed along in the nucleus of *boy*.

At the same time, it cannot be forgotten that there exists a cultivated, middle-class group whose children attend private school and do not learn the vernacular. There is an even larger group of middle-class speakers who attend public school, but go on to college and achieve a fairly strong command of the prestige dialect. The language of these upper groups becomes increasingly remote from that of ordinary people as the vernacular evolves.

We cannot then escape the inevitable question: Why? Every subjective reaction test shows that most ordinary people do think highly of the prestige dialect, and look down on their own vernacular. They hear the prestige dialect every day, but their dialect continues to become more and more different from it.

Possible explanations of the New York City vowel shift. We have already considered the possibility of an explanation from laziness and the principle of least effort, and suggested that it does not apply in the case we are considering here.

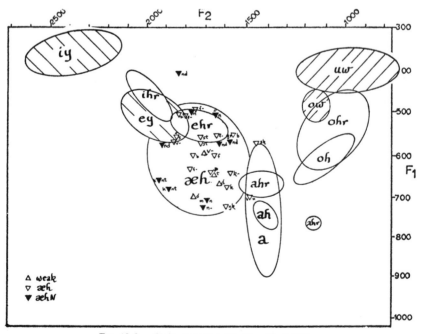

Fig. 12.8.   Chris Andersen, 73, New York City.

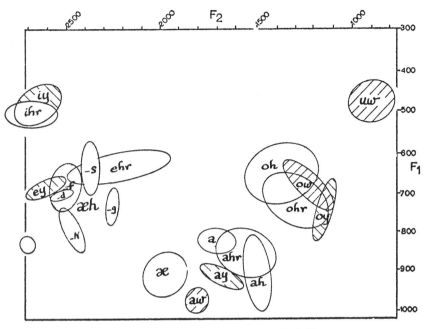

FIG. 12.9.   Margaret Morgan, 71, New York City.

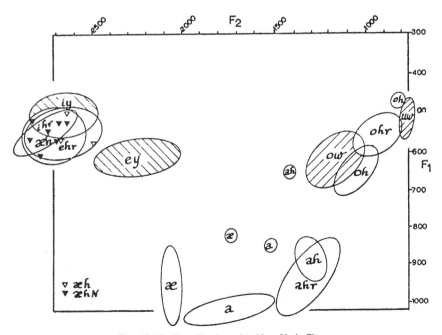

FIG. 12.10. Rose Bendato, 31, New York City.

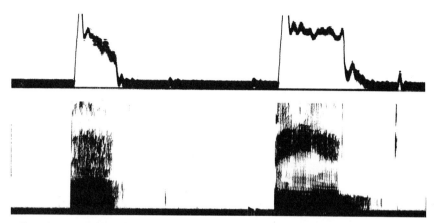

FIG. 12.11. Broad band spectrogram and amplitude display of *bat* and *bad* as spoken by R. Calissi, 42, New York City.

Figure 11 shows a spectrograph of two words, *bat* and *bad*, as pronounced in a word list by a 37-year-old New York woman. As we would expect, the vowel of *bad* is longer; the positions of the dark bands (formants) which mark vowel color are very different; but most importantly, the total amplitude displayed above shows how much more energy there is in the word *bad*, and how the energy level of this tense vowel is sustained throughout.

Does the change have any referential function? Does it increase the ability of New Yorkers to distinguish words? It does provide listeners with a clearer distinction between the auxiliary *can* and the verb *can*, and the article *an* and the name *Ann*, though these are very rarely in contrast. The only really useful distinction that the change provides is the increased contrast of *can* and *can't*, and as we have seen, this is easily overridden in neighboring dialects. As the change progresses, it also wipes out one or two useful distinctions with some painful consequences. For many New York children, the name *Ian* is hard to distinguish from *Ann*; we have a report of a family that was sharply criticized by the neighborhood children for giving their son a girl's name, $[$i:ən$]$.[19]

We have therefore considered a number of possible explanations for the continued raising of short *a* and been forced to reject them all.

1. There is no lack of communication with other dialects.
2. There is no advantage for the new form in distinguishing one word from another.
3. There is no prestige model on which the change is based; on the contrary, it is stigmatized.

[19]Another family in Philadelphia has a mother named *Ann* and a son named *Ian*. In telephone conversations with relatives in Massachusetts, they cannot tell whether someone up there is asking about *Ann* or *Ian*. The raising of /æh/ before nasals has also reached a high point in eastern Massachusetts.

4. The new form does not take less effort and is not easier to pronounce.

What then is the explanation? In searching for other motivating factors, we may want to look briefly at some semantic and grammatical changes, where the communicative pattern is somewhat clearer and even more paradoxical.

SOME REVERSALS OF POLARITY IN ENGLISH GRAMMAR

In general, grammatical change in progress is hard to find. The history of all languages indicates that grammatical change must be just as frequent as sound change, yet for various reasons it is usually not noticed until the change is fairly well completed. What we then see is the spread or diffusion of the pattern from one region to another.

We have recently begun to examine how speakers of other dialects react to these regional grammatical forms. The reader may want to address himself to two questions from our inquiry into syntactic dialects, Q-SCOM-III: (1) Somebody said, *I like liver* and then somebody else said, *So don't I*. What do you think he meant?

I do too _____
I don't _____
Other _____

(2) Someone said, *John smokes anymore*. Do you get the idea that
John hasn't been able to kick the habit _____
or John has quit _____
or John wasn't smoking for a while but now he is _____

One or the other of these forms will be strange to the reader. But both are regularly used by speakers in some region of the United States: the first in eastern New England, the second in the vast Midland area, from Philadelphia west (see Fig. 4). The question is how far general competence in English grammar will allow one to interpret and assimilate these forms and the rules that produced them. Some linguists have proposed that all regional variants can be fitted into an overall, pandialectal grammar of English (Bailey, 1972). We could find evidence for such a grammar if speakers of other dialects could quickly and accurately assimilate the alien rules once they were exposed to them. This might progressively involve the ability to recognize the forms as English; to evaluate their social status (nonstandard, or just regional); to interpret their meaning in context; to label the meaning out of context; to predict extensions of the rule into other environments; and finally, to use the form productively oneself. The entire inquiry gives us insight into the amount of information that is conveyed by these forms across dialect boundaries, or conversely, the ways in which they might form barriers to communication (Labov, 1972b).

Among the various kinds of grammatical change that we have studied, a surprising number concern reversals of polarity (i.e., positive-negative opposition), where on the surface at least, negative comes to mean positive or positive negative. It seems very unlikely that this is a change in the meanings of the expressions—that people who used to mean "yes" now mean "no." These are changes in the surface expression of meanings. The only issue is whether reversals in the surface are obstacles to communication: whether they lead others to think that these speakers mean "no" when in fact they meant "yes."

We are all familiar with the oscillation between "I couldn't care less" and "I could care less," and the fact that they mean the same thing. But it takes quite a bit of thought to figure out which of these is the original form, consistent with the ordinary meanings of *less* and *not*. We pose a similar problem to the subjects of our experimental design when we ask them Questions (1) and (2) above.

Does *So don't I* mean that the speaker does or does not like liver? The results for 139 subjects from Philadelphia, Kansas, and Utah point in the negative direction; 61% interpreted *So don't I* as "I do not." But the right answer is *positive*: As noted above, this form is used only in eastern New England, where it is quite general in the vernacular. Of 24 native New England subjects, all responded "positive"; none thought it meant that the speaker did not like liver, or were in any doubt about it.

When I first encountered *So don't I*, on Martha's Vineyard, I thought it was a comical expression invented by high school students. But it quickly appeared it had become a very general joke: When I talked to a high school class about dialect geography, the teacher signaled desperately from the back of the room not to discuss *So don't I*, which he had been unsuccessfully trying to eradicate. I heard reports from other New England areas, and recorded its use in Brunswick, Maine, but not until we began to carry out systematic testing with Q-SCOM-III, could we assert that this construction was an integral part of the vernacular. Twenty-one of the 24 native New England subjects identified this as a New England form, but only 8% of subjects from all other areas could locate it. Four-fifths of the New England subjects said that they would say it themselves, but again only a handful of others did so—and their other responses were so chaotic that they strongly indicate that their self-report was inaccurate.

The general rule operating here is that when a conjunction with *so* is formed, and conjunction reduction applies to remove all of the phrase except the auxiliary, that negative *n't* is added to the auxiliary. This seems to be acceptable with any auxiliary construction, including past, present, and future tenses, and various modals: *So can't I, so won't I, so didn't I*, etc. Most outsiders are puzzled by the apparent contradiction between the positive *so* and the negative *n't*.[20]

---

[20]If we search for the nearest syntactic parallels to *So don't I*, we may obtain some clues as to its origin. Tag questions also reverse polarity, as well as expressions like *Don't I though!* If this last is connected with *So don't I* (despite its very different stress pattern), we may want to argue that *So don't I* was in its origin an emphatic form, similar to the other strengthening forms noted below.

TABLE 4

Responses to *So Don't I* Questions from Q-SCOM
Inquiry on Syntactic Dialects

	Meaning			Regional identification			Use it oneself	
	Pos	?	Neg	ENE	Wrong	None	Yes	No
Philadelphia series[a]	40	8	53	11	17	68	2	24
Midwest series								
Kansas	3	1	20	0	1	22	0	16
Utah	3	0	11	0	0	15	0	3
Providence series								
Nonnatives	6	0	2	3	0	5	2	5
ENE natives	16	0	0	14	0	2	12	3
ENE natives from Philadelphia	8	0	0	7	0	1	2	6
All ENE natives	24	0	0	21	0	3	14	9

[a]Excluding subjects of eastern New England origin.

The overall report just given makes it seem that the regional form would be a strong source of confusion in communication across dialects. Only those who use it seem to know what it means, reliably recognize it as English, evaluate and interpret it properly, and say what it means. On the other hand, it seems that communication across the dialect boundary is not as difficult as it seems: A certain amount of information seems to have leaked across it without anyone realizing it.

The 139 subjects for the Q-SCOM test outside of New England may be divided into two groups: those who were interviewed in Philadelphia,[21] and two other groups interviewed in the Midwest. Table 4 shows a striking contrast between these two sets: Almost half of the Easterners were correct on the meaning of *So don't I*, but an overwhelming majority of both western groups thought it was negative. This can only mean that those Easterners who figured out the positive meaning of *So don't I* were helped by an unconscious awareness of this or some parallel change in grammar.

Other evidence from New England supports the view that unconscious learning of an alien grammatical form is possible. Sixteen of our 24 New England subjects were from a study carried out at Providence College; along with these 16 were eight students who were raised in other areas (mostly eastern). Six of the eight correctly thought that *So don't I* was positive, though only three of them were able

[21]The Philadelphia subjects included a large group from the Philadelphia area, and a wide range of others from eastern states, the Midwest, and the Far West. Most were college students who had a fairly broad geographic background, and were thus ideal subjects for testing the hypothesis of a pan-dialectal grammar. Eight of them were from eastern New England, and for the purposes of this discussion, they are grouped with the 16 native speakers interviewed in Providence.

to identify it as a New England form. They had assimilated the meaning of the grammatical construction without acquiring the ability to label it.

The contact between the Philadelphia sample and the Eastern New England group was obviously much more extensive than for the Midwestern groups. Sixty-three percent of the 96 Easterners had visited Eastern New England at least once; but only 7 of the 25 in the Kansas group had, and 3 of the 15 from Utah. The obvious inferences from geography are thus borne out by actual travel patterns.

So don't I thus forms a parallel to the regional sound patterns discussed above. It represents a form concentrated within a regional dialect which is known only vaguely to those in other areas. When we begin to speculate about the cause of a negative inversion of this type, we are apt to look to playful manipulation of language, the search for novelty, and so on. But the shift of a negative particle to a positive construction is not unique to current English grammatical changes. We also observe the same general process in a number of other constructions.

In our study of syntactic dialects, we have concentrated most intently on the use of positive *anymore*, as in Example (2) above. This construction is also regional: It is concentrated in the Midland area, indicated as one of the major dialect divisions of the United States on Fig. 4.[22] Everyone who uses this form agrees that it is positive, and furthermore that it means roughly ''nowadays.'' Example (2) means that John used to smoke less, and now he is smoking much more. When this construction is called to the attention of outsiders, from New England, New York, the South, etc., they find it very strange. But very few of them misinterpret it as negative. The more common misinterpretation is ''still''—that John smoked a lot before and still is doing so. More results of our inquiry into *anymore* are given in other publications (Hindle & Sag, in press; Labov, 1972b). Here we are interested in the fact that everyone seems to have some expectation that this negative polarity item, *anymore*, can be shifted into a positive context even if they do not do it themselves.

The movement of *anymore* seems to be part of a general movement of *any*. We have collected a wide range of examples which seem odd extensions to many, acceptable to a smaller number.

Three examples from my own observation will indicate the general picture:

(3) My daughter Joanna, at the age of 11: ''Ice cream? I hope there's any.''

(4) A druggist, responding to an inquiry about razor blades: ''I hope there's any left; they're going like hotcakes.''

(5) Myself: ''Unfortunately, we are missing any stops from here.''

When we included (4) in our inquiry into syntactic dialects, we found that 103 out of 107 subjects correctly interpreted *I hope there's any left* as ''I hope there's some left.'' How is this possible? The movement of *any* into positive contexts is part of a

---

[22]The Midland area was identified on the basis of regional words in Kurath (1949). In Kurath and McDavid (1961), it was found that a number of other phonological isoglosses were concentrated along the same line. The distribution of positive *anymore* in our own records and in articles in *American Speech,* show that this syntactic feature is another defining feature of the Midland.

general shift of indefinites to an emphatic meaning. This syntactic shift seems to have no geographic pattern. In the same way, we find a wide scattering of people who have shifted *never* from a negative indefinite to a simple negative emphatic past. In response to a negative sentence like *I didn't go to see Love Story last night*, these speakers can respond *I never either*, meaning "I did not do it either."

An even more general aspect of this emphatic adaptation of the indefinites *any* and *ever* is in negative concord, or multiple negation.[23] We can distinguish a series of stages in which the negative particle is used in progressively wider scope, adding emphasis to the negative meaning rather than reversing it:

(6) *a*. Nobody knows anything about him taking any money.
   b. Nobody knows nothing about him taking any money.
   c. Nobody knows nothing about him taking no money.
   d. Nobody don't know nothing about him taking no money.
   e. Nobody don't know nothing about him not taking no money.

In *(a)* there is only one negative in the surface sentence; in *(b)* the negative is copied in the first indefinite, within the clause; in *(c)* it spreads to the second embedded clause; in *(d)* the negative is copied onto the preverbal position in the auxiliary; and in *(e)* it spreads to the preverbal position in the following clause. Various dialects are limited to *(a)*, *(abc)*, or *(abcd)*; we have evidence for *(e)* only from one dialect: the Black English vernacular. But, on the other hand, native speakers of other dialects show an extraordinary ability to decipher the right meaning for constructions that they would never use and claim not to have heard. Only 25% of our subjects interpreted constructions such as *(6d)* as positive. However, *(6e)* is a much more difficult case: Here we have a sharp split between black and white. A majority of the white speakers thought that the sentence of the type *(6e)*, *There ain't nobody can't figure that out* meant that "everyone can figure it out." But a sizable minority, 46%, correctly thought that the negatives added up to a single negative message, even though this construction was quite outside of their experience.[24]

Negative concord is obviously not a regional, but a socially stratified pattern. It is similar to the sociolinguistic variables in the sound pattern of New York City where speakers of both dialects live in the same area. The simpler forms of negative concord, like *(6a,b,c)* are known to everyone, and even those who would

[23]Although the shift of *any* to certain positive contexts may be new in English, there is no reason to assert that negative concord represents a change in progress. Negative concord was a feature of Old English, and the main trend of modern times was to limit the application of this rule in the standard language. But for one reason or another, the extent of negative concord varies from one dialect to another, and we can use this rule as a testing ground for speakers' ability to decipher and interpret the rules of other dialects.

[24]We can contrast the white subjects' ability to grasp this extended negative concord with that of the blacks. Eight of thirteen black subjects interpreted the test sentence as negative, indicating that they saw the possibility of negative concord, as opposed to 11 of 13 for the extension of negative concord to preverbal position within the clause.

never use it themselves are fully able to recognize, evaluate, interpret, label, and predict its use. The extensions made of the process in other dialects may be unfamiliar to them, but they clearly demonstrate the ability to follow the process as it proceeds. The function of negative concord is reasonably clear: It is an emphatic process that strengthens the act of negation.[25] Similarly, the extension of the indefinite *ever* to *I never either* represents a process of strengthening. The shift of the indefinite *any* to positive contexts in *I hope there's any left* also appears to strengthen the negative presupposition: It is so unlikely that *any* are left that we'd be lucky to find even one.

These nonregional grammatical processes, which seem at first to represent a reversal of polarity, are part of a long-term drift in English in which the indefinites acquire emphatic meaning and relinquish the generality of their scope. It is this general meaning of the indefinites *any* and *ever* which makes this possible: They extend statements to consider the entire range of possible cases for which they might be true. *Any glass will break* means that "if you select one out of the whole class of glasses, no matter which, you will find that it will break" (Labov, 1972b). This general law is a stronger statement than *Glasses will break*: The extensions of *any* and *ever* to emphatic statements seem to be related to this generalization.[26]

On first glance, it seems as if the reversals of polarity are in direct conflict with the need for clear communication. But the strengthening of denials, assertions, hopes, and fears is just as important an aspect of communication as establishing the correct polarity. If a denial is made weakly, and not believed, it is worse than no denial at all. The communicative value of negative concord is attested to by hundreds of languages that have followed this path; English is not at all exceptional in this respect.

As the process of strengthening continues, the variable used to strengthen the message becomes weaker itself. As the word or grammatical form becomes used more and more often, each occurrence carries less and less significance; at the end of the line, when its use becomes completely regular, it carries no information at all and new devices must be found to carry the message. For speakers of Black English this has happened with ordinary negative concord within the clause, which is quite uniform within the vernacular.

We can observe this steady strengthening of messages and weakening of the variables in taboo words and obscenities. English has a special set of three "super-obscenities," of which *motherfucker* was long considered an outstanding

[25]In most dialects, negative concord is optional so that *no* alternates with *any*. We often see dramatic shifts when the need for emphasis arises. One speaker from Atlanta used no negative concord for 15 or 20 minutes, until she was asked if she measured when she cooked. "I don't measure nothin'!" she answered, and repeated this is a number of times to leave no room for doubt (Labov, 1972c, 177ff.).

[26]We frequently find that speakers shift to these indefinites to exaggerate a point, in a way that would be untrue if listeners took them literally. It is a standard rhetorical device to use "Nobody liked her cookies" to mean that some people did not like them, and the listener is invited to interpret this as emphatic rather than a claim that not one single person liked them.

example. Its free use has been most characteristic of the Black English vernacular. In ritual insults like the *dozens* and in the great epic poems of the vernacular, it becomes a part of the ritual itself, an essential element of the complex rhythm.

In ''The Sinking of the Titanic,'' the epic hero Shine meets a baby swimming in the water; the baby is crying.

> ''Shine say, Baby, baby, please don't cry,
> All you little motherfuckers got a time to die,
> You got eight little fingers and two little thumbs,
> And your black ass got to go when the wagon comes.''

The ritual character of *motherfucker* does not exclude its use in an aggressive move. In ''Signifying Monkey,'' for example, the lion kicks the sleeping elephant.

> ''Hey motherfucker, you better get up from under that god damned tree,
> And when you do, don't try to cop no plea.''

And on the other hand, the elephant's answer shows that *motherfucker* can be used as a relatively neutral term.

> ''The elephant opened one of his big bloodshot eyes,
> Said, 'Go ahead, chickenshit, go find some motherfucker your size.' ''

Faced with this range in use and meaning, what is one to make of the fact that members of the black community have been given up to six months in jail for calling a cop a motherfucker. In one Jersey City case, the judge insisted on taking this breach of the peace literally, stating that any red-blooded American would be provoked to violence by being accused of committing incest with his mother.

Let us assume that there is a dialect difference between the black defendant and the white judge: that progressive strengthening of insults has led to a weakening of this epithet so that it does not mean the same thing in the black community as in the white community. Can we assume that the dialect difference has been a barrier to communication? That the black speaker did not know that he would be provoking the cop by calling him a motherfucker? This is more than unlikely, considering the fact that in the black community *motherfucker* is also a ritual way of starting a very real fight. It seems more likely that the black speaker was deliberately using the dialect difference to sharpen his provocation, and the judge was deliberately making use of the difference to defend his action by interpreting a ritual epithet as a literal one.

The need to strengthen messages (with corresponding weakening of elements of the message form) is certainly a major factor in linguistic change. But it cannot be the only one. We would not find it so easy to make this claim for the *So don't I* of eastern New England,[27] and we must look for other kinds of communication that are being made here.

LOCAL IDENTITY

My first exploration of linguistic change in progress was on the island of Martha's Vineyard. One of the general sound changes of English had been reversed: The (ay) and (aw) in *right* and *out* was gradually being centralized to [ə ι] and [əv], heading back in the direction of the seventeenth century English which was used when the island was settled (Labov, 1963). The complex distribution of this sound change showed that it was favored in rural areas more than urban ones, by fishermen more than farmers, by men more than women, by Yankees more than Portuguese or Indians. But the one correlation which explained the most was whether or not the speaker expressed a positive attitude toward the island of Martha's Vineyard. Young people who had decided to leave the island for a career in banking or engineering did not show the sound change; but it appeared most strongly in those who decided to stay (or who came back). The centralization of (ay) and (aw) on Martha's Vineyard is an archtypical case of a sound change communicating *local identity*.

There is a great deal of evidence to show that many local vernaculars are heavily stigmatized. But this evidence is almost always *in response to some direct inquiry about language*. The stability and vigor of urban vernaculars argues for an opposing set of values that are not as easily elicited, but which have an even stronger effect than the standard values that appear in a test situation. One of these values is the need to assert one's membership in a local community, class, ethnic, or age group. It is one of the hardest to obtain objective evidence on, though we have recently tapped such responses in subjective reaction tests in south Harlem.[28] Some speakers are conscious of a pride in their local identity; others are not, or even reject it. But all speakers can feel the penalty of being excluded from their original group.

The function of slang in establishing local identity has been observed for many years. Its chief function seems to be identifying group membership. In any case, we find that groups resent the adoption of their own vocabulary by others; if they cannot prevent it, they will shift to other forms that are still their own.

The adolescent group known as the Cobras in south Harlem always used the

[27]Though it can be made; see Footnote 18.

[28]The subjective reaction tests asked for reactions on three scales: (1) What is the highest job a person could hold speaking in this way? (2) How likely would the speaker be to come out on top in a street fight? (3) If you got to know him, how likely would he be a friend of yours? Answers on Scale 2 were regularly the reciprocal of answers on 1. Responses on 3 were aligned with 2 for the lower-class speakers, but with 1 for middle class and the upper sections of the working class (Labov, 1972a, 250). For the lower-working class groups, friendship and toughness were associated with the vernacular, a reasonably positive configuration.

term *tip* to mean "go," as in *Let's tip*. We had heard *Let's tip* hundreds of times, and there was no doubt about its appropriate meaning and use. But when I used it one day on an outing with the Cobras, there was an immediate surge of amusement from the members and they pretended not to understand. Outsiders are allowed and encouraged to shift on some points of phonology and grammar, but there was a sharp reaction against anyone else wearing this linguistic mark of local identity.

Slang is one of the most conspicuous forms of linguistic innovation; most linguistic change operates well below the level of consciousness. Young people know that their slang is different from their parents; but they seldom realize that their sound pattern or their grammar has changed. *So don't I* has risen to the level of an overt stereotype in eastern New England. Teachers consider it to be one of the many mistakes in grammar that young people make because they do not know better. But as far as young people are concerned, it seems to function as one of the marks of local identity, a symbol of resistance to the standardizing influence of the teachers who would erase those marks if they possibly could.

INTIMACY

Vocabulary is fairly accessible to inspection; sound changes are more difficult to observe, and grammar even more so; but perhaps the most elusive of all linguistic changes are systematic shifts in the rules of discourse. When we are engaged in social interaction with another speaker, at the beginning or ends of our conversations, we are in a structural situation that makes it almost impossible to know exactly what we are saying or doing.

A good example of such a structural situation is leave-taking. For several years, I have been observing these forms: first, taking notes on what speakers actually say; second, asking speakers what they say. There is little connection between the two.

Most English speakers have come to realize that *good-bye* is much too formal for ordinary leave-taking. It implies distance and finality. They believe that they most often say *So long, 'bye, I'll see you*, or sometimes *g'bye*. But the most common form by far, on the telephone or in person, in England or in America, is never the majority form on any questionnaire. Most Americans react with amused disbelief or violent disgust when they are told that they use this form.

The normal, nonformal way of taking leave from someone in English today is to say *Bye-bye*. Table 5 is one of our many studies which support this observation. When attention is focused directly on this term, it seems to most English speakers to convey effeminacy or childishness. But when a person begins to try to observe his own usage, he often returns and admits (with shame and amazement) that he uses it.

There are four variants of this form that are used in successively less formal and more intimate exchanges:

[baɪbaɪ, babaɪ, bəbaɪ, bʊbaɪ]

TABLE 5

Forms Used for Leave-Taking in American English
and Intuitive Responses of Native Speakers

	Forms actually observed[a]			Intuitions on most common form observed[b]
	Male	Female	Total	
Goodbye	6.0%	2.0%	3.4%	08%
Goodbye now	1.2	0.0	0.4	04
Good'bye [gʊbaɪ]	4.8	1.3	2.5	
G'bye [gəbaɪ]	1.2	1.3	1.3	
	13.2	4.6	7.6	
Byebye now	2.4	4.0	3.4	
Byebye	41.7	43.3	42.7	08
Babye [babaɪ]	9.5	11.3	10.6	
Bubye [bʊbaɪ]	2.4	9.3	6.8	
B'bye [bəbaɪ]	1.2	0.7	0.9	
	57.2	68.6	64.4	
bye	13.1	19.3	17.0	04%
bye now	10.7	4.7	6.8	
	23.8	24.0	23.8	
So long	1.2	0.7	0.9	04
Take care	2.4	0.7	1.3	12
Goodnight	1.2	0.7	0.9	
Thank you	1.2	0.7	0.9	
See ya (later)				32
Other				28
Total	100.2	100.0	99.8	100
N	84	150	234	

[a]Data observed by W. Labov from October 1970 to November 1971.
[b]Questionnaire responses of 33 Columbia College undergraduates in 1970.

These are of course only three points on a continuum; the reduplicated form *bye-bye* offers a wide range of possibilities for stylistic variation. In contrast, the simple "bye" offers no unstressed syllable that can be reduced.

It seems that there has been a long succession of terms for leave-taking, which undergo similar processes of reduction. It is well known that *good-bye* is itself a reduction of *God be with you*. By the time a term is actually recognized overtly by the community, it has already become too formal for normal use. If speakers knew that they said *Bye-bye*, they would immediately begin to say something else.

One possible explanation for this behavior is that in our society no conventionally recognized form can be intimate enough to set the proper tone for the end of a conversation. A long succession of *O.K.*s, *all rights*, etc., show the two parties repeatedly assuring each other that they still stand in the same good relationship that they did at the beginning of the conversation. Any sign of stiffness or conventional behavior would demonstrate the contrary; most serious of all, of course, would be a firm *good-bye*.[29] The informality required in a final leave-taking is a necessary demonstration that the good feeling is spontaneous, and not merely a ritual event—though it is of course exactly that.

It follows that continual linguistic change is needed in order to communicate intimacy. No matter how informal a term may be, its repeated use in a ritual situation is bound to result in its recognition as a formal term, and new linguistic forms will be needed to replace it.

THREE MOTIVATIONS FOR SOUND CHANGE

These examples of grammatical change in grammar and discourse have shown us three modes of communication which are characteristic of linguistic change. A new form can be used to signal a stronger meaning than the older form; to display the speaker's membership in a local group; and to demonstrate greater intimacy than an older form. It should be clear that we have not proved that these messages are present in the various linguistic changes we have discussed. We have only suggested them, on the basis of some direct and some indirect evidence. The proof will require more subtle subjective reaction tests than we have carried out so far.

It would be easy to argue that all three messages reduce to one: that the more intimate message is required to strengthen personal ties, to strengthen a claim to personal identity, and to strengthen the force of a denial or assertion. But at this level of abstraction, every change may necessarily be a strengthening of some quality or other, and we find it more illuminating to focus on the three qualities being increased: force of expression, local identification, and intimacy. Let us now apply this thinking to the case that appeared so paradoxical in earlier sections: the evolution of the New York City vernacular in the face of strong social stigmatization.

There is no doubt that the term *strengthening* can appropriately be used in connection with the raising of tense and ingliding vowels.[30] We have observed that the most advanced forms tend to be the most highly stressed and most emphatically uttered within the body of spontaneous speech. The advancing forms are pronounced with more extreme positions of the nucleus of the vowel, with greater lip-spreading or rounding. There is reason to believe that the central target for

[29]Though people will say *goodbye* when they are taking leave for a long period of time, or permanently. For this very reason, *goodbye* is now inappropriate for normal, temporary leave-taking in which the parties look forward to meeting again as soon as possible.

[30]This formulation is that of Jules Levin, of UCLA, who sees strengthening as the general mechanism of sound change.

pronunciation of a given vowel lies at the upper edge of its distribution, rather than its center. The same reasoning can be adopted for the gradual lowering of diphthongal nuclei in the vowel shifts illustrated in Figs. 1, 2, and 3.

There is no doubt that the New York City vowel shift communicates local identity. That is precisely the basis for the stigmatization. It is another matter to show that there is a positive force behind local identity; that in some important way, speakers who say they do not want to be New Yorkers actually do desire this status. We have shown that speakers in south central Harlem associate the use of vernacular forms with someone who is more likely to be a friend of theirs, as well as someone who is apt to be tougher in a fight (Labov, 1972b). The same demonstration has not been made for the white vernacular, but it is a reasonable hypothesis.

Finally, we have no difficulty in showing that the more advanced forms are associated with more intimate conversation. For all New Yorkers, formal contexts discourage the use of the vernacular, and for this reason it is not possible to study it accurately with word lists and reading tests. Our best record of the vernacular is found in contexts where the speaker is deeply involved with his narrative, or reacting casually with intimate friends or family. In our interviews there are a number of dramatic shifts when speakers turn from formal to intimate speech. The fact that the older, more conservative forms of language are associated with formal situations means inevitably that the newer, more advanced forms will be associated with casual and intimate speech.

The view of language change that emerges from these last sections is quite different from the traditional view of the lack of communication and the absence of effort. It is clear that many linguistic changes are the result of isolation, and that some are the result of assimilatory shifts which lead to faster and easier articulation. The problem is to explain the sizable body of cases that cannot be accounted for in that way. We have suggested the possibility of a communicative function for change itself.

In Darwin's (1873) exposition of the parallels between linguistic and biological evolution, he argued that the survival of the fittest could be seen in language: that as words became shorter, they became better. It would be hard to find support for this idea among linguists. But language may be rebuilt and adapted in many ways, and it would be too soon to discount the notion that linguistic change has adaptive value. We have examined some of the indirect evidence that change is a form of communication in itself, by which the speaker lets the hearer know that he is not using the older, weaker form of assertion or denial; that he shares with him the marks of local identity which are reinforced by the newer form; and that he stands in the new, intimate relation that is signaled by the fresh and spontaneous use of the new form.

We must also consider that there are changes in language introduced by polite society which have the reverse effect: The speaker may use new polite and mitigating forms that weaken his assertion or denial; the speaker may shift to a neutral form and avoid the older marks of local identity; or the speaker may abandon the old and direct way of talking for the new formal approach which establishes a distance between him and his audience. We can find both grammatical and phonological examples of features which operate in this way. A New York City speaker, for example, will use the polite forms of network English to establish this weaker, more general, and more distant effect; when he introduces [r] pronunciation in increasingly formal speech, he abandons the new tense vowels of the vernacular. This introduction of a prestige pattern is also a form of linguistic change, of a well-recognized type which we may call "change from above." But on the whole, the history of language seems to be largely determined by "change from below," and it is this type of vernacular change that generates the profound paradoxes that we have tried to resolve here. From the point of view of polite society, "change from above" restores order to the chaos produced by "change from below." My own point of view is quite the reverse. I see the evolution of the vernacular as restoring and reopening lines of communication that have become clogged and confused by the rituals of weakness, generality, and formality.

Until recently we have concentrated our research on the study of vernacular change rather than its opposite, polite codification. To accept or reject the suggestions made here on the communicative value of change, it will be necessary to begin a careful study of the dynamics of this opposition, reexamining the rate of change at all points in the sociolinguistic pattern. It is not only working-class children who reject the models of polite society; every social group has a vested interest in linguistic change, except perhaps the few who are completely satisfied that they have said what they have to say.

For most of us, linguistic change is a necessary part of the continual effort to overcome the barriers that time and social practice place between us and our fellow speakers. We may not be able to account fully for change or predict its course, but through the study of change in progress, we seem to be coming to better terms with this omnipresent fact of social life; and be spared at least the long and bitter frustration of those who oppose without understanding.

REFERENCES

Bailey, C.-J. N. The integration of linguistic theory: Internal reconstruction and the comparative method in descriptive analysis. In R. P. Stockwell & R. K. S. Macaulay (Eds.), *Linguistic change and generative theory*. Bloomington: Indiana University Press, 1972.

Bloomfield, L. Language. New York: Holt, 1933.

Bright, W., & Ramanujan, A. K. Sociolinguistic variation and language change. In H. Lunt (Ed.), *Proceedings of the IXth international congress of linguists*. The Hague: Mouton, 1964.

Burgess, N. A spectrographic investigation of some diphthongal phonemes in Australian English. *Language and Speech,* 1969, **12**, 238–246.

Chomsky, N., & Halle, M. *The sound pattern of English*. New York: Harper & Row, 1968.

Darwin, C. *Descent of Man*. 1873.

Gauchat, L., "L'unité phonétique dans le patois d'une commune." In, *Aus romanischen sprachen und Literaturen: Festschrift Heinreich Morf.* Halle: Max Niemeyer, 1905.

Greenberg, J. H. Language and evolution. In, *Evolution and Anthropology: A centennial appraisal.* Washington, D.C. Anthropological Society of Washington D.C., 1959.

Greenberg, J. H. *Language, Culture, and Communication.* Stanford: Stanford University Press, 1971.

Herzog, M. I. *The Yiddish language in northern Poland: Its geography and history.* Bloomington, Ind.: Research Center in Anthropology, Folklore and Linguistics, 1965.

Hindle, D., & Sag, I. Some more on *anymore.* In, *Proceedings of the second conference on new ways of analyzing variation.* Washington, D.C.: Georgetown University, in press.

Hymes, D. Functions of speech: An evolutionary approach. In F. C. Gruber (Ed.), *Anthropology and education.* Philadelphia: University of Pennsylvania Press, 1961.

Jespersen, O. *Language.* London: Allen & Unwin, 1922.

Kurath, H. *Word geography of the Eastern United States.* Ann Arbor: University of Michigan Press, 1949.

Kurath, H., & McDavid, R. I., Jr. *The pronunciation of English in the Atlantic states.* Ann Arbor: University of Michigan Press, 1961.

Labov, W. The relation of dialect boundaries to communication networks. Unpublished paper, Columbia University, 1962.

Labov, W. The social motivation of a sound change. *Word* 1963, **19**, 273-309.

Labov, W. *The social stratification of English in New York City.* Washington, D.C.: Center for Applied Linguistics, 1966.

Labov, W. *Sociolinguistic patterns.* Philadelphia: University of Pennsylvania Press, 1972. (a)

Labov, W. Where do grammars stop? In R. Shuy (Ed.), *Georgetown monograph on languages and linguistics.* (No. 25) Washington, D.C.: Georgetown University Press, 1972. (b)

Labov, W. *Language in the inner city.* Philadelphia: University of Pennsylvania Press, 1972. (c)

Labov, W., Yaeger, M., Steiner, R., *A quantitative study of sound change in progress.* (Report on National Science Foundation Contract GS-3287.) Philadelphia: United States Regional Survey, 1972. (204 N. 35th St.)

Lambert, W. E. *Language, psychology, and culture.* Stanford: Stanford University Press, 1972.

Shuy, R., Wolfram, W., & Riley, W. K., *A study of social dialects in Detroit.* (Final Report, Project 6-1347) Washington, D.C.: United States Office of Education, 1967.

Sorenson, A. P. Multilingualism in the Northwest Amazon. *American Anthropologist,* **69**, 1967, 670–684.

Spielman, R. S., Migliazza, E. C., & Neel, J. V. Linguistic and genetic differences among Yanomama Indian language areas, 1973. (Mimeo)

Weinreich, U. *Languages in contact.* New York: Linguistic Circle of New York, 1959.

Weinreich, U., Labov, W., & Herzog, M. Empirical foundations for a theory of language change. In W. Lehmann & Y. Malkiel (Eds.), *Directions for historical linguistics.* Austin: University of Texas Press, 1968.

AUTHOR INDEX

Numbers in *italics* refer to the pages on which the complete references are listed.

A

Abelson, R. P., 195, 199, *200*
Aiba, F. H., 195, *200*
Arnold, T. W., 204, *219*
Austin, J. L., 15, *16,* 54, *66,* 113, *119*

B

Bailey, C. J. N., 243, *255*
Bar-Hillel, Y., 20, *44*
Bateson, G., 204, *219*
Bellugi, U., 126, 128, 135, *143*
Berlin, B., 102, *119*
Berlyne, D. E., 33, 34, 37, 39, 40, *44*
Bever, T., 47, *66,* 128, *142*
Bexton, W. A., 39, *44*
Birdwhistell, R. L., 203, *220*
Black, M., 93, *93,* 100, *119*
Bloom, L., 127, *143*
Bloomfield, L., 70, *80,* 222, *255*
Blumenthal, 70, *80*
Borsa, D. M., 33, *44*
Bourne, L. E., 113, *119*

Bowerman, M., 127, *143*
Braine, M. D. S., 126, 127, *143*
Brayman, W., 39, 40, *44*
Bright, W., 224, *255*
Broadbent, D. E., 30, *44*
Brown, R. W., 99, 109, *119,* 123, 124, 126, 127, 128, 131, 132, 133, 134, 135, 136, *143*
Bruce, D. R., 102, *120*
Bruner, J. S., 113, 117, *119*
Burgess, N., 227, *200*

C

Cabin, S., 199, *200*
Campbell, D. T., 107, *121*
Capec, M., 169, *183*
Carey, P., 47, *66*
Carey, S. T., 34, *44*
Carnap, R., 20, *44*
Carothers, J. C., 171, *183*
Carroll, J. B., 101, *119*
Casagrande, J. B., 78, *80,* 101, *119*
Castillo Vales, V., 110, *121*
Cazden, C. B., 135, *143*

257

SUBJECT INDEX

A

Aesthetics, 40 – 42
Alphabetic typography, *see* Printing
Ambiguity of sentences, 47 – 50
  and syntactic structure, 48

B

Balance theory, 190 – 191
Behaviorism, *see also* Persuasion
  and language, 68 – 70, 89 – 90
Beliefs, as related to understanding, 15
Body communication
  a demonstration, 214 – 217
Boredom, 38 – 40

C

Chimpanzee, *see* Language
Clauses, relative, *see also* Performative
    analysis
  nonrestrictive vs. restrictive, 60 – 61

Codability
  and memory, 111 – 112
Coding, 30
Cognitive dissonance, 189, 197
Color perception, *see* Language, effects on
Communication, levels of processing, *see*
    Levels of linguistic processing
Communication, 1, 3 – 4, 6, 145 – 150, 153,
    156 – 163, 185 – 187, 203, 205 – 214
  as control of behavior, 185 – 187
  definition, 1
  dyadic model, 205 – 208
  failures in, 6
  vs. instinct, 208 – 210
  interdisciplinary study of, 4
  multisensory process, 203, 211 – 214
  related to psychology, 3 – 4
  technical means, 145 – 150, 153, 156 – 163
    centralization and decentralization, 159 –
      161
    and international organization, 156 – 163
    traffic density, 147 – 149
    and values, 153
Communication media, 154 – 155, 166 – 183,
    see also Printing
  successive stages, 166 – 183